The social history of Canada

MICHAEL BLISS, EDITOR

Philosophy of railroads

AND OTHER ESSAYS, BY T.C. KEEFER

EDITED, WITH AN INTRODUCTION, BY H.V. NELLES

UNIVERSITY OF TORONTO PRESS

Toronto and Buffalo

ISBN (casebound) 0-8020-1911-0

ISBN (paperback) 0-8020-6157-5

Microfiche ISBN 0-8020-0250-1

LC 72-163835

Printed in the United States of America

These essays have been reproduced with the co-operation of the Public Archives of Ontario and the Metropolitan Toronto Central Library. The map on page 130 is courtesy of the Public Archives of Canada.

Contents

An introduction

BY H. V. NELLES

1

NOT VERY long ago the fact that Canada possessed more miles of railroad per capita than any other country was a matter of considerable national pride. Now, with even the publicly owned Canadian National Railways curtailing service and rolling up track, that boast is seldom heard. Gradually over the generations a system of transportation that at one time symbolized Canadian national achievement has been reduced to something akin to a public embarrassment.

From our post-industrial vantage point we might well wonder at the excitement evoked by steam engines and railroads a century ago. In our time railroads are accused of blighting and bisecting our cities, of monopolizing scarce land with rusting wastelands of track, of isolating towns and cities from their rivers and lakefronts. As a transportation service railroads linger on as a drain on the public treasury and a source of continuing disappointment for even the most determined, sentimental travellers. In the public mind railroads have become caricatures of corporate arrogance; their distinguishing characteristics – chronic bankruptcy and neglected facilities – impart to them the fascination of some decrepit, better forgotten, government department. How indeed could anyone ever have been enthusiastic about railroads?

We might wonder too at the curious mystique that once surrounded steam. As a source of motive power the steam engine has been supplanted by several generations of more efficient machines. Its epitome, the steam locomotive, if it stirs any recollections at all, usually brings back memories of noxious smoke, raining cinders, and deafening, earth-shaking noise. It must surely have been the arch-polluter of the century. How strange that enthusiasm generated by steam seems, now that the locomotives have been relegated to public parks or to museums of technology where they stand in rows, lined up like steel dinosaurs and looking every bit as unbelievable. Even the architecture of the railroad age is passing from view. The great cathedrals and smaller denominational chapels to Steam – the echoing railroad stations of cities and towns – have been torn down, or, in fits of nostalgia or shrewd economy, their tracks have been ripped up, their yards paved for parking, and they themselves have been pressed into unlikely service as art galleries, museums, liquor stores, or dominion-provincial conference centres.

Each year too the loosening hold of the railroad upon the popular imagination can be measured in the dwindling space allotted to the electric train in the toy sections of Christmas catalogues. The mystique of steam, which now maintains a furtive existence in the basements of aging train buffs, is surely beyond the immediate comprehension of a generation that has only an academic grasp of the uses of coal and thinks striped denim fashionable. Still, somewhere off on the edge of our consciousness, diesel locomotives go methodically about the dreary business of shunting box cars, driven, we are told, by men wearing sports jackets. Railroading, if it has not become boring in our time, has most certainly become ordinary – far from the stuff of which national fantasies are made.

This eclipse of the railroad has had its intellectual dimension as well. The possibility of now asking the formerly unthinkable question, 'would the economic development of the North American continent have been possible without the railroad?' suggests the distance we have come from the age of steam. It was once readily accepted that the rapid expansion of the railroad system gave shape and direction to agricultural and industrial growth in the late nineteenth century and that such a spectacular achievement would not have been possible without the railroad. That proposition (known as the axiom of indispensability) received one of its classic formulations in the first pamphlet reprinted in this collection. As T.C. Keefer phrased it: '... we may as well in the present age attempt to live without books or newspapers, as without Railroads.' It should not be surprising that, in another age preparing to live without all three, the axiom of indispensability could be severely challenged.

At the beginning of the 1960s the American economist Robert Fogel observed that the prevailing interpretation of the influence of railroads on American economic growth during the nineteenth century was still dominated by hypotheses spawned during that era. Guided by economic theory and armed with elaborate statistical techniques and counterfactual models, Professor Fogel and other 'new economic historians' concluded that the railroad contributed only marginally to American economic growth, that, in fact, it was quite dispensable. To quote Professor Fogel: 'despite its dramatically rapid and massive growth over a period of a half century, despite its eventual ubiquity in inland transportation, despite its devouring appetite for capital, despite its power to determine the outcome of commercial (and sometimes political) competition, the railroad did not make an overwhelming contribution to the production potential of the economy.' This astonishing generalization and the even more remarkable techniques employed to arrive at it provoked a debate that is about to enter its second decade. One of the results of this debate has been a theoretical clarification of what is meant by economic growth and what contributes to it. Henceforth, the contribution of the railroad to the growth process will be a matter of close argument and precise language, if not measurement.[1]

In Canada several generations of intellectuals have invested railroads with even greater transforming powers than they had been credited with in the United States. Railroads play a key role in the staple interpretation of Canadian economic development and the Laurentian interpretation of Canadian history. The transcontinental railroad in particular has been elevated to the status of a prerequisite of viable nationality. Here the arguments of the transcending economic importance of railroads are still accepted as Gospel and the assumptions of the railroad building era still stand as acceptable assessments of the importance of railroads.

Notwithstanding Pierre Berton's phenomenal success with the saga of the CPR, there are signs that this attitude of unquestioning acceptance is beginning to change. Following Professor Fogel's work on the Union Pacific, Peter George, an economist from McMaster University, argued that the Canadian Pacific Railway could have been built and would have provided a satisfactory rate of return on its investment with much less government assistance than it actually received. In more recent essays he has suggested that the economic (and perhaps the political) importance of the CPR has been grossly exaggerated.[2]

Plainly the age of steam and perhaps also the age of the railroad itself are behind us. Why then, at a time of mounting academic scepticism and public disillusionment with railroads, reprint these obscure railroad lectures, essays, and pamphlets? What useful purpose might their re-issue serve besides kindling a little harmless nostalgia?

When Keefer published his *Philosophy of Railroads* in 1849 there were less than sixty miles of primitive track in all of British North America. Thus its argument effectively takes us back to the pre-railroad era in Canada. From this vantage point we can view the coming of the railroad in its historical context. By implication, too, the *Philosophy of Railroads* reveals something of the initial opposition advanced against the construction of railroads in Canada and directly informs us of the convincing counter-arguments proffered on their behalf. How did the railroad acquire the revolutionary powers later attributed to it? Perhaps too by analysing the rhetoric of an enthusiastic promoter the railroad fever of the nineteenth century might be more readily understood.

In the second essay in this collection, a lecture entitled simply 'Montreal,' T.C. Keefer turns our attention from the general advantages to be expected from improved rail communication to the specific role of the railroad as an agent of urbanization and metropolitanism. At the Mechanics' Institute in January 1853 we encounter the engineer as strategist looking out beyond the rooftops of Montreal, surveying the natural hinterland of the city and planning a commercial strategy to capture it, and, most importantly, proposing the practical vehicle of realizing that ambition. This particular engineer also shows that by laying railroad track and by fulfilling metropolitan dreams, Montrealers would be raising the foundations of a wholly new type of urban community, an industrial city. With the buoyant confidence of the day, Keefer assures his audience that the disagreeable and dangerous aspects of city living could be made to melt away through the rational application of the same ingenuity that created the railroad. The lecture gives a splendid impression of the strategic role engineers conceived for themselves in nineteenth century Canadian society – they were in fact the doctors of technology. And in the final paragraphs we catch a glimpse of that soaring optimism liberated by railroad propagandists convinced of the connection between the moral and material progress of man.

But for all this excited rhetoric, what became of Keefer the civil engineer during Canada's first railroad boom in the 1850s? What happened to the railroad prophet in the railroad age? The controversy that flared up in May 1856 and drew from Keefer a little-known pamphlet entitled *A Sequel to the Philosophy of Railroads* turns our attention to his early professional career and helps us to place his promotional writings in another perspective. Reflection upon T.C. Keefer's unhappy experiences as a railroad engineer and upon his analysis of the engineer's predicament leads directly to a consideration of the development of the engineering profession in general. What conflicting roles was the engineer called upon to perform at this time? What were the engineers' relationships with promoters, politicians, mechanics, labourers, the community, and other engineers? Within what technical, economic, and political circumstances did the conception of engineering as a profession crystallize? Keefer's *Sequel to the Philosophy of Railroads* advances the discussion begun in the earlier pamphlet on a qualitatively different, more personal, and critical level. The *Sequel* might serve as a useful point of departure for consideration of hitherto neglected professional movements in the nineteenth century. It is an important document in the making of a Canadian profession.

The final essay in this collection brings us full circle: the prophet has become the avenging critic. During the fourteen years that separated the *Philosophy of Railroads* and the essay Keefer composed on 'Travel and Transportation' for Henry Youle Hind's *Eighty Years' Progress of British North America,* almost two thousand miles of track had been laid in the Canadas alone and Montreal had established rail connection with its western hinterland. At least the physical aspect of Keefer's vision had been realized, but what had been the result? In Keefer's mind did the actuality of railroads square with their promise? Looking beyond Keefer, how did Canadians perceive the impact of the railroad upon their society? The concluding essay on railroads is at once a lively description of the remarkable expansion of the Canadian railroad system in the 1850s and an indictment of railroad manipulation – a critique that was all the more pointed and perceptive because it was so intensely personal. If he could only brood upon the failure of railroads when he composed this essay on transportation for a volume conceived of as a celebration of progress, what had occasioned such bitter disappointment?

2

It would not be much of an exaggeration to suggest that the Keefer family history could serve as a guide to the major achievements in Canadian civil engineering from the canal era to the age of electricity. The patriarch of this first family of Canadian engineering, George Keefer (1773-1858), came to the Niagara district in 1790 with a group of New Jersey Loyalists. His father, a Huguenot, had perished in Sir William Howe's army during the Revolutionary War. George established himself as a cabinet-maker and surveyor and later as the proprietor of a sawmill and gristmill on Twelve Mile Creek.

There he met and befriended William Hamilton Merritt, a young merchant who would later be the moving spirit behind the Welland Canal. From this association and his financial backing of Merritt's scheme, Keefer achieved the distinction in 1823 of being named the first president of the Welland Canal Company. Hc was also favoured with the considerably more lasting and tangible reward of a magnificent waterpower concession along the canal upon which he quickly built a complex of thriving mills and storehouses. As George prospered in his new surroundings he also took pains to consolidate his family within the crusty landed and commercial élite of the peninsula. In this society, where military rank still marked the gradations of social distinction, George Keefer's progress can be charted in his steady rise from ensign to captain of the militia in 1815. Nor were these mere honorific commissions; he saw action at the battles of Chippewa and Lundy's Lane. For his services in war he was rewarded with a magistracy. Chance and ambition favoured him as he amassed the wealth, land, offices, honours, and social standing from which to launch a second generation of Keefers into prominence.

George Keefer's accomplishments as a husband and father were every bit as exceptional as his financial and social successes. Indeed, his four marriages into socially prominent families regularly confirmed both. By his first two wives George Keefer sired fifteen children, fourteen of whom survived to maturity. Counting the step-children acquired during the course of his many marriages, his household consisted of twenty offspring. Even more notable than this demographic explosion in the Keefer household was the pattern of occupational and marital selection in the second generation. As a rule the boys entered one or another of the professions and the girls married professional men from the United States. Three of George Keefer's ten sons became civil engineers, three took up law, one entered medicine, another became a teacher, and two chose commerce. The daughters chose as husbands two lawyers, a doctor, and an artist (the fifth girl died an infant). Almost without fail the children followed a professional career pattern by which commercial élites sustained family reputations and fortunes in succeeding generations. There, in the quest of the already established classes for lasting prestige, one discovers a powerful social force in the drive towards professionalism.[3]

Given George Keefer's interest in technical matters, the intimate connection between the family and the Welland Canal, the constant stream of American canal engineers that boarded in his house, and his ability to pay for the best schooling available, it was not surprising that his sons should be strongly drawn towards engineering as a career. From such a household sprang two of the foremost Canadian engineers of their day, Samuel Keefer (1811-90) and Thomas Coltrin Keefer (1821-1914), the author of these essays. Samuel was appointed the first chief engineer of the Department of Public Works after the Union and later served as inspector of railways and deputy commissioner of public works – in which latter capacity he oversaw the planning of the new parliament buildings at Ottawa. As a civil servant and then as a private consultant he had a hand in the construction of both the Victoria Bridge at Montreal and the suspension bridge across the Niagara gorge, the Canadian engineering marvels of the time. His younger step-brother, Thomas Coltrin Keefer, though better known for his writings, was also recognized as 'Canada's most celebrated hydraulic engineer.' He first made a reputation as a canal builder and manager; afterwards he designed, installed, and acted as a consultant for the waterworks of Canada's major cities. The eminence of these brothers attracted later generations of Keefers into similar lines of endeavour. Whenever transportation or engineering in the nineteenth century is discussed, the name Keefer is apt to crop up.

Thomas Coltrin Keefer, the eighth son in line, distinguished himself at Grantham Academy in St Catharines and was then sent to Upper Canada College, from whose seventh form he emerged in 1838 at the age of seventeen. For the next two years he worked and studied as an engineering apprentice on the Erie Canal, which was then (in the era before formal engineering courses on university curricula) the leading engineering school in the United States.[4] In 1840 he returned to Canada where, through family connections, he secured the positions required to launch a career. For five years he served as an assistant engineer on the Welland Canal; in 1845 his brother Samuel, now the chief engineer of the Department of Public Works, appointed him engineer in charge of the timber slide and river improvements at Bytown – his first assignment as a full-fledged engineer. Although he performed his duties competently he was dismissed from this post in 1848, ostensibly for reasons of economy. But it was rumoured in his defence that he had alienated some members of the new administration by opposing some politically necessary but professionally needless expenditures. Family influence could take him far, but it could not protect him against a change in government.

During the interval of unemployment that ensued, T.C. Keefer wrote the two essays which in large measure established his reputation as an engineer, the *Philosophy of Railroads* (1849) and the *Canals of Canada* (1850). The first pamphlet, which is reprinted in this collection, was commissioned by a group of Montreal merchants to promote western rail connections. The *Canals of Canada* was Keefer's entry in Lord Elgin's essay competition held to celebrate the completion – at long last – of the St Lawrence canals. Keefer's essay took the prize and its wide distribution immediately established its author as an expert on transportation and commercial questions. With the publication of these essays T.C. Keefer emerged from under his brother's shadow and became a minor public figure in his own right.

One can find no better expression of the idea of a commercial empire of the St Lawrence than the *Canals of Canada.* Keefer believed, as D.C. Masters observed, 'that the Almighty, with due regard for the theories of Mr. Bentham, had located the St. Lawrence in such a way as to promote "the greatest happiness of the greatest number." '[5] He dwelt at great length upon the capacity of the Great Lakes basin to produce in quantity the raw materials and foodstuffs needed in Europe, and upon the natural superiority of the St Lawrence River to collect this produce and speed it by the shortest, cheapest, fastest 'airline' to its trans-Atlantic markets. By airline he meant that the Canadian gateway to the western interior was in fact much closer to Europe than the projections of Mercator made it appear. This direct, short route, combined with the natural advantages of the river (now fully equipped with splendid new canals), ensured that the St Lawrence would soon outdistance its lesser American rivals. Further downriver, he argued, navigation improvements would consolidate Montreal's strategic position as the entrepôt of the system. Both the success of the new canals and the prosperity of the colony depended upon encouraging the flow of trade on the St Lawrence.

Inasmuch as he drafted this paper during the turbulent year 1849, T.C. Keefer could not avoid concerning himself with the proper economic policies to accomplish these objectives. What was to be done now that the system of imperial preferences, upon which the canals had been predicated, had been repealed? Keefer's answer was a policy of qualified free trade in agricultural products between Canada and the United States, linked with free international navigation of the St Lawrence and its canals. By this he did not mean to imply absolute free trade between the two countries. That, he admitted, would prevent Canada from ever developing its own manufacturing industries. 'What manufactures we have,' Keefer claimed, 'are mainly the offspring of our tariff ...' Therefore he advocated a policy of moderate protection 'for those manufactures only which require little manual labour, and of which we produce raw materials.' But high tariffs, like absolute free trade, were to be avoided. Free trade in agricultural products would, he maintained, maximize the utility of the expensive canal system while moderate, selective protection would assist in the gradual industrialization of the colony. Taking the long view Keefer believed that these two policies would be 'the readiest method[s] of *obtaining* reciprocity, and of rendering us *independent* of it.'[6] And he warned Montrealers against trying to capture their Upper Canadian hinterland through prohibitive trading regulations aimed at American competitors. That city's dominance of the western interior could only come from improved communications and aggressive commercial activity. The only thing to be gained by restrictive legislation would be the undying emnity of Upper Canadians. Commerce would take its natural course if men possessed the wisdom to act in harmony with natural forces like the great river.

The *Canals of Canada* strove to reconcile the most contentious commercial issues of the day: free trade and protection could be resorted to simultaneously and in the long run, when reciprocity on a broad range of goods was a possibility, the independence of the Canadian economy and the integrity of the state would in no way be threatened by closer continental trading relations. The ingenuity and apparent technical authority of this essay, rather than the originality of its ideas, won Keefer new patrons. William Hamilton Merritt immediately recognized that these impressive literary talents ought to be enlisted in his own campaign for a reciprocity treaty. At the same time Keefer's opinions on the ways in which Montreal might reconstitute its faltering commercial empire after the repeal of the Corn Laws and the Navigation Acts caught the attention of the Montreal merchants – most notably the Honourable John Young – who seized the opportunity to bring this young engineer's pen and expertise to the aid of their own commercial ambitions. For the next several years Keefer served two not always compatible masters: reciprocity and Montreal metropolitanism.

Merritt secured Keefer temporary employment surveying the St Lawrence rapids in 1849. Then, when the time was right, he recommended him to Israel D. Andrews, the energetic American consul general for New Brunswick, as an able Canadian collaborator in the fight for reciprocity. Accordingly Keefer spent the better part of two years gathering trade statistics and drafting memoranda on the volume and character of Canadian-American commerce which Andrews incorporated in his two *Reports* issued in 1850 and 1852. It was a pleasant enough time – the food and drink were unsurpassed – but the life of research assistant and lobbyist did not particularly suit Keefer's more active engineering temperament. Afterwards he harboured bitter memories of this phase of his career when, like so many of Andrews' associates, he failed to get paid for his work.[7]

Keefer found the role of consulting engineer to the Montreal commercial interests much more to his liking. To the merchants the author of the *Philosophy of Railroads* and the *Canals of Canada* was an obvious ally in the unending struggle for more government assistance. He could be relied upon to apply his engineering knowledge to those physical problems which impaired the growth of Montreal commerce and at the same time report his findings in an engaging, authoritative, and thoroughly readable style – a rare combination of skills. The Honourable John Young became his patron and commissioned him to report upon a number of harbour and river works which might improve downstream navigation. His most important assignment, also obtained through the influence of Young, required him to locate the best site and recommend the most appropriate construction technique for a railroad bridge to connect Montreal Island with the south shore. The Victoria Bridge was subsequently built on the site he selected (but not according to his specifications) by Robert Stephenson, the British engineer. Much later the omission of Keefer's name from the tablet marking the opening of the longest tubular bridge in the world stirred up a brief nationalist controversy as to who was its true author, Stephenson or Keefer. Some hint of this debate can be detected in the editorials from the Toronto *Leader* reprinted with the *Sequel to the Philosophy of Railroads* in this collection.[8]

In short, Keefer was expected to mobilize the new steam and iron technology behind Montreal's commercial ambitions. As an engineer he sought to demonstrate in convincing style how the harbour and river ought to be improved, where the bridges and railroads should be built – all at public expense of course – and how these improvements would serve the interests of Montreal. Besides expounding these themes in his numerous technical reports, Keefer also delivered two popular lectures at the Mechanics' Institute, one of which is reproduced here, on the relationship of Montreal to its western and northwestern hinterland.

Important as all this was, Keefer aspired to greater responsibility and glory. He was, after all, an engineer (he invariably identified himself as T.C. Keefer, CE). Instead of merely writing and talking about railroads he desperately wanted to build one. For a time it seemed that through the good offices of his influential Montreal friends he might get the opportunity. In 1851 the Montreal merchants hastily got up two railroad companies to be first in the field should a western trunk line ever be built. The provisional directors of the Montreal and Kingston and the Kingston and Toronto railways then instructed Keefer to undertake preliminary surveys for the route. It appeared that he would play a leading role in planning and building the very trunk railroad he had proposed in the *Philosophy of Railroads*. In a couple of months of furious activity Keefer gathered up the required data and issued two glowing reports which the directors printed in support of their application to the legislature for a charter. But with that Keefer's association with the project ended. Again he became a casualty of politics. To his bitter disappointment he was not retained as chief engineer of the project when the Grand Trunk Railroad absorbed these two corporations in 1852.[9]

Perhaps as consolation he was retained to design and oversee the construction of Montreal's municipal waterworks. This assignment, which occupied most of his time from 1852 to 1856, opened up a new and important phase in his career. Though he would continue to be best known for his views on railroads, the only detailed engineering work he would ever personally undertake derived from his experience building this more prosaic but equally necessary public utility in Montreal. Although he encountered some difficulty with the municipal politicians at the outset and then construction problems inflated costs well above his initial estimates, Keefer's waterworks won praise from his fellow engineers. Walter Shanly, a friend but sometimes also a jealous rival, pronounced the project 'a magnificent thing – the finest thing of the kind on the continent. He is getting everything up in the best style.'[10] Building the waterworks for Canada's largest city immediately established Keefer's reputation as an hydraulic engineer. Thereafter he was in constant demand as a consultant on similar projects all over British North America. During the late 1850s and all through the 1860s Keefer drew up engineering studies for waterworks in Toronto, Hamilton, Halifax, Quebec City, Dartmouth, London, and St Catharines and for harbour works in Saint John and Richibucto. That, aside from writing a few promotional reports for several small and basically speculative canals and railroads, was the extent of his practical engineering career. He would never fulfil his first ambition – the building of a major railway – but he did succeed in becoming Canada's leading authority on municipal water systems.[11]

It was more as an essayist and spokesman for an emerging engineering profession than for any remarkable development work of his own that T.C. Keefer came to be identified in the public mind as one of Canada's foremost engineers. Standing as he did on the sidelines of the really spectacular building projects of the day, equipped with technical ability and a sharp pen, and animated by disappointed ambition, Keefer launched a full-scale critique of the railroad boom. After having been denied the rewards and honours he thought rightly his, Keefer turned to exposing the scandalous behaviour of the railroad promoters and his fellow engineers. As a remedy for these abuses Keefer proposed to establish engineering as a profession alongside medicine and the law. But in his case, and I suspect in many others, the element of personal disappointment in the drive towards professionalism should neither be overlooked nor underestimated. After all, the idea of a professional was a weapon to be used against those who called themselves engineers or performed engineering functions by men who considered the title and the activity exclusively their own. They wanted the jobs – at the time regrettably held by unworthies – the opportunities, honours, and, of course, the material rewards. It was even better that the interlopers actually were, or could be made to appear, scoundrels. At the very least the concept of professionalism offered the consolation of a sense of moral superiority to losers such as Keefer. The last two essays in this collection date from this phase in Keefer's development as a professional engineer.

Keefer pursued patronage relentlessly. He identified his personal success at place-seeking with the promotion of the interest of the entire profession. By the time he reached middle age the assiduous cultivation of influential people brought Keefer some of the rewards – honorific and monetary – which he so eagerly sought. In 1851 he played a marginal role in assembling the Canadian exhibits for the Crystal Palace Exposition held in London. Eleven years later Keefer served as Canadian commissioner at the second London International Exhibition. He became in effect the political spokesman of Canadian engineering and material progress at world's fairs. For the 1878 Paris Exposition Keefer assembled the Canadian exhibit, drafted the triumphant catalogue of accomplishments that went with it, served as executive commissioner of the Canadian delegation, and – the greatest honour of all – he acted as one of the jurors in the engineering competitions. For his service to his country and to engineering Keefer was decorated with the Legion of Honour by France and a Companionship in the Order of St Michael and St George by Great Britain.

He was also instrumental in organizing his fellow engineers and the intellectual community of which he felt himself a part into societies to promote the advancement of knowledge and professional conduct. He helped to found among others the American Society of Civil Engineers, the Canadian Society of Civil Engineers, and the Royal Society of Canada. In recognition he was elected first president of the Canadian Society of Civil Engineers in 1887, the following year served a term as president of the American Society of Civil Engineers, and in 1898 was honoured with the presidency of the Royal Society of Canada. McGill University conferred an honorary doctorate upon him in 1905 and six years later he was made an honorary member of the prestigious Institute of Civil Engineers of

Great Britain. Thus he lived to receive some of the highest honours that the profession he had helped to build could bestow. Although his actual achievements were modest, to many people Keefer personified the best qualities of the engineering profession. An urbane, erudite, physically attractive public figure, he was one of those individuals whose wide personal esteem brought welcome dignity to an emerging profession.

Although he never actually built any railways, he never lost his affection for them and never stopped promoting them. In 1869-70 he urged a Pacific railroad upon the newly confederated dominion in a series of letters to the Montreal *Gazette.*[12] When, as president of the American Society of Civil Engineers in 1888 he addressed the annual meeting at Milwaukee, he lectured his colleagues on the engineering wonders of the recently completed Canadian Pacific Railway. Even in his remarkable 1899 presidential address to the Royal Society of Canada, in which he projected an ecstatic vision of the tremendous industrial future that lay ahead for Canada in the hydroelectric age, the one prospect that particularly excited his imagination was that of smokeless, high-speed, electric trains racing noiselessly between clean, well-lighted cities.[13]

That in outline is the career of the affable, cultivated, aggressive, and slightly pompous author of the pamphlets, essays, and addresses in this collection. It was a career crowned with honour to be sure, but it was also not without its bitter disappointments and cruel ironies. A man renowned for his judgment on railways, Keefer had no practical experience with them. The archetypal engineer, he was more of a representative and promoter of the profession than an accomplished builder. Although he dismissed politicians as corrupt, meddlesome intriguers bent upon furthering the cause of friends and lining their own pockets over advancing science and human welfare, he owed his entry into the profession, his official posts, and his later decorations to political influence. And despite the fact that he wrote voluminously on a variety of subjects in the course of a long life, he continued to be best known for his first, slim pamphlet, the *Philosophy of Railroads.*

3

In the mid-nineteenth century, before the role of the engineer had been narrowly defined and his conduct ringed with a code of professional ethics, the civil engineer was expected to perform a number of duties which, in a more highly organized, specialized society, would normally fall outside the province of the profession. Public relations was one of those tasks. If the railroad promoter could not do it himself, he would commission an engineer to draw up a glowing assessment of the practicability, permanent worth, and miniscule cost of his project. The object of such a document was, of course, to whip up enthusiasm for the undertaking and thereby assist in the raising of money. Usually the engineer would take an armchair survey of the district through which the canal or railroad would run; he would collect voluminous data on landforms, crops, and commerce; take note of the technical problems to be met; and provide an estimate of the cost. His report of supposedly objective facts, concluding always with booster-like enthusiasm for the future of such a work, would be printed in pamphlet form and distributed widely to soften up private investors and politicians in charge of the public purse. Keefer's *Philosophy of Railroads* is a splendid example of this genre.[14]

T.C. Keefer first spoke on the subject of railroads in July 1847 when – ironically – he accurately predicted the collapse of one. On that occasion he pointed out in a series of public letters (reprinted in his pamphlet) that the little portage railway from Montreal out to the head of the Lachine Rapids would be of no benefit to either the city or its owners. 'The Lachine Road will be a partial failure,' he boldly explained before it opened, '*because the route is too short* and the expense very great. The cost of furnishing and managing will be as great as for a road ten times its length, while only one-tenth of the fare can be exacted.' To his mind the sooner it failed the better. Then Montrealers could provide themselves with the kind of transportation they genuinely needed.

Keefer argued that the continued prosperity of the city depended upon forging a rail link with Toronto, thereby outdistancing Americans in the competition for the western trade. Until that point in time Montrealers – to the extent they had interested themselves in railroads at all – had concentrated first upon building portage roads to facilitate the movement of goods around rapids (such as the Montreal and Lachine railway on the island and the Champlain and St Lawrence on the south shore) and then, inspired by John A. Poor from Portland and A.T. Galt from Sherbrooke, upon promoting a line eastward towards Portland in Maine (the St Lawrence and

Atlantic). Besides improving communications with the agricultural districts of the eastern townships, the St Lawrence and Atlantic promised Montreal an all-important winter outlet to the sea. Without denying the value of the Portland line, Keefer insisted that western railroads were its necessary complement. What use would a road to tidewater be if American cities had already penetrated Upper Canada with railroads and drained off its commerce to other Atlantic ports? Montreal, if it hoped to remain competitive, could not depend upon its canals alone to bring down this trade from the west, nor could it hope to force the trade of Upper Canada through the canals to its wharves by law. The merchants of the city would have to reach out beyond their puny Montreal and Lachine line and capture the business of the west and the Ottawa district with railroads.

In 1849, amid talk of a possible Main Line project linking the Maritime colonies with Canada West, the directors of the Montreal and Lachine line recognized the advantages of proposing a western extension of their route. The most they could expect would be to be included as a link in the Main Line – with all the benefits of public assistance that implied – and the least would be to have their charter bought up – at a considerable premium – by whoever undertook to build such a route. They turned to their former critic, the then unemployed T.C. Keefer, to draw up a pamphlet that would persuade a sceptical public of the need for more railroads and the legislative assembly to grant their project a charter and generous financial support. The *Philosophy of Railroads* was the memorable result.

In less than a year the pamphlet went through three editions and a revised fourth edition in French was published in 1853. According to a contemporary biography of T.C. Keefer, the wide circulation and extensive reprinting of the pamphlet in numerous newspapers '... contributed more than any other to aid in the railway agitation which secured the completion of the Great Western, the Toronto Northern, Port Hope, Cobourg, Ottawa, and Grand Trunk Railways.'[15] Apparently, too, Keefer's essay also saw service in the promotion of several Maritime and New England railroads. But whatever the direct impact of the *Philosophy of Railroads* may or may not have been is beside the point for the moment; it was one of the most successful pamphlets of its kind and in Canada the source of much that was thought and spoken on the subject of railroads during the 1850s. For those reasons alone its contents warrant consideration.

What did Keefer intend by the word 'philosophy' that adorns his title and pivots the concluding sentence of his superb opening paragraph: '... blockaded and imprisoned by Ice and Apathy, we have at least ample time for reflection – and if there be comfort in Philosophy may we not profitably consider the PHILOSOPHY OF RAILROADS.' What followed this arresting introductory passage – whose themes of confinement and consolation echoed Boëthius – was most certainly not a treatise on either the physics, metaphysics, ethics, or aesthetics of the steam railroad. At the same time Keefer's concern went deeper than the mere utility of railroads. In his own words, he set out to 'investigate the Railway System in its applicability to new countries – to define its limitations by shewing where and why its application becomes justifiable ...' By philosophy, then Keefer seems to have meant something like knowledge of the logic of the railroad system. He sought to introduce the *idea* of railroads, in particular the conception of the railroad as a train of consequences as opposed to a simple line of track. In the long run the social, economic, and moral implications of the railroad would be more far-reaching than its modest appearance would at first suggest – an argument that he summed up in the memorable sentence: 'Steam has exerted an influence over matter which can only be compared with that which the discovery of Printing has exercised upon the mind.' The aim of the *Philosophy of Railroads* was to establish a direct linkage between the railroad and the noblest ideals of the age, and to illuminate the process through which steam technology would necessarily advance the material improvement and moral perfection of man – thus the felicity of that pretentious word, philosophy.

In thesis and tone Keefer's essay closely resembled Andrew Ure's much more famous, similarly titled, apology for the British factory system published fourteen years earlier, *The Philosophy of Manufactures*. This uneven work is justly remembered for both its naïveté and insight concerning the functioning of the well-ordered industrial kingdom to come. In his celebrated third book on the 'Moral Economy of the Factory System' Ure defended factory production against its numerous critics in what has been described as a 'lyric poem' on the inherent progressivism of industrialism. No less an agency than Providence, Ure claimed, had assigned to man 'the glorious function of vastly improving the productions of nature by judicious culture, and of working them up into objects of comfort and elegance with the least possible expenditure of human labour – an undeniable position which forms thc basis of our Factory System.' Operating from that premise Ure explored the benefits and requirements of industrialization, insisting that reason demanded the subordination of some human impulses – in this case the capriciousness and rebelliousness of the working classes and the reactionary envy of the aristocracy – to the imperatives of that system.[16] Keefer's tract was in fact the thesis of Ure's third book applied to railroads.

Keefer had obviously heard of Ure's previous work and it is entirely possible that he had read it. But his brief pamphlet was by no means a direct copy of *The Philosophy of Manufactures,* however derivative its spirit may have been. After the statement of title and theme, the resemblance between the two essays ends. Of the two Keefer's was much the shorter, primarily because he devoted no space whatever to the mechanics of railroading – probably because he kept in mind his popular audience and free distribution. Nor was the *Philosophy of Railroads* as defensive in tone or as concerned with the problem of industrial discipline as its counterpart. Although both men were philosophers of the stultifying, utilitarian ethics of what Lewis Mumford has identified as the 'paleotechnic phase' of industrialism, Keefer displayed a humanity, grace, humour, and concern with the intellectual development of society entirely lacking in Ure's work.[17] The sacrifices demanded in the name of progress by Keefer were far less stringent than the regimentation, righteousness, and self-denial insisted upon by Ure. Though Keefer's focus was more narrowly colonial and pragmatic, his values were perceptibly broader. In general, the basic difference between the two essays was one of context. Both authors professed faith in the capacity of technology to promote commerce and civilization: whereas Ure wrote in defence of a system against its critics, Keefer wrote to urge the adoption of the railroad system where it did not exist.

Keefer's task consisted of describing the revolutionary potential of railroads, of showing how they acted as the indispensable agents of advancing civilization, and, lastly, of convincing his countrymen that they could afford to build them. The goal of his philosophy was action. He composed his essay to inspire enterprise and overcome inertia: 'to disseminate popular information upon a too unpopular subject, and to turn a portion of that earnest and eager covetousness of foreign prosperity back upon our own neglected resources.' Here again we are reminded that the philosophy of railroads had to be learned; it was not self-evident. What qualities did railroads possess that made them so infinitely superior to the existing means of transport? What would railroads contribute to the march of progress in general? And, more pertinently, where should the track be laid and how should construction be financed? Those were the questions T.C. Keefer retired to his study to answer on behalf of his patrons in the Montreal business community.

Why did the railroad constitute a qualitative leap forward in the history of transportation? Because it brought distance, and therefore time, under human control. The steam engine imparted to movement through space the regularity and consciousness of time associated with the mechanical clock. In the revealing cliché that has been applied to every major transportation improvement since, the railroad 'annihilated' distance. The amazing speed of the steam locomotive – in less than a generation the pace of the civilization accelerates from fewer than ten to more than fifty miles per hour – seemed to bring distant places closer. Toronto would be less than a day instead of a week or more away; that was a form of control. And steam released man from the bondage of nature. Motion no longer depended upon animals or the wind; nor could the seasons impose a ban upon the movement of goods. When the canals were locked in ice, the carriages and waggons over their hubs in mud, when storms raged and calm prevailed, the train pressed rhythmically onward, impelled by its own man-made demon. The regularity, control, and speed of the railroad vastly improved the capacity of economic man, whether a farmer or merchant, to respond quickly to price fluctuations in distant markets. Steam and iron united in the railroad strengthened the power and extended the sway of the invisible hand of the market system.

What civilizing wonders would the railroad work upon the backwoods society of the Canadas? To illustrate his answer Keefer borrowed one of the best-known scenes from Washington Irving's *Sketch Book*. He would create a pastoral Sleepy Hollow of his own inhabited by a race of amiable but unenterprising Rip Van Winkles.

Then, by introducing a railroad, he would transform the valley into a prosperous, enlightened seat of industry. Steam would bring this quaint community, whose venerable churchyard was slowly filling up with tombstones, suddenly to life; the impatient screech of the whistle would drive out the self-satisfied indolence of former days. New crops must be cultivated first to feed the construction crews and then the wants of the distant city. In due course a bustling town springs up in the valley itself. And just as surely as the railroad had quickened activity in Sleepy Hollow it also broadened the outlook and elevated the conduct of its inhabitants. 'While the physical features of our little hamlet are undergoing such a wonderful transformation,' Keefer observed as he shifted attention from the click of the loom, the rushing shuttle, the hum of the spindle, the thundering trip-hammer, and the roaring of steam, 'the moral influence of the iron civilizer upon the old inhabitants is bringing a rapid "change over the spirit of their dreams." ' Wave upon wave of new people, styles, products, and ideas that flow into the valley over these rails bury the parochialism of its citizens and set new dreams and ambitions stirring. Tranquillity, Keefer seemed to be saying, was in reality the outward appearance of ignorance, suspicion, and domination, particularly in matters related to exercising the franchise. The 'iron civilizer' provided an antidote to what he called this state of primitive, but not innocuous, simplicity that prevailed in Sleepy Hollow:

> Poverty, indifference, the bigotry or jealousy of religious denominations, local dissensions or political demagogueism may stifle or neutralize the influence of the best intended efforts of an educational system; but that invisible power which has waged successful war with the material elements, will assuredly overcome the prejudices of mental weakness or the designs of mental tyrants. It calls for no co-operation, it waits for no convenient season, but with a restless, rushing, roaring assiduity, it keeps up a constant and unavoidable spirit of enquiry or comparison; and while ministering to the material wants, and appealing to the covetousness of the multitude, it unconsciously, irresistibly impels them to a more intimate union with their fellow men.[18]

Such then were the moral and material forces unleashed by the railroad.

Obviously, therefore, Canadians would have to equip themselves with railroads. They could not afford to live without them. Of course the railroads would come in time; but, Keefer asked, under whose direction would they be built and to whose profit would they redound? Montreal stood at a crossroads; it could either seize the opportunity presented by the railroad or be left behind in the race. If the merchants continued to dream that the St Lawrence would become the main artery of commerce for the continent and that Montreal would serve as its entrepôt, then the canal system would have to be immediately complemented by a trunk railroad. Otherwise, the lamentable history of the Erie Canal's effect on the St Lawrence would be repeated in the railroad era. American cities would drive roads deep into Montreal's natural hinterland – as they were already doing – and once again Upper Canadian business would be drawn to the ambitious ports of the American eastern seaboard.

Nor would the railroads compete with the canals if they were properly laid out. For example, just at the time the colony's major export, wheat, brought its best prices the canals were frozen solid. Business losses on that account alone, Keefer calculated, were sufficient to build fifty miles of railroad a year. In summer the trunk road would generate sufficient local business along its route through the promotion of trade and manufacturing to sustain itself. In due course it would win the higher quality business of a much increased through traffic. The first priority then lay in connecting Montreal with Toronto and the Great Western system beyond Hamilton.

But who would build such a line and how would it be financed? Canadians (especially Montrealers) would have to take the initiative, formulate plans, mobilize their collective resources, and seek out foreign investors. A trunk railroad of this magnitude would not and should not be built for them by outsiders. And a shortage of capital, which was the normal negative response to grand railway projects, was of less hindrance, Keefer insisted, than timidity and doubt: 'Zeal and enterprize, directed by a knowledge of our subject, are more rare and efficient commodities than the mere possession of capital; because they will carry capital and all other things with them.' Keefer and men like him could supply the expert knowledge and help in the kindling of enthusiasm, but that would not be enough. The businessmen and substantial citizenry of the towns would have to divest themselves of their stand-offish individualism and learn to combine in associations or corporations to undertake this enormous responsibility. The 'habit of association' characteristic of Americans, Keefer argued, accounted in part for their remarkable success with the railroad system. Nevertheless, even if private companies did not exist or could not command the confidence necessary to accumulate the savings of the community for productive purposes, all was not lost. Those corporations that did exist, municipal corporations, could step into the breach. If the society was unfamiliar with the capital requirements of business and the forms of business organization, those familiar corporate bodies close at hand could be modified to perform the required role. A number of American states had constructed successful rail systems under various forms of public enterprise before the appearance of a well-developed private system of capital formation. In Canada, too, wealthy individuals, in co-operation with local and provincial governments, could just as effectively plan a system, raise the necessary funds, and build the railroad themselves. The assembly had already provided a Guarantee Act to secure the interest on the bonds of railroads that might become links in a Main Line route; similarly, the municipalities could pledge the credit of their citizens to worthy railroad ventures. All that was missing to bring these elements successfully together, Keefer observed, were entrepreneurs of vision and courage supported by informed public opinion. He hoped that the *Philosophy of Railroads* would inspire both.

The essay is notable as much for its style as for its argument. Keefer was no mere compiler or artless scribbler. He was a master of what used to be called rhetoric and the essay as a whole is a model of persuasion. Keefer's favourite device is the goading comparison; if others had measured up to the task, what could possibly be holding back Canadians? Whenever he wants to capture attention or clinch an argument he merely juxtaposes information (all of it carefully selected) of Canadian and American conditions. Familiar literary borrowings and allusions strengthen the impact of the argument and lighten its mood. His imaginative reconstruction of Sleepy Hollow and his ability to transform it so easily draws upon and is deepened by Washington Irving's popular success. Vanity and stubbornness, if they cannot be observed in ourselves, can be recognized readily enough in others – especially literary characters. Similarly, Keefer's delightfully overdrawn caricatures of Canadian intemperance and indulgence contrasted with the frugality and industry of 'leaner brethren' and 'rectangular cousins' to the south recalls to mind Sam Slick working up to one of his swaggering, didactic harangues. Of course T.C. Keefer and Thomas Chandler Haliburton shared an identical purpose: the encouragement of their reluctant fellow colonists to get on with the really important business of building railways.

The first, second, and third editions of the *Philosophy of Railroads* did not differ substantially one from the other. Besides an expansion of the appendices, the main addition to the third edition of 1850 consisted of the second last paragraph of the text in which the Canadian reader is shamed – even frightened – into activity for yet another time by the example of the 'restless, early-rising, "go-a-head" people' of the United States. It is a minor but illuminating point, but in the same edition Keefer quietly removed the evidence from Appendix L which seemed to suggest that the British railroad bubble had burst in 1849 – which of course it had! The main revisions came during the preparation of the French edition in 1853. The fact that the essay was being republished by a rival to the Grand Trunk, the projected route of which passed through some French-speaking counties along the north shore of the Ottawa River, explains most of the alterations from the earlier English versions. Naturally enough most of the glowing references to the southern route which hugged the St Lawrence and the lakeshore were dropped. But so were the passages recommending railroads as a speculative investment. For the benefit of his new audience Keefer installed some new appendices emphasizing the value of railroads to farmers, and a conclusion complimenting the progressive municipalities of Upper Canada for taxing themselves to obtain the railroads they needed. This latter insertion, coming where it did in the text, introduced an interesting ambiguity (intentional or not?) as to who the people 'inquiet, matineux, marchant en avant' might be – Americans or Upper Canadians.

4

After the success of the *Philosophy of Railroads* was crowned by the Governor General's prize for the *Canals of Canada*, T.C. Keefer, engineer and essayist, enjoyed a brief vogue in Montreal. In due course he was invited to repeat his literary triumphs in a series of popular lectures (the first of which is reprinted in this collection) at the Montreal Mechanics' Institute. Never one to conceal either himself or his views with an excess of modesty, Keefer eagerly seized the occasion to address the yeomanry of the city on the subjects closest to his heart: railroads, metropolitanism, and progress – the transportation philosopher's trinity.

Keefer's genius both as a writer and as a speaker was his knack of sizing up his audience – in this case the artisans, shopkeepers, workingmen, and their wives assembled in the gaslight before him – and making a direct connection between his views and their concerns. He carefully tailored his message, both its style and substance, to its context. Here at the Mechanics' Institute, for example, he would speak to plain, practical men such as himself and he would do so in straightforward, unadorned language. Although he would address himself to their meanest commercial desires, he would do so in such a way as to gratify their noblest images of themselves. 'It is usual, I know, on these occasions to make the subject a scientific one, to take up some of the -isms or the -ologies, and expound them,' Keefer began. 'If I am guilty of any innovation in meddling with the domestic affairs of this City, my apology is that having been honored with a request to address you, I am more anxious to benefit than to amuse you. We are a practical people, and we live in an eminently practical age, and what more edifying, what more profitable subject can the Mechanics of this City discuss, than the causes which favor or which threaten the prosperity of Montreal.' Whether it was before an audience of academicians, engineers, politicians, or shopkeepers, T.C. Keefer was a master applicator of what Sam Slick liked to call 'soft sawder.'

There was no better way to begin than by expressing absolute faith in the will of the people. What was progress, after all, if not the realization of the enlightened self-interest of rational, honest, hardworking men such as those gathered in this very hall? If only that popular will could assert itself then the prospects of the colony and the civilization were truly boundless. The problem, of course, was that a number of obstacles, man-made and natural, appeared to stand in the way. As a first step in overcoming these impediments men had to be made aware not only of their best interests but also of the instruments that were at hand to fulfil their ambitions. The process of education, it turned out, was especially important for the working classes, misled and mystified as they had been by the shameless ignorance, idleness, and personal indulgence of their political and social leaders. 'We live in a country, thank God! where almost every man has some influence ...'; therefore, it was possible for ordinary men to command politicians to do their bidding. Thus Keefer shrewdly pointed out, as he moved in from the general to the more particular, 'if the working classes study the resources and wants of their districts and devise any enterprise for its welfare, they can carry it because they have the votes.' Democracy and technology were allies in the liberation of the progressive spirit. But the time was short. As is the case with most inspirational orations, an undercurrent of challenge and doubt imparted a sense of urgency to Keefer's secular sermon to the mechanics of the city. While Montrealers wiled away their hours amid the January snows curling on their canal basin their rivals were busily engaged in the interior carrying off their commerce. Beyond the proverbial allusion lay the threat of biblical judgment.

What was the message Keefer wished to leave with the workingmen of the city? It was simply: Wake Up! There are railroads, canals, factories, and futures to be built. And where did their duty lie? It consisted chiefly in demanding strategic public works and taxing themselves to get them.

The future prosperity of the city depended, Keefer argued, upon the immediate and forceful assertion of an informed, intelligent public opinion. Keefer believed that the democratic principles of politics also ought to be applied to the community's economic affairs: 'Nearly all great public works, here and elsewhere, are to be ascribed to the efforts of a few individuals generally deemed visionaries, humbugs, or rogues, by their contemporaries; but, in these latter days, our wants accumulate so rapidly that we should no longer wait for the appearance of apostles or champions of progress to lead us on; this was the feudal, the despotic system, but if we are capable of governing ourselves, we ought to be able to prescribe for ourselves and order what we want.'

At the risk of interrupting T.C. Keefer in full flight it should perhaps be noted that another interpretation can be put on his insistence upon public involvement in transportation improvements. It might be repeated that, in a relatively backward but economically ambitious society in which capital markets are poorly developed and entrepreneurship scarce, the state is often compelled to perform those functions that in a more thoroughly developed economy might be undertaken by individuals or companies. Where private means are inadequate or the task is too great the only corporate bodies, the colonial and municipal governments, must be mobilized to do the job. Keefer correctly believed that undertakings as expensive as railroads could not be built without political aid and initiative. Therefore popular feeling had to be stirred up for necessary projects and then directed upon the legislature or city hall to secure the required charters and funds. We might, therefore, substitute the meaning 'aroused and manipulated public opinion' for the 'independent public initiatives' referred to in his text. But of course in Keefer's mind – and every other promoter then and since – the two meant the same thing.

Like a canny merchant Keefer proposed to begin his discourse by taking stock. Where did Montreal stand? What would it require to maintain its commercial hegemony in the years ahead? The answer, of course, was a predictable list of harbour and navigation improvements, bridges, canals, and western railroads. There is no need to go into the particulars. The thrust of the argument in the public lecture on Montreal is much like that in the *Philosophy of Railroads;* namely, that Upper Canada was the natural hinterland for the city and that its American rivals were already drawing off that trade with new railroads. Rather than try to defeat this invasion with 'class legislation' or trade restrictions that required Upper Canadian commerce to pass through the hands of the Montreal merchants, Keefer insisted that Montreal should quickly get about building its own railroads and improving its communications. That way the commerce of the interior would come down to the city *naturally* through the best, most convenient, and most efficient channels.

Three qualities set Keefer's lecture apart from his pamphlet and justify its reprinting. First, the lecture was intended to whip up popular enthusiasm not for the Grand Trunk scheme but for a short-lived competitor, the St Lawrence and Ottawa Grand Junction Railway, that planned to strike west through the Ottawa country to Lake Huron and Georgian Bay. Secondly, in the lecture Keefer was led to reflect upon the urban dimension of metropolitan expansion. As surely as the new technology would tighten Montreal's grip on its commercial hinterland, it would also transform the city itself. And, finally, in the last few moments of his address Keefer expanded upon his idea of progress, the unifying theme of all his written work.

During the previous summer the government of the united Canadas had finally approved construction of a trunk railroad – the project, it will be remembered, that the *Philosophy of Railroads* had been written to promote. But the railroad authorized by Francis Hincks' administration would be built and owned by English contractors on terms T.C. Keefer found disagreeable. Thus by the time he delivered this lecture in January 1853 Keefer was no longer associated with the Grand Trunk project. In this procession of events Keefer had also changed his tune somewhat. Now he contended that the Grand Trunk, being situated so close to the St Lawrence River, would be of no great use to Montreal. 'We must look after the backing,' he warned, 'otherwise the benefits will be too superficial – we will be all front without the proper depth and solidity.'

What Montreal really needed, Keefer now maintained, was a railroad that would penetrate what he called the back country and tap the lucrative trade of the Ottawa Valley:

> The location of the Trunk Line on the front, as a provincial work for through travel and the mails, therefore not only justifies but creates a necessity for another line in the rear, which can neither be called a parallel nor a competing one: for it will do a business, and create a business which cannot and will not be done by the Trunk Road. Such a route is now absolutely essential for the protection of the interests of this City as a means of preventing the tide of the Ottawa trade from flowing toward the St. Lawrence and thus placing it in dangerous proximity to the Ogdensburgh road.

It will come as no surprise to learn that T.C. Keefer was then the chief engineer for a railroad that proposed to do just that, or that his second lecture to the mechanics of Montreal was a lyric account of the agricultural and commercial possibilities of the Ottawa Valley.

But Keefer's plans for the St Lawrence and Ottawa Grand Junction Railway did not end at Bytown. From there a second railroad would be driven westward through the forest and rock of the Shield to the shores of Georgian Bay. Equipped with these two railroads and a fleet of ships the city of Montreal could thus capture the trade of the American midwest, the Upper Lakes region, and, ultimately, the North West. The engineer's vision was that of the commercial empire of the St Lawrence restored[19] – and more, for beyond Bytown a transcontinental destiny beckoned the merchants of the city. In the meantime, should money prove tight, construction of a short line into the Ottawa district would suffice as a necessary first step.

In both the *Philosophy of Railroads,* which he wrote for the Montreal and Lachine Railroad, and his lecture on Montreal, for the St Lawrence and Ottawa Grand Junction Railroad, Keefer strove to turn the attention of the Montreal commercial classes westward. In his view far too much effort and enthusiasm had been spent obtaining rail connections with the sea and too little on gaining access to the interior. Keefer believed that the success of a city depended upon the amount of territory it could bring under its control, and, therefore, the volume of trade it could oversee. Because he understood the relationship between improved communications and the process of urban growth Keefer valued western railroads more highly than eastern ones – and the more the better.

It is also worth noting that although his early pamphlets and lectures were written to promote two very different projects Keefer conceived of both railroads within the same metropolitan frame of reference. His plans for both the Montreal and Lachine and the St Lawrence and Ottawa Grand Junction railways aimed at the ultimate restoration of Montreal's inland commercial empire. But was this dwelling upon metropolitan aggrandizement merely a device to enlist public money behind a private interest? Boosterism has always been the quickest, most reliable route to public favour. Notwithstanding the 'soft sawder' already referred to, there is a certain innocence about Keefer and a grandeur about his vision that sets him apart from the ordinary run of promoters. Despite his reputation as a man of science, Keefer was more convincing as an artist, as a poet of metropolitanism. He gathered up the scattered ambitions and random thoughts of various groups in the city and spun them into an integrated heroic vision. No doubt as far as the financiers employing him were concerned Keefer was little more than a spellbinder. His supposed expertise gave their projects credibility; his vision added a glow of respectability and public service, and his artistry suffused their designs with urgency. Though they might delight in the poet's creation they nevertheless remained outside of it. Not so Keefer; he was a dreamer among schemers, dreaming dreams that other men found useful.

On this occasion Keefer afforded his audience a brief glimpse of a new city by the mountain. Keefer recognized that the technology that promised to restore Montreal's hegemony over its Upper Canadian hinterland would also fundamentally change the city itself. Metropolitan success implied new forms of urbanization. The railroad and the forces it represented would irresistibly transform the compact, commercial city by the river into an industrial metropolis. Once again Nature had amply prepared the city for this role. Montreal might not be situated upon fathomless beds of coal, but it did command a source of energy probably just as good, the St Lawrence River. Keefer confidently predicted that 'The water power of the St. Lawrence capable of driving ... millions of spindles will sooner or later be called into activity. Our magnificent rapids cannot much longer be allowed to flow uselessly to the sea – the admiration of travellers – the toys and playthings of romantic maidens – the gigantic rocking horses of annual flocks of tourists who come and go as regularly as the wild geese.' Montreal was destined to become the manufacturing centre of the colony; it would supply, not just forward, the necessities, luxuries, and services required by an ambitious, productive people. Then the warehouses by the harbour would be joined by teeming factories; chimneys would vie in height with church steeples, and a whole new class of industrial workers would mingle with the labourers, teamsters, mechanics, craftsmen, and merchants in the streets. It was a prospect at once bright and forbidding.

Obviously T.C. Keefer and men like him did not peer ahead into gloom. He did not conceive of industrial cities as 'mere man-heaps' and 'machine-warrens' like later critics would.[20] The future consisted largely of light and hope. But why? As his address ought to remind us, the commercial city harboured horrors too. There was much that required improvement before the coming of industry. Although they might vary with the seasons, fire, disease, misery, and destitution were permanent residents of the commercial town. As Keefer mordantly observed: 'Fire is the only thorough scavenger for a city badly drained: and it is perhaps fortunate that the same poverty which causes our early towns to neglect their drainage also builds of combustible materials, thus providing the future fuel for the purifying process.' Inspired by what Asa Briggs has called the 'sanitary idea,'[21] technology would be able to purge the city of its perils. For example, water and sewage systems – both interestingly enough the inventions of the civil engineer – would dramatically improve standards of public health and public safety. In short, Keefer hoped that the rational, scientific principles upon which the railroad, the factory, and the industrial city ultimately rested would find a social application as well. Keefer saw the causal link between the railroad and the factory, but he would have strenuously denied that slums and what they stood for were to be necessary conditions of industrialism. Quite the contrary; economic growth impelled by science and technology seemed to offer the first real hope that poverty, illiteracy, and squalor might be eradicated. 'Ignorance and prejudice will flee,' Keefer beamed, 'before advancing prosperity.' With the factories humming and the trains steaming back and forth with the produce of the country and the goods of the city, men would be able to attend to the hitherto neglected physical and moral needs of their society. Decent almshouses could be provided for the poor and libraries stocked to satisfy the popular yearning for knowledge; riverside parks and geometric public squares would then import light, freshness, and dignified perspectives into the dingy, crowded city. As far as Keefer could see into the future, the new Montreal, the industrial city that would develop naturally upon a foundation of technics, metropolitanism, and the civic gospel, would represent a vast improvement over the old cramped and contaminated commercial town in which he and his audience presently lived.

Keefer's optimism sprang primarily, of course, from a profound faith in the inevitability of progress. For him history was the record of man's advancement, however unsteady and halting during certain eras, towards an earthly paradise. Surely the signs and portents that mid-Victorian man lived in a specially chosen age, one during which the entire civilization was bounding forward towards the goal with unsurpassed speed, could not be mistaken by even the meanest intelligence: 'And may not we be entering upon those latter times, when many shall run to and fro and knowledge shall increase? and may not the vast, the almost incredible extension of the Railway system, the Electric Telegraph, and the Ocean Steamer over all the Christian Earth, be a forerunner – a necessary and indispensable forerunner – to that second great moral revolution, the

Millenium ... [?]' Had not Britain carried the civilizing power of her language, culture, and commerce to the four corners of the globe? Did the agents of Anglo-Saxon ascendancy, science and improved communications, not harken back to the last great flowering of human achievement, Imperial Rome? And could it be denied that the new science and the new steam highways were vastly superior to the old? Mankind stood, therefore, upon the threshold of a new imperium infinitely grander than the noblest civilization of them all. Should not the humble mechanics, the men listening to his closing words, draw strength and pride from the knowledge that they were not just part of this triumphant procession, but that they were its driving force?

And shall not the mechanic, even the pioneer of progress, lift up his eyes from the work bench and look ahead? Has he, the humble instrument in a mighty revolution, no right to think on such things? ... as you ply the busy hammer or wield the heavier sledge some of you may dream that you are fast driving nails into the coffin of prejudice, of ignorance, of superstition and national animosities; that as you turn down the bearings or guide the unerring steel over all the 500 parts of a locomotive engine, fancy will picture you cutting deep, and smooth, and true, into obstacles which have so long separated one district, one family, one people from another – and ... you may exult in the reflection that those huge drivers will yet tread out the last smouldering embers of discord, that those swift revolving wheels – by practically annihilating time and space and by re-uniting the scattered members of many a happy family – will smooth the hitherto rugged path, fill up the dividing gulf, break through the intervening ridge, overcome or elude the ups and downs of life's chequered journey, and speed the unwearied traveller upon his now rejoicing way.

T.C. Keefer was not so much a prophet of the idea of progress as one of its hot gospellers.

In recent, less self-assured times, the elements and underlying assumptions of this idea of progress have attracted a great deal of critical attention.[22] According to Laurence Fallis, Jr., the historian of this faith in mid-nineteenth century Canada, its central tenants were:

> ... that growth and development were central to the historical process and that the movement of Canadian history was linear and progressive; second, that Canadians possessed the resources – physical, economic, social and human – to carry out successfully a program of sustained internal development; third, that Canadians through the use of science and technology would master the new environment and place the secrets of Nature at the service of man; fourth, that education would provide an enlightened citizenry so essential to the realization of the dreams of the social utopians; and finally, that the favourable moral climate of North America would encourage social amelioration and moral regeneration.[23]

In most respects Keefer might be considered a representative spokesman for this persuasion. But there is a hint in what he preaches of a slight deviation from the conventional North American canon. Some time ago Rush Welter distinguished between the European and American variants of the idea of progress.[24] He suggested that Europeans conceived of progress as a revolutionary process, as a drastic disruption of the present and a qualitative stepping upward to a new level of consciousness. Americans, on the other hand, routinely thought of progress as the mere unfolding of the present. That did not require any great revolutionary effort. *America was progress,* whereas Europeans could only visualize progress being unleashed by a radical reformation of society. In Europe the idea of progress was by its very nature revolutionary, but in an American context it was essentially conservative.

What is especially interesting about Keefer's only partially formulated conception of the idea of progress in this context is the fact that his millennium was neither as secularized nor as firmly attached to his present as Rush Welter would have us believe the American idea was. The Christian and at times apocalyptic quality of Keefer's thought is perhaps stronger than one might expect from an otherwise secular, thoroughly North American, writer. Keefer's rhetoric, for example, draws heavily upon Fundamentalist allusions; he connects the sacred and the profane by juxtaposing biblical quotations with business aphorisms. His thought, at this point, becomes blurred. Keefer avoids direct consideration of the revolutionary-conservative, imminent-inherent problem. However incomplete, his discussion ought to remind modern readers that the

Canadian idea of progress has not yet been studied in a comparative context. What was derivative and what was unique about the gospel being proclaimed by men like T.C. Keefer at mid-century?

The lecture on 'Montreal' forms a perfect companion piece to the *Philosophy of Railroads.* It focuses attention upon the utility of the steam railroad within the context of an actual metropolitan strategy. Secondly, it anticipates some of the internal economic and social changes that Montreal would undergo as a direct consequence of projecting a communications system out upon its hinterland. Finally, the revivalist conclusion of the address brings the doctrine of progress to the surface, the ideology upon which so much of T.C. Keefer's thought depends.

Both essays might be taken as typical illustrations of Keefer's buoyant, pre-railroad frame of mind. His optimism knows no limits and the promotional spirit completely dominates his critical faculties. But, as we shall see, in the years that were to follow disappointment would temper his enthusiasm and sharpen his judgment.

5

We are a little ahead of ourselves. In tracing the development of Keefer's thought from the *Philosophy of Railroads* forward to his lecture on Montreal we have lost sight of T.C. Keefer, the practising civil engineer. A man's ideas, after all, ought properly to be considered in their social context. It is essential, therefore, to examine Keefer's engineering career up to and beyond his lectures to the Mechanics' Institute. How did the railroad philosopher and poet fare as an engineer once railroad construction got under way? How did his vision of the railroad system stand up against its unfolding actuality? The near pessimism of the final two selections provides an illuminating contrast to the indiscriminate boosterism of the first two essays. As T.C. Keefer surveyed the headlong rush to build railroads during the 1850s, ironically he found more to damn than to praise. Gradually, the philosopher of the railroad became its most trenchant critic.

When in late 1850 the Montreal merchants organized themselves into two companies with the expressed purpose of planning a trunk railroad to the west, their choice of a chief engineer fell upon

T.C. Keefer.[25] Basically he was retained to carry out a preliminary survey of the route and to draft an attractive report on the practicality of the project which would be printed, as usual, to elicit government aid. Thus, in his own mind at least, the author of the *Philosophy of Railroads* seemed destined to become chief engineer of the colony's most important railroad.

Excellent social connections and success as a pamphleteer were in fact his principal qualifications for the job. As far as his colleague Walter Shanly was concerned Keefer owed his appointment more to social and literary distinction than to any demonstrable technical competence or previous experience. Shanly fumed that Keefer could '... get any Road he wants because they think him H[oly] since he wrote his books.' Shanly, who was toiling manfully for the shaky Bytown and Prescott Railway at the time, was highly annoyed that Keefer should automatically be assigned the preliminary responsibility of surveying the route, especially since he knew that Keefer did not have the slightest idea where to begin. 'Tom Keefer has got no regular appointment,' Walter explained to his brother Francis; 'He merely has been employed to run a line of levels from Kingston to Toronto – preparatory to application for a charter – for which he receives £ 250 – a nice little sum as the whole thing will not take him more than two months. He is allowed assistants enough to do all the work – & he himself will not I suppose walk over a mile of the ground.' Although he was a close friend of Keefer's, Walter Shanly nevertheless grumbled to his brother that these jobs were not awarded on the basis of merit and experience – that is, to Walter Shanly: 'He came to me when on his way up to commence the work and actually did not know how to begin locating a railway ... Now there is nothing wrong with an Engineer who has never been on Railway work not knowing the practice of it – but it is absurd that where I could get the superintendence for [a] 50 mile Line, Tom could get 500 – in Canada.'[26]

The eventual report of Keefer's survey of the Kingston-Toronto section would corroborate some of Shanly's allegations. As puffery for a charter it was no doubt solid enough, but as an engineering document it was vague and evaded particulars. The general principles of locating the line came through clearly, but it left a great deal of latitude on the exact placement of the rails and stations. Keefer explained that he proceeded by finding the most northerly limit of navigation on the rivers running into Lake Ontario and then connected these points. The resulting route ran in a sweeping arc well inland from the lake. Although this route would be longer he argued that it possessed distinct advantages over a more direct path. It would open up the back country; it avoided the hills and deep gullies along the front; and it afforded gentler grades along its entire length. His route, he freely admitted, would not be the cheapest, but in the long run it would generate more traffic for itself than the lakefront route and would prove to be more economical to operate. Keefer's report resembled the *Philosophy of Railroads* more closely than it did a detailed engineering study. Its tone was predominantly promotional. That, of course, was its intent. It was prepared not so much with a view to guiding the grading crews as it was to inspiring legislators and municipal politicians along the proposed route.[27]

But from this first assignment Keefer clearly expected to be retained as chief engineer during the all-important design and construction phases of the work. His employers, however, may have had plans of their own. In his history of the Canadian National Railways, G.R. Stevens concluded that the Montreal and Kingston and the Kingston and Toronto railways were in fact nothing more than ground staking companies. Galt, Holton, and the rest of the Montreal group had merely contrived to plant themselves in such an advantageous position that their charters would have to be bought up – at a handsome profit to be sure – when the genuine railroad builders arrived on the scene.[28] What this thesis lacks in supporting evidence it makes up for by the fact that this is what happened. When Francis Hincks, representing the Canadian government, struck a bargain with the famous British railroad contractors, Peto, Brassey, Jackson and Betts, to build the Grand Trunk line (from which he too is alleged to have profited), these two ephemeral railroads standing in the way were quickly swallowed up by the new company. If such a strategy existed beforehand it would appear that Keefer had not been privy to it. Again the evidence is indirect and all *post hoc.* Francis Hincks' Grand Trunk reorganization of 1852 neither enriched Keefer nor satisfied his ambition. In fact it did him considerable harm. The owners could make peace with the newcomers – after extortionate terms of sale had been extracted from them – but Keefer never! *His* project had fallen into the hands of British contractors. He could never come to terms with them – any terms. Disappointment and outrage swept him well beyond the bounds of discretion.

When the Grand Trunk proposals came before the Assembly in 1852 T.C. Keefer launched a stinging attack upon them in the press. Many of his charges later proved to be well founded, but they were no more palatable to the new proprietors on that account. He argued that the new British owners would build and operate the railroad without reference to local needs. 'Thus after paying the highest price for a road constructed in defiance of local wishes, it will be thrown back on our hands, having been managed "by reference to the board at home," damaged in reputation, and not improbably, worn out in track and gear, by the cupidity or indifference of temporary non-resident tenants.' The scheme not only offended his nationalism, it also affronted his sense of professional propriety. He objected to the position of Peto, Brassey, Jackson and Betts as both principal owners and contractors for the road. That, he suggested bluntly, opened up unlimited possibilities for what he liked to call 'chiselling.' Moreover, instead of saving money by amalgamating with the Great Western beyond Toronto the new company proposed to build an expensive, duplicate line of its own. Finally, in language that foreshadowed later criticisms of Macdonald's railway policy, Keefer warned against the tremendous powers of patronage that Francis Hincks would inevitably exploit: '... wielding that power through a project which extends throughout the entire length and breadth of the land, he can defy the whole army of politicians – who can only oppose principle to *interest,* agitation to a *con*sideration.' From the outset, then, he condemned the absentee ownership, manipulation by contractors, and political intrigue which in his mind would bedevil the project and would most certainly spell the ruin of respectable Canadian railroad proposals thereafter: 'We tremble for the name and fame of Canada when we reflect with what hot haste this Jackson business has been spurred on ... The public character of Canada is to be prostituted in the London stock market, and used as an engine to extract their means from distant and confiding men and women.'[29]

Keefer may have been right, but he was on the wrong side. The Grand Trunk scheme went through and the project which he liked to think he initiated went ahead without him. Peto, Brassey, Jackson and Betts had engineers of their own and it was unlikely that either the railroad company or the politicians whom he had maligned would hire him as their engineer. Keefer's impetuosity succeeded only in cutting him off forever from the Grand Trunk project. By contrast, the Shanly brothers, who appear to have thought along much the same lines as Keefer in the matter, kept quiet about it and did very well for themselves.[30] After 1852 Keefer was merely a spectator. He had the waterworks contract for an income and for interest's sake he continued to serve the disaffected Montreal merchants as the chief engineer of their unlikely rival to the Grand Trunk, the St Lawrence and Ottawa Grand Junction Railway Company. But these assignments could hardly erase his disappointment.

While he nursed this private grievance against the project he pressed a more substantial monetary claim against the company. The Grand Trunk had absorbed the charters and obligations of its Canadian precursors but it had failed to pay T.C. Keefer for the work he had done on the preliminary surveys of the route and the Montreal bridge. After repeated appeals he had received a reduced payment for his surveys but nothing at all for his report on what would become the Victoria Bridge. Meanwhile, as Keefer brought his small private request for relief before the public, the Grand Trunk itself tottered on the brink of collapse. Costs had outrun estimates, waste and scandal had been rife, and the stock could not be sold in England; the project would fail unless the government advanced an immediate guarantee of the interest on some £ 900,000 of the company's bonds. At length, in June 1855, the government of Sir Allan MacNab agreed to extend the terms of the Guarantee Act and provide the required aid, but its support was contingent upon the receipt of a favourable report on the progress of the road from independent engineers.[31]

In the summer of 1855 Keefer's name had been mentioned in connection with this examining board. He was one of the few engineers in the country who had no immediate vested interest in the project and he could, therefore, be counted upon for an objective, third-party opinion. Keefer had made far too many enemies, however, to be given this delicate assignment. In addition, an impartial investigation was the last thing desired by a government whose politics were railroads and a railroad whose business was politics. The engineers' report was to be so much window-dressing got up not so much for the benefit of the Canadians (who knew well enough what was going on) as for the potential British bondholders. Once again Keefer found himself shut out in the cold.

As a contribution to the brief and marginal controversy that blew up over the appointment of the government engineers, T.C. Keefer compiled a curious little pamphlet which he called *A Sequel to the Philosophy of Railroads.* It was more than just the petulant reply of wounded pride to a vicious newspaper attack – though there was enough of that in it. The title implied a logical connection between the two pamphlets and the circumstances that inspired each. If the purpose of the *Philosophy of Railroads* had been to reveal the moral and material implications of the idea of railroads, its *Sequel* was a treatise, teaching by example, on the ethics of their construction. As he stood gloomily on the sidelines, permanently alienated from his own project, Keefer had been led to contemplate some of the corrupting forces unleashed by railroads and the role the *professional* civil engineer might play in eradicating them. It is this aspect of the controversy and the pamphlet that gives them a wider significance. Disorganized, incoherent, and particular though the *Sequel* might be, it does provide a convenient point of departure for an examination of the professional impulse among Canadian civil engineers.

The facts of the controversy are straightforward enough. When T.C. Keefer failed to receive the appointment a friend of his in the legislature asked why. Some time later the Honourable John Ross, who had formerly been both a member of the government and president of the Grand Trunk Railroad, replied explaining that Keefer was thought to be an inappropriate choice because he had a claim outstanding against the company whose affairs he would be required to look into. From a private source Keefer also learned that another reason advanced to explain his unsuitability for the job was that he had refused to work with the chief engineer of the Department of Public Works. William Killaly is known to have had a strong aversion to the Keefer brothers (his one time rivals and critics) and T.C. Keefer's contempt for Killaly is readily apparent in these appended documents.[32] Keefer candidly admits that he considered Killaly on trial. To subordinate himself to a civil servant was in Keefer's mind as dishonourable as bearing a brief for the company. The latter is precisely what he accused the engineers who were subsequently appointed of doing. The real reason for his being overlooked, he suggested, was that he refused to acquiesce in the cozy relationship that had grown up between the government and the company, the civil servants, the company engineers, and the contractors. He would submit a professional, honestly critical report; that, he claimed, would never be accepted by either the government or the company. It would have been, however, in the best interests of the country.

Keefer's letters of explanation and a report of his lectures given at McGill brought forth a bombastic counterattack from the Toronto *Leader,* the government organ and stalwart defender of the Grand Trunk Railroad against all comers. In substance the *Leader*'s editorial argued that the real reason behind Keefer's rejection was not his self-proclaimed impartiality but his incompetence. It proceeded to document his alleged failures. The *Leader* refused to print Keefer's equally detailed rebuttal; however, the *Globe* did. Keefer effectively refuted the specific charges and in the process heaped a good deal more abuse and sarcasm upon the manner in which the Grand Trunk had been constructed. For this he was rewarded with a classic *ad hominem* attack which was in some particulars beside the point but in others painfully close to the mark. Where, the *Leader* wanted to know, had Keefer gained the practical experience necessary to undertake the duties for which he thought himself fit? 'It is notorious that he left no trace of his labors behind him. His work was incomplete, and entirely valueless [in locating the route of the Grand Trunk], and he knows better than anyone else, that the line was not taken because it could not be found ... The fact is, that Mr. Thomas Keefer has lived on the reputation of his pamphlets and his projects.' The *Sequel to the Philosophy of Railroads* was Keefer's only reply to this assault.

By collecting the letters and lectures that stated his side of the argument he obviously aimed at clearing his name and vindicating his position. But in pulling all of this material together under that title Keefer also intended a comment upon the way in which railroads suborned politicians, journalists, and even engineers. The real issues could not be debated rationally in such a libellous, partisan atmosphere, nor could the real interests of science and society be treated as long as civil engineers continued to be junior partners in 'the firm of Grab, Chisel & Co.' In these circumstances Keefer proposed a non-partisan status for engineers beyond the immediate control of governments and corporations.

These *Leader* editorials, Keefer's letters of explanation, and his lectures to the students at McGill expose some of the seamier aspects of Canadian railroad building in the 1850s. Taken together they offer several perspectives upon the venality and pettiness of nineteenth century railroad politics. To that extent they also help to reconstruct the troubled atmosphere within which the idea of professionalism emerged.

Keefer's role as an outsider – though not exactly an impartial one – enabled him to see things clearly and to say things more directly than those caught up in the rough and tumble of the boom. Of course he was also a very disappointed man. Yet another opportunity of reconciliation with the railroad interest (which incidentally he eagerly sought) had slipped through his grasp. Publication of the *Sequel to the Philosophy of Railroads* tended only to widen the gulf between himself and those in command, and to reconfirm his spectator status. But the critique of railroad politics that he developed in his lectures rested upon something more substantial than bitterness. He was genuinely repelled by the corrupt alliances that had grown up between politicians, contractors, and civil servants, primarily because the discreditable results threatened to undermine completely the early promise of the railroad. In earlier, happier days, of course, he had not been so morally fastidious. Now he did not just want a piece of the action for himself; he wanted to be a railroad engineer to be sure, but on totally different terms than those that prevailed. His alienation led him to wonder how all of this might be changed.

The huge new undertakings and parallel growth of the great contracting firms, Keefer argued, had dwarfed the engineer. Only a few unpleasant options remained open. He could either work in a minor capacity for a contractor, fret out an insecure and insignificant career in the public service (Keefer had done both), or, if he was ambitious, he might launch a contracting enterprise of his own like Casimir Gzowski. But his usual employment was that of a junior partner in the firm of Grab, Chisel & Co., or as a pawn of venal politicians. Only the greatest engineers, men like the Stephensons and Telfords, ever escaped this vortex. Keefer did not blame the hapless engineers; he knew at first hand the insecurity and family obligations that forced them to place their jobs ahead of their conscience. He simply wanted to draw public attention to the predicament in which all engineers found themselves: '... to secure an honest Engineer,' Keefer reported gloomily, 'you must first establish honesty in the Corporation or Government which appoints him; because it is a melancholy fact that appointments have been made, not in ignorance, but *because* dishonesty was a primary qualification, a necessity, and because one Engineer could be made a scapegoat for many politicians ...'

There were objective standards according to which bridges should be built and railroads laid down. However, politicians, promoters, or contractors could always find good reasons – usually the lining of their own pockets – for deviating from them. Invariably, the engineer, whose duty it was to protect the community by guarding these standards, had to submit to the force of circumstances. How could this apparently inevitable drift from the *Philosophy of Railroads* to its *Sequel,* from the idea of railroads to its debasement, be reversed? What steps could be taken to enhance the engineer's power in this brawling jungle of private interests? Keefer's answer was the twofold one of public education and professional status.

Only an 'enlightened, a moral and above all, a vigilant constituency' could guarantee the integrity and intelligence of government and corporations in these matters. 'If the people, therefore, complain that they are plundered and deceived, they have themselves to thank for it, in their indifference to the character and motives of adventurers who, unasked, thrust themselves upon them, and by the aid of their prejudices, bigotry and a suborned press, obtain control of their affairs.' Keefer hoped that publicity and political action would in due course replace bad men with good men: 'The best antidote to this incompetency in politicians and their proteges, with respect to engineering subjects, is to supply each political party with a sufficient amount of engineering ability, so that when they have no higher motive than the credit of their party, they may at least have the means of making a good appointment ...' Indeed, Keefer thought it necessary that engineers themselves, even though they might be better employed, should become candidates: 'Had there been even a few Engineers in our Parliament (as is the case in the British) there might have been a little less of folly – and something more than folly – perpetrated there.' Doctors and lawyers had entrenched themselves politically; next it would be the engineers' turn. A little courageous political involvement by engineers and greater public vigilance would, in Keefer's view, go a long way towards bringing order out of chaos. But in themselves they would not be enough.

The civil engineer had also to be accorded professional status. Without the respectability, security, independence, and power of a recognized professional, Keefer argued, the civil engineer could not perform the duties expected of him. If he had to guarantee the mechanical soundness of public works the engineer required at least the same status as the doctor, for example, who held similar responsibilities over the individual's welfare. And the foundation of independence was financial security:

When engineers whose services are sought after assume the same position as lawyers and doctors, decline to be chartered by any party, but take as many clients or patients as they feel they can do justice to, it will not be in the power of the Government or a corporation to dismiss them to begin the world anew, when past the spring time of life, and laden with the support of a family. This position once established, the engineer is no longer necessarily a wandering Bedouin, but, by being able to have a fixed habitation he has some inducement to store, and having secured independence of position he may sustain independence of character.

With security he could not be tempted; with stature he would command respect and be trusted in the exercise of power.

The ideas expressed in Keefer's lectures were not particularly original. He made no claim for them on that account. His modest observations upon the condition of engineering concluded with a conventional appeal to faith in liberal measures (such as public education) and élitist institutions (such as professions). Nor was his treatment of his subject especially comprehensive. There is little to be found here on the topics of entry into the profession, professional education, or any detailed discussion of a code of ethics. In his defence it might be noted that he would devote the better part of his later career to founding and maintaining two vital professional associations whose preoccupations were just those sorts of problems.[33]

The point is, however, that the very appearance of these lectures, particularly the context within which they came to light, is important evidence concerning the professional impulse. A cynic might observe that as far as Keefer was concerned professionalism was a way of displacing unscrupulous rascals and installing in their place trustworthy, upright men such as himself. Much of the emphasis upon income security might be seen as a function of Keefer's all too regular unemployment during these years. But that surely is only part of the truth. Professionalism was most certainly a weapon in a power struggle, a weapon mobilized by men of a certain class and used against other men of their class and other classes. In particular cases it was a struggle over jobs, to be sure. But professionalism might also be seen as a group striving, as a collective response to a new problem. T.C. Keefer might be looked upon as a representative young man from the established classes, equipped with an education that already distinguished him as someone of privilege, attempting to carve out an influential niche during the first stages of the industrial revolution in Canada. How was privilege to maintain itself in the future without a broad financial or political base? The answer: by commanding knowledge in an age when, as Keefer himself reminded his student audience, 'Knowledge is power.' Possession of both, of course, made the case for some sort of social distinction as well.[34]

The *Sequel to the Philosophy of Railroads* introduces a modern reader to a society in which everything is in flux, in which roles have not yet been defined, and in which work has not yet become fully divided or bureaucratized. Economic and technological forces have destroyed the old familiar relations between proprietors, master builders, craftsmen, and labourers, and altered the distinction between things public and things private. But new patterns have not yet emerged. In looking into the past the historian tries to rediscover the social and economic context that gives rise to social movements and within which they gain a foothold and contend for power. Keefer's *Sequel,* in its own partisan, idiosyncratic way, should help us to understand the complex circumstances and antagonistic environment from which the conception of a professional civil engineer evolved.

6

The final article in this collection, a railroad chronicle published in 1863, brings to a fitting conclusion the cycle Keefer began fourteen years earlier with the *Philosophy of Railroads.* In the interim the railroad madness had descended upon the Canadas with a fury Keefer himself found bewildering. By 1860, 1900 miles of railroad were in operation and many more were planned or under construction. In retrospect what did Keefer think about the impact of the railroad upon Canadian society – about the way Canadians had taken his *Philosophy* to heart?

An invitation from Henry Youle Hind to contribute an essay on transportation to a volume entitled *Eighty Years' Progress of British North America* provided Keefer with the occasion to record his reflections.[35] Hind, a noted explorer, essayist, editor of literary and scientific periodicals, geologist, chemist, and professor at Trinity College in Toronto, had assembled a distinguished group of authors to compile what Laurence Fallis has called the most significant tract of progress written in nineteenth century Canada.[36] Hind wrote two articles himself on the geography and economy of British North America, while others contributed essays on natural resources, the history of education in the Canadas, and the progress of the Maritime colonies. Keefer responded with a lengthy history of 'Travel and Transportation' (slightly less than half of which is reprinted here) that was in some respects curiously out of harmony with the ruling spirit of the volume.

Hind's compendium, as its title and more particularly its subtitle suggest, was to be a hymn to progress. 'From the days of Herodotus, to the middle of the last century,' Hind observed in his preface, 'the world made little progress. It is true that great empires rose one after another upon the ruins of their predecessors; but so far from there being anything like real progress, the reverse seems to have been the case. It has remained for the present age to witness a rapid succession of important inventions and improvements, by means of which the power of man over nature has been incalculably increased, and resulting in an unparalleled progress of the human race.' Nowhere on earth was proof of that proposition more apparent than in North America. But as a rule commentators contented themselves with recording the achievements of the United States. This neglect of the British North American provinces, Hind remarked, was thoroughly unjustified, for in the eighty years since the American Revolution their progress had been, in many respects, more prodigious:

> ... they have at least kept pace with their powerful southern neighbours, and ... though laboring under some disadvantages, they have in eighty years increased tenfold, not only in population but in wealth; they have attained to a point of power that more than equals that of the united colonies when they separated from the mother country. They have, by means of canals, made their great rivers and remote inland seas accessible to the shipping of Europe; they have constructed a system of railroads far surpassing those of some of the European powers; they have established an educational system which is behind none in the old or the new world; they have developed vast agricultural and inexhaustible mineral resources; they have done enough, in short, to indicate a magnificent future – enough to point to a progress which shall place the provinces, within the days of many now living, on a level with Great Britain herself, in population, in wealth, and in power. If in the next eighty years the provinces should prosper as they have in the eighty years that are past, which there seems no reason to doubt, a nation of forty millions will have arisen in the North.[37]

It was up to Keefer, therefore, to recount the ways in which successive communications improvements opened up the interior and unleashed these progressive capabilities.

No one seemed better qualified for the assignment than T.C. Keefer. He was, as we have seen, Canada's foremost advocate of the railroad, chief symbol of the progressive spirit which Hind's volume was designed to celebrate. Keefer had played a role, albeit a controversial one, as chief engineer of several railroads; so he appeared to speak with authority. He was also a recognized authority on the canal system. Finally, he was a man of strong opinions who knew how to write. Yes, Keefer would do the job and settle some old scores at the same time.

For ninety pages or so Keefer's essay proceeds as one might expect: forest trails turn into macadamized roads; canoes and sailboats give way to steamships; canals ascend the great rivers; the electric telegraph spins out its web, and accordingly the pace of commerce and settlement pick up. Then the 'iron civilizer' makes its appearance. It is at this point that this excerpt begins, and the whole tone of his article changes. How curious it is, in an ode to transportation progress, to find the greatest railway of the province pronounced a 'magnificent,' 'complete and disastrous' failure. In a most unexpected turn of events, instead of contributing to the general progress of civilization, railroads seem to have led to its demoralization.

There is no need to rehearse Keefer's lamentable tale in any detail. Besides being a standard source of useful information, it is also one of the more spirited, revealing passages in Canadian railroad history. After a century it may still be read with profit. The classic sections on the 'Grand Trunk Railway' and 'Railway Morality' have not yet been superceded.

Keefer recounted with obvious relish Francis Hincks' mysterious dealings with the firm of Peto, Brassey, Jackson and Betts that led, in his mind at least, to the betrayal of the Grand Trunk idea. Having been a victim himself, he drew some considerable personal satisfaction from the self-evident moral and financial bankruptcy of the revised scheme. Keefer then exposed the corrupt methods of the British and American railroad buccaneers who descended in droves upon the lobbies of the legislature during the 1850s. Nor did the supposed innocents, the colonial small fry of political knaves and posturing local magnates, escape his ridicule. Indeed, there are moments of high comedy to be found here. And, finally, disappointed to the point of distraction, Keefer concluded abruptly with a grumpy, not wholly rational, attack on street railways – perhaps the most revolutionary transportation improvement of his time, the one that would have the greatest social impact of them all.[38] In short, as Keefer told the railroad story after the fact, it was one of unrelieved villainy, robbery, and moral lassitude.

Keefer offered a number of explanations for the failure of the Grand Trunk and other railroads to live up to their earlier promise. In the case of the Grand Trunk he continued to believe that it had been a mistake to hand over such an important public work to foreign, private enterprise. The source of much later difficulty could be traced back to that first, fatal decision. Secondly, the foolhardy extension of the project at both ends had unduly encumbered the profitable sections of the road later. So too, the overgenerous terms by which the Grand Trunk leased and bought out connecting lines weighed down the entire enterprise when it became an operating proposition. But the greatest mistake, from which so many others inevitably stemmed, was to allow the railroad to be built and owned by the same contracting company:

The system under which the road was constructed was a vicious and illegitimate one, the order of things being reversed from that in well-regulated corporate enterprises. The only way in which an honest and efficient construction of any railway can be guaranteed, is that where *bona fide* shareholders elect their directors, who appoint the engineer and solicitors, and invite competition before the contract is given out. Thus those who expect to become the owners of the property have some control over its formation. But in the case of the Grand Trunk, the contractors assumed the risk of floating off the shares and bonds in consideration of getting a contract upon their own terms, with a board of directors, and an engineer and solicitor, of their own selection (and deriving their fees and salaries through them), to carry them through those all-important preliminary stages when the future shareholders are irrevocably bound, and in too many cases have their interests sacrificed, to those of the contractor.

From this set of circumstances the alternate skimping and extravagance, the plundering, the incompetent management, and all the rest naturally flowed. The Canadian people had been fleeced in the Grand Trunk job; looking around, Keefer could not see that their experience with other railroads had been appreciably better.

Most, if not all, of the responsibility for this state of affairs rested with Canadians – at least Canadian politicians. Keefer concluded that railroads had been thrown down in too great haste principally because they had been used to gull credulous investors. With the full knowledge, even connivance of the responsible political authorities, a magnificent system of transportation had fallen into the hands of corporate charlatans. It would have been better had Canadians taken their time and built their railroads as public works when they were needed. But that chance had been missed. In the present situation all one could do was hope that adjustments in the rate structure would produce enough local traffic to make the big railroads break-even propositions before they ruined the reputation and credit of the colony.

This story of folly and political corruption is familiar enough. The only real problem that it raises is the one of reconciling it with Keefer's expressed belief in the doctrine of progress.

Notwithstanding the gloomy, discordant tone of the essay, Keefer had not lapsed into pessimism. It can be argued, I think, that he had not lost his faith in progress, and certainly not his confidence in the intrinsic progressiveness of technology. What he had lost was his confidence in men. Keefer's ideal railroad existed only in the mind of God. He no longer looked out on the world with the same rosy, wide-eyed optimism of the *Philosophy of Railroads.* While he continued to pin his hopes upon invention and the infinite possibilities of new machines, he tempered that enthusiasm with reservations about man's ability to use them intelligently. Even though technology marched forward, judging from the experiences of Canada in the 1850s, it was by no means certain that human nature had kept pace. Science would continue to open up dazzling opportunities, but these hopes, like the railroad, could still be squandered or discredited by greed. Technology had ordained progress, but it had not eliminated original sin.

Surely the very existence of sin was a contradiction in the progressive universe? Perhaps, but under firm control it could be tolerated. And by implication the instruments of constraint were again public opinion and professionalism. The *Sequel to the Philosophy of Railroads* had argued the case for professional recognition; the essay on 'Travel and Transportation' supplied the evidence for its necessity. That is clearly part of the underlying connection between the two essays. If the record was anything to go by, Keefer implied, inventions could not be trusted to ordinary men or conventional procedures. A whole new class of professional men had to be created within the social system to mediate the inevitable struggle between intentions and temptations. Properly organized and duly recognized, this group of professionals would warrant the trust of the community and protect its interests in these all-important technical matters. But such a group could only be effective when politics had been purged and the conditions of public probity reinforced. Thus, informed public opinion was an essential ally in the professionals' struggle to unfetter man's progressive capacities. These measures could not eliminate, but they would curb, his baser impulses. This then was the basis of Keefer's continuing optimism.

This collection offers an interesting sample of one man's thought as it developed during the middle years of the last century. It opens with an expression of hope, the *Philosophy of Railroads.* The lecture on 'Montreal' that follows particularizes those expectations, and in passing reveals the philosophical foundation upon which they rest. The *Sequel to the Philosophy of Railroads* brings us back down to earth, to a world of careers and grasping personal ambitions as well as transcending metropolitan dreams. As a defence against the delinquencies it exposes and the final essay amply documents, Keefer makes a case for social reform based upon professional institutions and vigilant public opinion.

At one level these essays say a great deal about nineteenth century railroads and in their context they offer some insight into nineteenth century Canadian society. At another level they represent a cycle, from enthusiastic idealism to realism, in one man's thought. And on yet another level they introduce us to the historian's problem of establishing relationships between ideas and the material conditions within which they appear.

Finally, these essays, pamphlets, and lectures should be read with questions in mind. The ethos which we see here in the process of formation is, for the most part, behind us. T.C. Keefer's lyric advertisements to a generation that had yet to learn about the properties of the steam railroad, seen in the context of his own experiences with and strictures against the railroad builders of the day, should assist in our re-examination of the railroad as a factor in nineteenth century Canadian social and economic history. Critical reflection upon Keefer's disappointments as an engineer during this first great Canadian railroad barbeque and his compensating professional drive thereafter should serve as yet another reminder that the professions in Canada still lack their historians and, on that account, our social and intellectual history is the poorer.

NOTES

1 Robert Fogel, *Railroads and American Economic Growth: Essays in Econometric History* (Baltimore, 1964), pp. 1, 15, 207-8, 235; for a bibliographic survey of the controversy, see Paul A. David, 'Transportation Innovation and Economic Growth: Professor Fogel On and Off the Rails,' *Economic History Review*, 2nd series, XXII, 1969, pp. 506-25.

2 For the most recent interpretation of the Canadian Pacific as Canadian nationalism, see Pierre Berton, *The National Dream* (Toronto, 1970), and *The Last Spike* (Toronto, 1971); for Peter George's views, see 'Rates of Return in Railway Investment and the Implications for Government Subsidization of the Canadian Pacific Railway: Some Preliminary Results,' *Canadian Journal of Economics,* I, 1968, pp. 740-62; 'Recent Developments in the Quantification of Canadian Economic History,' *Histoire sociale,* IV, 1969, p. 88; and his introduction to the reprint of H.A. Innis' *A History of the Canadian Pacific Railway* (Toronto, 1970).

3 Biographical information on the Keefer family can be found in Rev. Robert Keefer's *Memoirs of the Keefer Family* (Norwood, Ont., 1935); Henry J. Morgan, *Sketches of Celebrated Canadians* (Quebec, 1862), pp. 648-55; G.M. Rose, *A Cyclopedia of Canadian Biography* (Toronto, 1886), pp. 226-8; and *The Macmillan Dictionary of Canadian Biography,* ed. W.S. Wallace (3rd ed., Toronto, 1963), p. 359. For George Keefer's role in building the Welland Canal, see H.G.J. Aitken, *The Welland Canal Company* (Cambridge, Mass., 1954), pp. 28, 42-3, 52-3; J.P. Merritt, *Biography of the Hon. W.H. Merritt* (St Catharines, 1875), pp. 58, 63-8; and T.C. Keefer, *The Old Welland Canal and the Man Who Made It* (Ottawa, 1911), p. 13. On the social context of engineering professionalism in the United States, see Monte A. Calvert, *The Mechanical Engineer in America, 1830-1910* (Baltimore, 1967), pp. 8-10.

4 Daniel H. Calhoun, *The American Civil Engineer* (Cambridge, Mass., 1960), pp. 24-9, 47-53.

5 'T.C. Keefer and the Development of Canadian Transportation,' Canadian Historical Association, *Annual Report,* 1940, p. 37; see also George A. Rawlyk, 'Thomas Coltrin Keefer and the St. Lawrence-Great Lakes Commercial System,' *Inland Seas,* XIX, 1963, pp. 190-4.

6 *The Canals of Canada, their prospects and influence* (Toronto, 1850), pp. 33, 48, 66, 110-11, his italics; see also his later pamphlet, *Free Trade, Protection and Reciprocity* (Ottawa, 1876).

7 *Report on Reciprocity between Canada and the United States,* 31st Congress, 2nd Session, Senate Executive Documents, no 23; *ibid.,* 32nd Congress, 1st Session, Senate Executive Documents, no 112. For contrasting views of Andrew's role in the negotiations and

marginal comment on Keefer's participation, see D.C. Masters, *The Reciprocity Treaty of 1854* (Toronto, 1963 ed.); Irene D. Hecht, 'Israel D. Andrews and the Reciprocity Treaty of 1854: A Re-appraisal,' *Canadian Historical Review*, XLIV, 1963, pp. 313-29; D.C. Masters, 'A Further Word on I.D. Andrews and the Reciprocity Treaty of 1854,' *ibid.*, XVII, 1936, pp. 159-67; and W.D. Overman, 'I.D. Andrews and Reciprocity in 1854: An Episode in Dollar Diplomacy,' *ibid.*, XV, 1934, pp. 248-63. Keefer gave his own account of his activities in his plea for redress, *A Sketch of the Rise and Progress of the Reciprocity Treaty; with an explanation of the Services Rendered in Connection Therewith* (Toronto, 1863).

8 T.C. Keefer, *Report on a Survey for the Railway Bridge over the St. Lawrence at Montreal* (Montreal, 1853); *Report on the Dredging in Lake St. Peter and on the Improvement of the River St. Lawrence between Montreal and Quebec* (Montreal, 1855); A Montrealer, *The Canadian Engineer of the Victoria Bridge* (Montreal, 1860); A Canadian, *The Victoria Bridge at Montreal, Canada. Who Is Entitled to the Credit of its Conception? or, A Short History of Its Origins* (London, 1860); James Hodges, engineer to Messers. Peto, Brassey, and Betts, Contractors, *Construction of the Great Victoria Bridge in Canada* (London, 1860); and L.T.C. Rolt, *George and Robert Stephenson* (London, 1960), pp. 299-317.

9 See below, part 5.

10 Public Archives of Ontario, Francis Shanly Papers, Walter Shanly to Francis Shanly, 8 Dec. 1853. See also *Rapport sur une exploration préliminaire faites dans la vue de fournier de l'eau à la ville de Montréal* (Montreal, 1852); *Letter of the Chief Engineer in reply to a Resolution of Council for Information Respecting Water Works* (Montreal, 1856).

11 For details of this phase of his career, see John Charles Dent, *The Canadian Portrait Gallery*, IV (Toronto, 1881), pp. 134-7; the several biographical dictionaries listed above in n. 4; the bibliography (though not a complete one) of Keefer's writings in Royal Society of Canada, *Proceedings and Transactions*, 1894, Series I, XII, p. 46; and his obituary in *ibid.*, 1915, pp. x-xii.

12 6 April, 12 and 14 July 1869; 22 Jan., 2 Feb. 1870.

13 'The Canadian Pacific Railway,' American Society of Civil Engineers, *Transactions*, no 394, XIX, 1888; 'Canadian Waterpower and Its

Electrical Product in Relation to the Undeveloped Resources of the Dominion,' Royal Society of Canada, *Proceedings and Transactions,* 1899, presidential address.

14 Keefer would perform these largely literary services a number of times in his career; see, for example, *Reports of the Directors and Chief Engineer of the St. Lawrence and Ottawa Grand Junction Railway Company* (Montreal, 1853); *Report ... of a Survey of the Georgian Bay Canal Route to Lake Ontario by Way of Lake Scugog* (Whitby, 1863); and *The Canada Central Railway* (Ottawa, 1870).

15 Morgan, *Sketches of Celebrated Canadians,* p. 650.

16 *The Philosophy of Manufactures: or an Exposition of the Scientific, Moral, and Commercial Economy of the Factory System of Great Britain* (London, 1967 ed., originally published in 1835), pp. 1, 55-6, 278.

17 In this respect Keefer's little tract might be compared with other heavily technical manuals of the day, such as Nicholas Wood, *A Practical Treatise on Railroads, and Interior Communication in General* (London, 1832 ed.); R.M. Stephenson, *Railways: An Introductory Sketch, with Suggestions in Reference to their Extension to British Colonies* (London, 1850). For Mumford's critique of industrialism, particularly Ure's contribution to the ethos, see *Technics and Civilization* (New York, 1963 ed.), pp. 151-211.

18 On the recurring Sleepy Hollow metaphor in American literature, see Leo Marx, *The Machine in the Garden: Technology and the Pastoral Idea in America* (New York, 1957), pp. 11-33.

19 Keefer wrote: 'This route, when made, must become one of the great lines of this continent. It is a route worthy of this City. If Portland could project and successfully urge forward a route through the Mountains to Montreal – the latter with double her population may with confidence cope with an undertaking not more than double the extent. The particular and indeed supreme importance of this route when opened to the Western trade is that it would place Montreal on the route of the great American trade from West to East and vice versa.' On the concept of commercial empire, see of course D.G. Creighton, *The Empire of the St. Lawrence* (Toronto, 1956 ed.); for metropolitanism, see J.M.S. Careless, 'Frontierism, Metropolitanism and Canadian History,' *Canadian Historical Review,* XXXV, 1954, pp. 1-21.

20 Lewis Mumford, *The City in History* (London, 1966 ed.), pp. 508-48; see also his *Technics and Civilization*, pp. 163-82.

21 *Victorian Cities* (Harmondsworth, 1968 ed.), pp. 20-1.

22 Following J.B. Bury's groundbreaking study, *The Idea of Progress* (London, 1920), the bibliography of this fascinating subject has grown to enormous proportions. In recent years it has been of special interest to American intellectual historians. For a good short introduction to the literature, see the notes to Clarke Chambers, 'The Belief in Progress in 20th Century America,' *Journal of the History of Ideas,* XIX, 1958, p. 197 ff.

23 'The Idea of Progress in the Province of Canada, 1841-1867,' unpublished PH D thesis, University of Michigan, 1966, preface; see also his article of the same title in W.L. Morton, ed., *The Shield of Achilles* (Toronto, 1968), pp. 169-83.

24 'The Idea of Progress in America: An Essay in Ideas and Method,' *Journal of the History of Ideas,* XVI, 1955, pp. 401-15.

25 For details of the formation of the Montreal and Kingston and the Kingston and Toronto railways, see A.W. Currie, *The Grand Trunk Railway of Canada* (Toronto, 1957), pp. 3-30, and O.D. Skelton, *The Life and Times of Sir Alexander Tilloch Galt* (Toronto, 1966 ed.), pp. 27-48.

26 Francis Shanly Papers, Walter Shanly to Francis Shanly, 9 Feb. 1851, and same to same, 16 May 1851.

27 *Report of the Preliminary Survey of the Kingston and Toronto Section of the Canada Trunk Railway* (Toronto, 1851), pp. 4, 9-10, 15, 25, and *Report on the Montreal and Kingston Section of the Canada Trunk Railway* (Toronto, 1851).

28 For G.R. Stevens' interpretation of these events, see his *Canadian National Railways,* I (Toronto, 1960), pp. 68-9, 73-82. He styles these companies 'squatters on the route.'

29 Keefer's letter is quoted at length in Morgan, *Sketches of Celebrated Canadians,* pp. 652-3.

30 Walter Shanly was named engineer in charge of the Toronto and Guelph division of the railroad, and he in turn found a place for his brother. But then the Shanly brothers had a habit of containing their rage; see especially Walter to Francis, 3 Aug. 1853.

31 For details, see Currie, *The Grand Trunk Railway of Canada*, p. 38 ff., and J.M.S. Careless, *Brown of the Globe*, I (Toronto, 1959), p. 215 ff.

32 One evening early in 1851 shortly after Killaly had been appointed to to the post of chief engineer of the Board of Public Works he dropped in on a friend of Walter Shanly's to enquire as to Shanly's engagements. The government had decided to go ahead with the Montreal-Toronto railroad, Killaly reported, and it would need an experienced engineer to oversee the job. He had decided upon Shanly, the correspondent explained, among other things 'just to keep the Keefers out.' Shanly of course agreed with Killaly's assessment; namely, that he (Shanly) was '... the only Canadian Engineer who has any practical knowledge of Railway work – and I certainly *ought* to get the place if such a place is created.' Apparently Killaly's opinions on the Keefers were delivered, the correspondent explained, 'after he became drunk – so you may take it at its value.' Walter Shanly to Francis Shanly, 24 Feb. 1851.

33 Canadian Society of Civil Engineers, *Charter, Bylaws and List of Life Members* (Montreal, 1887); for Keefer's role, see the founding meeting, 24 Feb. 1887, p. 7; see also Canadian Society of Civil Engineers, *Transactions*, I, 1887, for Keefer as first president. The second president was Keefer's older brother Samuel; see II, 1888, pp. 9-44, for Samuel's survey of the profession in Canada.

34 In addition to Calhoun, *The American Civil Engineer*, and Calvert, *The Mechanical Engineer in America*, the following would serve as useful reference points in the study of the Canadian professional movements; H.M. Vollmer and D.L. Mills, *Professionalization* (Englewood Cliffs, NJ, 1966); W.J. Reader, *Professional Men* (London, 1966); W.H.G. Armytage, *A Social History of Engineering* (London, 1970 ed.), and R.H. Merritt, *Engineering in American Society, 1850-1875* (Lexington, Ky., 1969).

35 The full title of the work is as follows: *Eighty Years' Progress of British North America; Showing the wonderful development of its national resources, by the unbounded energy and enterprise of its inhabitants; giving in historical form, the vast improvements made in agriculture, commerce, and trade, modes of travel and transportation, mining, and educational interests, etc., etc.* (Toronto, 1863). An identical second edition was published the following year.

36 'The Idea of Progress in the Province of Canada,' p.11; in *The Shield of Achilles*, pp. 171-2.

37 For biographical information on Henry Youle Hind, see Wallace, *The Macmillan Dictionary of Canadian Biography*, pp. 321-2, and Henry

J. Morgan, *The Canadian Men and Women of the Time* (Toronto, 1898), pp. 464-5. The quotation is from the preface to *Eighty Years' Progress of British North America*, pp. 4-5.

38 This is doubly ironic in view of the fact that in the 1880s T.C. Keefer would himself be the proprietor of a small street railway in Ottawa. On the social impact of street railways, see, for example, Peter Goheen, *Victorian Toronto* (Chicago, 1970), and Sam Bass Warner, Jr., *Streetcar Suburbs* (Cambridge, Mass., 1962).

1 PHILOSOPHY OF RAILROADS

Philosophy of Railroads
published at the request of the
directors of the Montreal and Lachine Railroad
by Thomas C. Keefer, civil engineer

[This reprint of the *Philosophy of Railroads* follows the third edition jointly published in 1850 by Armour & Ramsay printers of Montreal and Andrew H. Armour and Company of Toronto. The modified conclusion of the fourth, French edition, printed by John Lovell in Montreal in 1853, has been appended for purposes of comparison.]

OLD WINTER is once more upon us, and our inland seas are 'dreary and inhospitable wastes' to the merchant and to the traveller; – our rivers are sealed fountains – and an embargo which no human power can remove is laid on all our ports. Around our deserted wharves and warehouses are huddled the naked spars – the blasted forest of trade – from which the sails have fallen like the leaves of the autumn. The splashing wheels are silenced – the roar of steam is hushed – the gay saloon, so lately thronged with busy life, is now but an abandoned hall – and the cold snow revels in solitary possession of the untrodden deck. The animation of business is suspended, the life blood of commerce is curdled and stagnant in the St. Lawrence – the great aorta of the North. On land, the heavy stage labours through mingled frost and mud in the West – or struggles through drifted snow, and slides with uncertain track over the icy hills of Eastern Canada. Far away to the South is heard the daily scream of the steam-whistle – but from Canada there is no escape: blockaded and imprisoned by Ice and Apathy, we have at least ample time for reflection – and if there be comfort in Philosophy may we not profitably consider the PHILOSOPHY OF RAILROADS.

NEW commercial enterprises, however well supported by dry and accurate statistics, are not often undertaken upon imperfect information – through the respresentations of theorists or politico-economical writers – or even when supported by bright analogies, and the most authentic records of the success of similar undertakings amongst similar communities. It is true, that well-established systems become the subjects of stock-jobbing and speculation by parties ignorant of their uses or real value; but their origin and maturity are the work of the well-informed few, whose foresight has been rewarded frequently before it has been acknowledged. In older countries the feasibility of public projects and their value as speculations are more speedily ascertained than in our young and thinly populated Province, and any attempt to transplant a system, or found arguments for the latter from the experience of the former, is at once met with disparaging and 'odious' comparisons. The intrinsic merit of the question – the absolute instead of the comparative value of our own projects – are not often investigated, because the nature of such investigations are not familiar to us, while they have long since become unnecessary and are therefore not canvassed in those countries where an established system exists.

Thus it is with the Railway System in Canada. We see, and to our cost, feel its effects around us; – we acknowledge its importance, the great results it has achieved, and the substantial expression of public opinion in its favour in the hundreds of millions which have been freely devoted to its extension in other civilized countries.[1] We have talked about it for years – we have projected a great deal, and done very little, because the public – the real estate owners large and small – have not taken up the subject. Our Representatives have lately acquitted themselves nobly in this matter, but they have rather led than followed public opinion, and have themselves been acted upon by a 'glorious' minority, to whom the actual and efficient execution has hitherto been confined, and who have contended with the chilling influences of popular apathy, ignorance, and incredulity.

An attempt to investigate the Railway System in its applicability to new countries – to define its limitations by shewing where and why its application becomes justifiable – to disseminate popular

1 See Appendix N.

information upon a too unpopular subject, and turn a portion of that earnest and eager covetousness of foreign prosperity back upon our own neglected resources – will it is hoped be received with public favour – or at least with public charity.

At the outset it may be objected that there is an insufficiency of disposable circulating capital in Canada, to construct a tithe of the length of projected Railways, and that *therefore* the discussion is premature. The premises will be admitted to any reasonable extent, but the conclusion, instead of the discussion is, we hope to show, premature.

The population, soil, and wealth of Canada are not inferior to Vermont, New Hampshire, Michigan, Georgia, and other States which have Railways; and the local resources of some portions of our Province, where Railroads are wanting, are at least equal to those in Ohio and many other States where these advantages have been enjoyed for years. Whatever is or was the condition of the circulating capital in the States mentioned, they have *found a way* to build their roads. This we believe has been done through the energy and perseverance of the local proprietors of real estate, who have convinced capitalists that they could have no better security for their investments, than that contingent upon the certain increase of population, wealth, and traffic, in rising countries like our own; – and thus have they secured improvements from which the land is the first to benefit, and without which its value in Canada is stationary; and this too, under circumstances when to stand still is to recede. The projectors of the Welland Canal were not Rothschilds; yet the untiring perseverance of one gentleman secured the construction of a work which for importance has no parallel in America.

There is a greater amount of unemployed capital amongst our agricultural and trading population than is generally supposed; and of fixed capital and absolute wealth there is more than sufficient both to need and to warrant the construction of all the roads proposed. A very considerable class of the stockholders in New England roads are farmers, with investments from £50 to £500.

Railway stocks, unlike most others, are a species of real estate immoveably attached to the soil, and have therefore become of late years favourite channels for investment with all classes of capitalists.[2]

2 See Appendix A.

Banks may fail – commerce may languish or be partially diverted – manufactures be rendered unprofitable – even the earth may for a time refuse to many a return for the capital invested in it; but as long as there are men to profit or to lose by speculations, there will be people to sustain a Railway; and if universal ruin be inevitable, *they* will be the last public works to succumb to the general prostration. The cart road is succeeded by the turnpike, this again by the macadam or plank roads, and these last by the Railway. The latter is the perfected system and admits of no competition – and this characteristic pre-eminently marks it out as the most desirable object for investment in the midst of an enterprising and increasing population.

With an *assessed* value of about thirty-five millions of dollars – with cultivated lands worth thirty-six millions of dollars, and an annual crop, valued at ten millions of dollars, in Upper Canada alone – with population, production and wealth, doubling in about ten years, we offer a security upon the industrial character and the increasing wants of a progressive people, for all judicious commercial investments. We therefore believe – although we could not borrow a dollar for any other purpose – that as the unavoidable customers of a well placed Railway, we have only to secure its receipts to those from whom we ask assistance and take those necessary preliminary steps which none but ourselves can take, in order to obtain the capital required to construct our works. This can scarcely be contested from the experience of the past, because the value of Railway investment is of comparatively recent discovery – and is even now but partially appreciated. Did we not find it so difficult to foresee the inevitable future instead of looking backward, we must acknowledge that with the same future as past progress, there will have taken place in the natural order of things, *before* such works as we propose to consider *could be* brought into perfect operation, such an improved change as is now only demanded by the most incredulous in order to secure their sanction to a Railway System for Canada.

What we need most is that faith in the works themselves which will produce sufficient fruit to bring them within the munificent provisions of our late Railroad Act. It is to present something of the 'substance hoped for,' and the unseen evidence required to produce these works, that these remarks have been offered to the public.

The initiative must be taken by us: we cannot expect the accumulated capital of commerce or of older countries to seek out *our* investments. We must do as others do – lay our projects before the money holders, and shew our earnestness and confidence by taking stock to the extent of our means; – but, above all, we must inform ourselves and them fully of the grounds upon which we found our expectations. Zeal and enterprize, directed by a knowledge of our subject, are more rare and efficient commodities than the mere possession of capital; because they will carry capital and all other things with them.

Let us take a case of which Canada (we are proud and sad to say) presents more than one instance. A well cultivated district, in which all the lands are occupied (perhaps by the second generation) with or without water power, but situated twenty to fifty miles from the chief towns upon our great highway, the St. Lawrence, and without navigable water communication with it. The occupants are all thriving and independent farmers, the water power is employed only to an extent to meet their local wants, and the village is limited to the few mechanics, and the one store required for this rural district. The barter of the shopkeeper is restricted by the consumption of his customers, and he becomes the sole forwarder of the surplus product of the district. There is no stimulus for increased production – there are less facilities for it: the redundant population have all been accustomed to agriculture, and as the field for this is unrestricted, they move Westward to prevent a subdivision of the homesteads, and to become greater landowners than their fathers. There exists the well known scarcity of labourers for the harvest, because there is no employment for them during the remainder of the year; and they have not yet been led by necessity to that subdivision of labour and that variety of employment which are the results of an increasing and more confined population. Each farmer has his comfortable house, his well stored barn, variety of stock, his meadows and his woodland; he cultivates only as much as he finds convenient, and his slight surplus is exchanged for his modest wants. Distance, the expense of transportation, and the absence of that energy which debt or contact with busier men should produce, have prevented any efforts to supply the commercial towns on the part of the contented denizens of our 'Sleepy Hollow.' To themselves, to the superficial observer, their district has attained the limit of improvement. If they have no water power, or one limited to the supply of the needful grist or saw mill, it is clear to their minds that they were never destined for manufacturing people; and if they have abundant water power, their local market would not support one manufactory, while land carriage, want of people, money, and more than all *information,* precludes the idea of their manufacturing for a distant market. It is still more evident, from their position, they are not to become a commercial people and build up large cities; they, therefore, jog along with evident self-satisfaction – the venerable churchyard is slowly filling up with tombstones – and the quiet residents arrive at the conclusion that they are a peculiarly favoured people in having escaped the rage for improvement. They are grateful that their farms have not been disfigured by canals or railroads, or the spirits of their sires troubled by the hideous screech of the steam-whistle.

We will now suppose, (we would we could more than suppose), that two of our cities should be moved to unite by the iron bond of a Railway, which in its course will traverse the district just described. Excitement prevails in the 'Hollow'; – sleep has deserted her peculiar people – the livelong night is passed in mutual contemplation of farms 'cut up' or covered over – visions of bloody skirmishes between 'Far downs' and Corkonians – of rifled gardens and orchards, of plundered poultry yards and abducted pigs. The probable mother of a possible child bewails her future offspring 'drawn and quartered' on the rail by the terrible locomotive, and a whole hecatomb of cattle, pigs and sheep, are devoted by imagination to this insatiate Juggernaut. The Engineers who come to spy out the land are met with curses both loud and deep – the laws of property are discussed – the delinquent Member for the County denounced – until a handsome Rodman, by well-timed admiration of Eliza Ann, the rural spokesman's daughter, succeeds in obtaining comfortable quarters for his party, with board, lodging, and washing, at 12s. 6d. per week. The work has commenced; the farmer is offered better prices for his hay and grain than he ever before received: – even milk and vegetables – things he never dreamed of selling – are now sought for; his teams, instead of eating up his substance as formerly in winter, are constantly employed, and his sons are profitably engaged in 'getting out timber' for the contractors; he grows a much larger quantity of oats and potatoes than before – and when the workmen have left, he finds to his astonishment that his old friend the storekeeper is prepared to take all he can spare, to send by the Railroad 'down to town.'

And now some of the 'city folks' come out and take up a water privilege, or erect steam power, and commence manufacturing. Iron is bought, cut into nails, screws and hinges. Cotton is spun and wove, and all the variety of manufacturers introduced, because here motive power, rents and food are cheaper, and labour more easily controlled than in the cities, while transportation and distance have by the Railroad been reduced to a minimum. A town has been built and peopled by the operatives – land rises rapidly in value – the neglected swamp is cleared and the timber is converted into all sorts of wooden 'notions' – tons of vegetables, grains, or grasses, are grown where none grew before – the patient click of the loom, the rushing of the shuttle, the busy hum of the spindle, the thundering of the trip-hammer, and the roaring of steam, are mingled in one continuous sound of active industry. While the physical features of our little hamlet are undergoing such a wonderful transformation, the moral influence of the iron civilizer upon the old inhabitants is bringing a rapid 'change over the spirit of their dreams.' The young men and the maidens, the old men and the matrons, daily collect around the cars: they wonder where so many well-dressed and rich-looking people come from and are going to, &c. – what queer machines those are which they see passing backwards and forwards. They have perhaps an old neighbour whose son had long since wandered off, and now they see him returned, a first class passenger with all the prestige of broadcloth, gold chains, rings, gloves, and a travelled reputation: the damsels rapidly impress upon 'the mind's eye' the shapes of the bonnets, visites, &c., of that superior class of beings who are flying (like angels) over the country, and *drink in,* with wide-mouthed admiration, the transcendent splendour and indescribable beauty of 'that 'ere shawl.' All are interested, all are benefited, *cuique suum.* Is he a farmer? he has a practical illustration of the superior cheapness of transportation by increasing the load – the cart is abandoned for the waggon – for he sees the Railroad, notwithstanding the great cost of the cuttings, embankments, tunnels, bridges, engines, cars, and stations, carrying his produce for a less sum than his personal expenses and the feeding of his horses would amount to. Is he a blacksmith? he determines his son shall no longer shoe horses, but build engines. Is he a carpenter? he is proud of his occupation as he surveys the new bridge over the old creek. Even the village tailor gathers 'a wrinkle,' as he criticises the latest effort of Buckmaster or Gibb, whilst the unconscious advertiser is swallowing his coffee. Thus curiosity and emulation are excited and the results are discernible in a general predilection for improved 'modes.' A spirit is engendered which is not confined to dress or equipage, but is rapidly extended to agriculture, roads, and instructive societies, and finally exerts its most powerful influence where it is most needed – in the improved character is gives to the exercise of the franchise. This right is now enjoyed by too large a class, whose chief contact with public affairs has been limited to an occasional chat with ambitious retailers of dry goods, groceries, hardware, and political mysteries – or to a semi-annual sitting in a jury box, unconsciously absorbing all the virtuous indignation of some *nisi prius* wrangler, whose 'familiar face' is shortly after presented to them at the hustings, generously proffering to defend or advocate anything for four dollars per diem and a prospective Judgeship. He is opposed, perhaps, by the public-spirited shopkeeper, who, with mortgages, long credits, tea and tobacco – aided by a 'last call' to all doubtful supporters – incites the noble yeomanry to assert their rights as 'free and independent electors.' If the 'natives' can overcome these prejudices of local associations, or if the lawyer's 'collections' and 'notes' are sufficiently diffuse, ten chances to one the greatest talker is elected, and an improved judicature, instead of an improved country, is the result.

Nothing would be a more powerful antidote to this state of primitive, but not innocuous simplicity, than the transit of Railways through our agricultural districts. The civilizing tendency of the locomotive is one of the modern anomalies, which however inexplicable it may appear to some, is yet so fortunately patent to all, that it is admitted as readily as the action of steam, though the substance be invisible and its secret ways unknown to man. Poverty, indifference, the bigotry or jealousy of religious denominations, local dissensions or political demagogueism may stifle or neutralize the influence of the best intended efforts of an educational system; but that invisible power which has waged successful war with the material elements, will assuredly overcome the prejudices of mental weakness or the designs of mental tyrants. It calls for no co-operation, it waits for no convenient season, but with a restless, rushing, roaring assiduity, it keeps up a constant and unavoidable spirit of enquiry or comparison; and while ministering to the material wants, and appealing to the covetousness of the multitude, it unconsciously, irresistibly, impels them to a more intimate union with their fellow men.

Having attempted to illustrate the influence of a Railway upon a district supposed to have culminated, let us proceed to notice some of the general characteristics of the system before we apply the results of our investigations to our own particular wants.

We are not backward in importing improvements or transplanting systems *which we understand:* at the same time, those which are new to us, we have curiosity enough and distrust enough to challenge until their principles are defined – when, with the materials before him, with a particular individuality, each man arrives at his own conclusions as to the practicability of their proposed application to this country. It is to this broad principle of 'common sense,' judgment, or whatever you will, we prefer to appeal rather than to the 'availability' or elasticity of statistics.

Steam has exerted an influence over matter which can only be compared to that which the discovery of Printing has exercised upon mind. These two great discoveries – pillars of cloud and fire which have brought us out of the mental wilderness of the dark and middle ages – have combined to supply the mind with daily food and illustrate the value of time.[3] Men have now virtually attained antediluvian longevity; ideas are exchanged by lightning – readers and their books travel together but little behind their thoughts – while actors, materials, scenes and scenery are shifted with the rapidity and variety of the kaleidoscope.

The extraordinary expansion of the Railway System, within the last thirty years, is to be ascribed to the improved appreciation of the Value of Time; since it is *now* universally admitted, that distances are virtually shortened in the precise ratio in which the times occupied in passing over them are diminished.

Speed, economy, regularity, safety, and convenience – an array of advantages unequalled – are combined in the Railway System. These we will notice separately.

3 Steam Printing.

SPEED

The importance of speed in the transport of goods is annually increasing; even now the more valuable descriptions of merchandize take the rail in preference to the slower and cheaper route by canal; and since the cost of transport upon a Railway varies in an inverse proportion with the business of the road, it is annually becoming less, so that economy of time and economy of transport are becoming less and less antagonistical, and are approaching each other so rapidly, as to render the establishment of any line of demarcation exceedingly difficult if not impossible.

ECONOMY

Compared with all other land communications, their freighting capabilities may be inferred from the consideration that a horse usually draws from fifteen to thirty hundred weight on a good turnpike or macadamised road (exclusive of vehicle), four to six tons on a plate rail tram road, and fifteen to twenty tons on an edge rail including the waggons; – the friction on a level Railway being only from one-tenth to one-seventh of that upon the roads above mentioned. If this be the effect of the rail alone, it is needless to enlarge upon its power when travelled by an iron horse, with which hunger and thirst are but metaphorical terms, which knows no disease nor fatigue, and to which a thousand miles is but the beginning of a journey, and a thousand tons but an ordinary burthen.

But it is in a more extended sense than the mere *cost* of transport that the economy of the Railway is vindicated. While upon the best roads travelled by horses, the cost and time of transportation increases rapidly with the distance, it is clear that there is a point from whence the transport of certain articles becomes unprofitable or impracticable. Milk, fruits, and vegetables, for immediate use, will not bear ten or twelve hours jolting over fifty miles of the best turnpike to reach a market; while fresh meats, fish, eggs, cattle, pigs, and poultry, lumber, staves, shingles, and firewood, and many other necessaries of life, either could not afford the time or the cost of a hundred miles transport by horse-power. The production of these articles, therefore, is very limited in certain districts; but wherever a Railway takes its track their extensive production becomes at once a new element of wealth, and the Locomotive a public benefactor – making 'two blades of grass grow where only one grew before.' Thus the essence of a Railway system is *to increase its own traffic,* adding twenty-five per cent to the value of every farm within fifty miles of the track, doubling that of those near it, and quadrupling the value of timbered lands through which they pass. Railroads are in one respect more economical carriers than canals, in as much as they are both freight and toll receivers, and are therefore content with one profit.

REGULARITY

The superior speed and safety of Railway travel over the most expeditious water communications are scarcely more important than its extraordinary regularity; to which latter circumstance it is chiefly owing that in every country the Railway has been selected for the transportation of the mails. This monopoly of mails and passengers enables them to transport goods proportionally cheaper – thus becoming powerful rivals to the most favourable water communications. From this principle of regularity, Railways in the winter season have no competitors; and, working the whole year round, without delay of lockage, wind or tide, fog, frost, or rain, they, with a full business and fair 'grades,' can compete with ordinary canals in price, while they can make two trips, to one on the canal, in less than half the time.

SAFETY

The comparative safety of Railway travel with that upon steamboats is best appreciated by the reflection, that the causes which endanger human life upon the former are limited to collisions or leaving the track – both to be avoided by ordinary care: whereas in the latter, explosion, fire, collision, or wrecking, are attended with imminent risk to all, the only choice often being – the *mode* of death. Explosion of a locomotive boiler, besides being exceedingly rare, is scarcely ever attended with any danger to the lives of the passengers. The remarkable safety of well managed Railways may be further illustrated by the statement of Baron Von Reden, that upon the Railways of Germany only one person in every twelve and a quarter millions of passengers was killed or wounded from defective arrangements of the road, one in every nine millions from his own misconduct, and one in every twenty-five millions from his own negligence. The Germans are undoubtedly a prudent people.

CONVENIENCE

The convenience of the Railway System lies chiefly in its adaptation to its peculiar traffic; – artificial navigation is restricted to favourable ground and supplies of water, but modern improvements have enabled the Locomotive to clamber over mountains and penetrate the most remote corners of the land; there is therefore no limit to the number of its auxiliary branches, which can be multiplied and extended until their ramifications give the required facilities to every wharf and every warehouse – to the solitary mill or factory, or to the most neglected districts as an outlet to otherwise worthless products.

Having noticed some of the characteristics of Railways, we for the present will proceed to examine their capabilities as rivals or auxiliaries to canals and rivers – their winter operation – their effect upon manufactures – the comparative merits of long and short lines – 'through' and 'way' travel – and other advantages or peculiarities.

We have said that Railroads, with fair grades and a full business, can compete successfully with ordinary canals. We do not mean that any Railroad can compete with canals connecting long lines of navigable waters such as we have in Canada, where the canals are of a size to prevent transhipment or the navigation so sheltered as to permit boats to be towed its entire length; but we do believe, that wherever a transhipment is unavoidable and the Railroad is called upon to transport from one end of the canal route to the other, it will, with ordinary grades, be found the most eligible. We make this comparison assuming that a paying rate of tolls be placed upon the canals as well as on the road, and we base it upon the consideration that the road can do all which the canal would do, and a great deal which the latter would *never* do, viz., carry passengers, mails, fruits, vegetables, milk, fish, &c., which would never take the canal; and that it would be in operation when the canal was useless. This assertion involves the capacity of Railroads, and it is not difficult to prove that a Railway would transport far more in a twelvemonth than the majority of the English or American Canals and some of our own. It would be unfair to select such very imperfect navigations as the Rideau for a comparison, because, having no towing path the attendance of tug boats is required with every barge, or fleet of barges the lockage of which is an additional delay while its employment is a heavy expense; and because the absurd size of the Grenville locks nullifies half the capacity of those upon the Rideau. We will therefore take the best Canal and Railroad in America, and see what they have done. The number of tons which arrived at the tide water by the *Erie Canal,* was in the years

1846	1,107,270	
1847	1,431,252	Total, 3,722,859 tons of 2000 lbs.
1848	1,184,337	

On the *Reading Railroad*, in the years

1846	1,233,141	
1847	1,350,151	Total, 3,799,524 tons of 2240 lbs.
1848	1,216,232	

The length of the Erie Canal is 363 miles – opening to the Great West.

The length of the Reading Railroad is 94 miles – opening to a coal district.

The difference in estimating the tonnage makes more than ten per cent additional in favour of the Railroad. This statement simply shews the down freight or movement in one direction; – had the Railroad been as favourably situated for up freight as the Canal is, greater proportional superiority would have been shown by the road, which having a double track the up movement would not be delayed by down freight as on the canal. As it was, however, in 1847 the 'total movement' on the road in tons of 2000 lbs. amounted to upwards of 1,700,000, which if we compare with an equal length of the Canal will still maintain the supremacy of the Railway. The number of tons of coals transported in 1847 upon the York and Newcastle Railroad in England was 1,620,163. The freighting capabilities of a Railroad will be better understood, by giving a short account of the road which we have just compared with the Erie Canal.

This road employs about seventy locomotives and over five thousand freight cars; it has six side tracks at the Delaware Terminus and seventeen wharves in that river with a double track upon each; a storage for 195,000 tons of coal, and room for the simultaneous lading of ninety-seven vessels of 700 tons burthen each. Three or four engines are constantly employed in distributing cars to their respective wharves, and the Company's principal workshop employs several hundred men. An engine upon this road has drawn 150 iron coal waggons in one train, of 1268 tons weight, over a distance of eighty-four miles in eight hours and three minutes. The cost of the road has been $11,500,000; the gross earnings in 1846 were $1,889,713, and the net earnings $1,037,795. Of the gross earnings, $1,600,667 were for freight upon coal. The actual cost of transporting coal per ton over the whole distance of ninety-four miles, including the expense of bringing back the empty cars, was *thirty-eight and nine-tenths cents,* or less than two shillings currency; being four and one-tenth mills per ton per mile. At this rate the cost of transport of a barrel of flour the length of the Erie Canal (363 miles) would be ninepence currency, or fifteen cents, which is about the actual cost to the carrier on that Canal. Of course no tolls to the road are included. The gross receipts of this Railroad for July, 1846, exceeded $240,000. There is a Canal (competing with the Railroad for the same traffic) which has lately been enlarged, and the cost of which is about half that of the Railroad while it only does about one-third of the business, and has been at times rendered useless by freshets.[4]

We will not go so far as to say that a Railway could now compete with an established work having such wonderful advantages as the Erie Canal, but we feel confident with the present experience in these works that if the Canal were not in existence and a choice of communication were now to be made, the Railway would be selected. The lateral Canals of the State of New York it must be remembered, do not pay any dividends; the receipts and disbursements being about equal notwithstanding the great advantages which they derive from their connection with the Erie Canal. The extraordinary extent of sheltered and inland navigation in America render the Canal system more applicable to this country than to many others, but it cannot be denied that the mania which followed the unparalleled success of the Erie Canal induced an extension of the system into districts, particularly in the more northern climates,

4 See Appendix G.

where the Railway would have been more applicable. The Railway route from Albany to Buffalo is 326 miles; the cost of these roads, including the late relaying with heavy rails, has been $12,302,507 92.

Cost of the Old Erie Canal	7,143,789 86
Enlargement to September, 1848	19,086,490 80
Total	26,230,280 66

Several millions of the cost of the enlargement have been for interest paid during its suspension. We may however assume that, before the enlargement of the Erie Canal and the remodelling of the Railways be completed, the State of New York will have expended above forty millions of dollars (including the Railroad) for her communications between Lake Erie and the Hudson River. We will leave our readers to judge what sort of Railroad facilities this sum would have ensured.

The existence of the Railroads has proved of the greatest service to the Erie Canal not only in furnishing rapid communications between all points of this great thoroughfare, but in securing the forwarding of freight when frost or accident obstruct the navigation.

The navigation of the St. Lawrence is subject to the great drawback of being occasionally closed when the business is most urgent and most heavy. To obviate the great loss and inconvenience of wintering over large supplies at Montreal the Portland Railroad[5] has been undertaken. But the scheme will be incomplete, and the St. Lawrence route under great disadvantages until a Railway is extended from Lachine to Prescott or Kingston, securing to the Western producer the certain transmission of his produce should frost or accident to the St. Lawrence Canals (of which we have had no less than two instances in the last summer), detain it at Prescott.

5 [This railroad was in fact two railroads: the Atlantic and St Lawrence on the American side of the border, and the St Lawrence and Atlantic on the Canadian side. Portland merchants built the former and Montreal merchants the latter. For detail, see O.D. Skelton, *Life and Times of Sir Alexander Tilloch Galt* (Toronto, 1966 ed.), chap. 2.]

The necessity for this step will soon be so apparent that the Government will be compelled to lend every possible assistance to the project. Our shipping being limited, a sudden rise of prices produces a corresponding rise of freights and want of vessels, and as the result a portion of our exports will be sent through the more numerous and better supplied channels of our neighbours. In these critical times of high prices shippers cannot risk delay and will take the route that offers the most chances of getting on: moreover they want the means of communicating with their produce and business depots after the suspension and before the opening of navigation.

Perhaps the impression exists that a Railway upon this route could not compete with the river; but for through passengers up and all business passengers down – mails – all winter travel and freight, and all *way* passengers and freight, the River would offer no competition to the Railway, because the cars from Montreal would reach Kingston almost while the steamer was passing through *one* of the Canals; while in the spring, autumn, and in case of accidents, the latter becomes a necessary auxiliary to the former.

The Hudson River Railroad has been undertaken, upon the most substantial and expensive scale, by the side of a river where water transport has been brought to a perfection unequalled in the world, *because* New York can no longer do without a winter communication with the interior. The New York Railroads, situate along the line of the canals, transported in the fourteen months ending December 1848, 57,188 tons of freight, paying the Canal tolls, which amounted to $107,786. The Albany and Schenectady – the last link with the Hudson – received from this source alone $14,000 in the months of May and April, 1848.

It is a mistake, therefore, to suppose that Railroads will not carry freight by the side of a water communication – especially in winter. The State of New York only permits her Railroads to take freight from the canals by paying canal tolls. If these restrictions were removed we should see a greater freighting business done by the Railroads: but as it is – freight is carried by them in every month in the year to the extent of upwards of 1000 tons in each of the summer months, and as high as 11,500 tons in the month of December.

It is the assertion of the best authorities and the result of the best experience, that freight and travel upon every highway are quadrupled in a remarkably short space of time by the construction of a Railway.

Canada loses every year, by the want of Railroads and a winter market, enough to construct fifty miles of Railway. If we look at the price of flour for the last six years, we will see that it has been highest in the winter months (from October to May); and we have not forgotten when in 1847, we with nearly half a million of barrels of flour for exportation in Montreal alone, were regaled with accounts of winter sales at double the usual rates, in Boston, New York and other Atlantic ports, from which *for the want of Railways alone* we were shut out – not even having the privilege of paying the American duty.

As soon as the Western farmer secures his crop his whole time is required to get in the new one before the frost – for he sows fall wheat. Necessity alone makes him thrash out and take a portion of his grain to market. The winter is his idle season – then is his most convenient time for thrashing and bringing his produce to sale. The Eastern farmer sows spring wheat, but as the snow forms his best and cheapest road – the winter is also his proper time for coming to market. The same is the case with the farmer in the back Townships who has no summer road – he must wait for the snow and frost to bring out his grain to the best advantage. The chief part of their produce, therefore, lies on their hands with that on those of the miller until the ensuing season. Our mills must therefore stand still because like the bees we are sealed up in the winter, idly consuming the fruits of our summer's industry. With a Railway we could make flour in winter of a better quality and cheaper proportionally, because we have more time, cooler weather, and cheaper transport of the wheat – while our chances of high prices would be better and risk of souring less.

Nothing would tend more to the extension of Manufactures, particularly the numerous and valuable ones of Wood – the only description we would for some time export – than the existence of Railways; – nothing would more rapidly build up, what every country should have, *a home market* – place the consumer near the producer – keep our surplus population at home – promote the growth of wool – the cultivation of hemp – the settlement of waste lands – the employment of our unlimited water power – and the expansion of national enterprise.

If we would *now* have manufactories, (cotton for instance,) we must lay in our winter stock of raw material in November and allow our manufactures to accumulate until April or May before they can be distributed: while in New England, the train which takes up the wool to the water power upon Monday returns with the manufactures of that wool in the same week. These quick returns beget small profits, with which under our system it is vain to attempt competition. When we consider the amount of unprofitable capital 'winter killed' – the loss of winter prices on the seaboard – the cost of transport by waggons – the feeding of horses, and the rate paid in the towns for a scant supply of articles, valueless in the country, we repeat again – Canada loses by the want of Railroads and winter markets enough to build fifty miles of Railway every year!

There are some who, while they admit that a Railway from Montreal to Prescott would be desirable and profitable on account of the delay in ascending the canals, &c., yet believe that a road from thence to Kingston, Toronto, and Hamilton could not compete with the lake and river. We need not consider the question beyond Hamilton, because it is admitted upon all hands that the Great Western route is the best unoccupied one for a Railway in America. We start then with the assertion that a Railway from Montreal to Hamilton, passing through such towns as Brockville, Kingston, Belleville, Cobourg, Port Hope, and Toronto, would be more profitable than if it were to stop at Prescott.

Long lines are always more desirable and profitable than short ones for the same reason that long rivers discharge more water – by draining a greater area. The expenses of management do not increase proportionally with the distance while the powers of competition are diminished by it. Thus while a locomotive would only gain five hours upon a steamer descending from Prescott, it would gain at least sixteen hours upon one descending from Hamilton to Montreal in fair weather, and more in foul. So far from the lake and river being injurious to the interests of the road they are invaluable to it. They protect it from the competition of Southern roads by forcing the traffic to keep the North side of the lake – *and it has no more northern outlet.* And lastly, the route of one good natural highway is the proper place to put a superior one upon (as all will admit a Railway to be), for there we are sure to find people, wealth, and business.

It is no objection to this route that it seems to be unilateral: that is, that it would run along the lake shore drawing apparently only from the land side. If there were a more northern route to be proposed there would be some force in this objection; but from the peculiar position of Canada, this road would traverse the vital portion of the whole Province collecting the business without effort where it has accumulated at the towns and cities which are the only outlets of the back country. On the one side of the road there will be water – but it must not be forgotten that the road by being brought occasionally near the water, will do the business of the back country as effectually as if it bisected it, and that the water *may* supply a greater business to the road than any tract of land, however rich or populous, which could reasonably be tributary to it. This will especially be the case in spring, fall, and perhaps even winter, as the lake is always open above Kingston harbour.

This road would do the business of over 400,000 people in Upper Canada alone, occupying an area of 14,440 square miles, giving a population of about twenty-eight to the square mile.

Now it is the estimate of the most competent authorities, that a Railway of this length draws to its support, from the inhabitants of any district through which it passes, a net income of between ten and fifteen shillings per head on the total population tributary to it. The net earnings of the Massachusetts Railways exceed sixteen shillings and threepence per head for each inhabitant of that State. The New York and Erie Railroad passes for 425 miles through a grazing country, with a population of 532,000 persons, supposed to be dependent upon it, and the estimate of net earnings per head upon this route *(founded upon the experience of those portions in operation)* is twelve shillings and six pence per head. The area tributary to this road is 12,000,000 of acres, and the population twenty-eight to the square mile. The area tributary to a road from Montreal to Hamilton would at least equal this – the population be as dense, the cost of construction much less per mile, the line shorter, and the *'grades'* far superior, as any one familiar with the two routes will acknowledge. In locating such a road, not the shortest or most direct route, but the most probably productive one should be adopted; because the local capital is centered in the towns and villages and therefore the way travel from the one to the other – the supply of necessaries from the country, and from the east and west to the towns, will be the most certain and profitable business of the road.

The articles for which the Erie Railroad is an outlet are chiefly the products of a grazing country – milk, butter, cattle, calves, sheep and pigs. Of the former article, milk, so important is the business that a special train known as the 'milk-train' is run each morning for the supply of the citizens of New York, whose daily wants are thus administered to from cows feeding beyond the Shawangunk Mountains and drinking the waters which flow into the Delaware.[6] The freight *upward* to this grazing district is chiefly groceries, salt, *lumber,* iron, *flour and meal,* dry goods, salted provisions, &c. Now, if the construction of a Railway of 425 miles, through such a mountainous, difficult, expensive, and thinly settled region is profitable with the Erie Canal and its parallel Railroads within a few miles on the north, and the Pennsylvanian Canals and Railroads on the south, competing for the business, are we not justified in asserting that it is not only prudent and profitable but *imperative upon us* to commence at once a Railway route from Montreal through the easy valley of the St. Lawrence to Hamilton – a route which can have no competitor north of the St. Lawrence? It will be said that the Erie Railroad counts much upon the Western trade to be reached at Lake Erie. This argument would apply equally to the Canada road. But we maintain that our own local and provincial resources, our freights, passengers, and mails, will, before it can be completed if now commenced, support our own road. We consider all roads depending *chiefly* upon 'through' travel as inferior investments: there must be a good country and a local business – either existing or being developed – dependent upon the road; – resources which cannot be diverted. How can we depend upon a business over which we have no control? Of what value will the Champlain road be hereafter, unless incorporated in a line from Highgate to a ferry at Montreal? Of what value is the Lachine road *now*? Only seventy-four miles of the New York and Erie Railroad were in operation at the last official returns – and upon this distance the number of *way* passengers was 259,774, while the *through* passengers were only 28,324. The receipts from *passengers* $125,722, and from *freight* $185,190, and a dividend of $133,437 was announced. Even upon the great thoroughfare from Buffalo to Albany, the number of *way* passengers between Auburn and Rochester, one of the longest routes, is greater than those going 'through,' while upon the

6 See Appendix B.

Syracuse and Utica, and Utica and Schenectady they are nearly equal.[7]

Upon the Western Road from Albany to Boston the *way* passengers are more than nine times as numerous as the *through.* The *freight* receipts in October last were about four times those of *passengers.* In short, the business of the New England roads is almost wholly *local,* or business *created by the road and derived from residents who cannot abandon it; therefore these roads are the best paying ones in America.*[8]

The 'through' freight or travel has the choice of many routes and should only be viewed as auxiliary and occasional support, of which we have as good grounds for expecting our share as our neighbours.

We have thus endeavoured to show that it is not necessary for us to have a guarantee of the through travel from the West, or to wait until we ascertain whether the St. Lawrence will become a favourite route Eastward and from the Ocean, before we would be warranted in commencing a main arterial road from our chief seaport to our principal Western town; but that on the contrary, such a work will be one of the chief and now indispensable means for the attainment of so desirable and vital an object. We have also in the introduction suggested that we are not too poor to afford such a work, but rather that we are too poor to do without it, and that the initiative must be taken at *some time* and by *somebody* amongst ourselves, before we can expect capitalists to suggest what we seem so indifferent about. If we first do all we can, the experience we will obtain in the effort will enable us to do more than we at first hoped. We must first assert our own confidence in the project before we invite that of others. We have offered no illusive estimates, held out no flattering inducements: we believe the deliberate judgment of the country has never been pronounced upon this question – that it has never even been

7 The route being divided into so many Corporations, a passenger who goes *over one* road is set down as 'through,' although he does not travel half through the State. Even on this direct line between the East and the West, the 'through' passengers are not believed to exceed one half of the total number which pass from Buffalo to Albany. See Appendix P.

8 See Appendix E.

exercised upon it; and that it is only necessary to present the elements required for the investigation to ensure that attention and decision which so important a subject merits. The details we leave to local Corporations; – of these the number would probably be half a dozen, having a length of road sufficient to bring them within the provisions of the Railroad Act of last Session.[9]

The little commonwealth of Massachusetts, with an area of 7500 square miles and a population of about 800,000, has expended $50,000,000 in building 1000 miles of Railway, the most important of which now yield to their enterprising projectors an average of seven per cent; and she is now extending these feeders at the rate of 300 miles per annum.[10] Canada, in area, in population, in fertility of soil, water power and mineral wealth, is vastly her superior, and can surely *with such securities procure the means of constructing one iron track, which can have no competitor north of the St. Lawrence.*

The partial failure of our Portage Railways, particularly the Lachine, have undoubtedly had a prejudicial effect upon the Railway movement in Canada. It is difficult to conceive how or why any other result could be anticipated for a Railroad less than ten miles long, situate almost wholly in a valuable suburb, with a turnpike on one side and canal and river on the other, and which with its present length must lie buried one-third of the year in the snow.

Before the Lachine Road was in operation, the writer of these remarks published in a newspaper the following opinion:

> The Lachine is the last of the projected Railways about Montreal; this will be soon in operation and in its present shape *must prove a partial failure;* the sooner the better as thereby there will be a strong interest enlisted in the extension of this road to Upper Canada, as the *only* means of procuring a profitable return. The Lachine Road will be a partial failure *because the route is too short* and the expense very great. The cost of furnishing and managing will be as

9 [The Guarantee Act of 1849 provided a provincial guarantee of the interest, not to exceed 6 per cent, on an issue of bonds equal to one-half the total cost of any railway over seventy-five miles long. It was passed primarily to assist the struggling St Lawrence and Atlantic Railroad.]

10 See Appendix A and H.

great as for a road ten times its length, while only one-tenth of the fare can be exacted. The cab fare to the Montreal Terminus will be, (in addition to the fare on the cars) as much as coach fare direct to Lachine; and as the difference in time, between the train and a coach, will be confined to a few minutes, (the Corporation of Montreal compelling slow speed through the town for Locomotives,) the Company must always compete with the inordinate number of public conveyances in that city for less than an hour's drive over an excellent road – or drive them off by low and unprofitable fares. The expense of land damages, fencing and stock for this road must run up the cost per mile proportionally very much higher than upon roads of greater length and through less valuable property.

In that article, (advocating the commencement of a Railway from Montreal to Toronto), were some remarks which will apply with peculiar force to the present position of Montreal.

Montreal being then not only the Metropolis of Canada, but as she still is, the first Commercial City of British North America, the writer felt that the initiative of any great public enterprize should emanate from that quarter; and as the whole question was one of such peculiar importance to her citizens as a community, he took the liberty of criticising with no unfriendly *animus* their apathy upon the subject. Whether it was contempt for the production, or the apathy spoken of, the article was not then (July 1847) copied into any of the Montreal newspapers. In the hope that, chastened by affliction, they may now permit a fellow Canadian to offer some suggestions upon a subject with which he has been for many years professionally interested, he ventures to republish some further extracts from that article:

Montreal, our beautiful capital, with all its splendid buildings, noble wharves and fine steamers, is yet far behind any city of its population in any part of America. It is difficult at this day to account for the apathy of that city to those simple questions of improvement upon which the prosperity, health and comfort of its citizens depend. However satisfied they may feel with their present condition, it is obvious that ere ten years have passed the question of 'to be or not to be' must be determined by her citizens. They think ships will come to Montreal, houses and rents go up and flour stay up, *because* Montreal is the Seat of Government. So is Washington the Seat of Government of twenty millions, and yet it is not New York, Philadelphia, Baltimore, Boston, New Orleans, Cincinnati, Buffalo, or Albany, all of which without being National Seats of Government, (yet not without Railroads) are far ahead of Washington. Toronto, *since* the removal of the seat of Government from that place, has improved more rapidly than ever, and Kingston has not; because with cities (as with men) there must be some *inherent* properties upon which their success will depend, and which *must be intrinsic* in order that they may not be diverted. Toronto has a back country, but Kingston has not; the former depends upon her farmers in the rear – the latter upon her commerce, which anchors alone retain in her harbour. And now what are Montreal's advantages? On the north and south shores of the St. Lawrence, and to the westward between the Ottawa and the St. Lawrence, lies a country as rich as America can boast of – but where is Montreal? Upon an Island – an *island* to this hour. The Capital of Canada can be approached from the wealthiest and best half of the Province, at two seasons of the year, only by *scows* breaking the ice before them. On the south shore a miserable flat bar Railway has been in operation for several years, but its Terminus is nine miles from that city; – constructed because the nature of the ground seemed to invite the experiment, upon the cheapest principle, and depending upon the curiosity of strangers for its support, the only Railway using Locomotives in Canada is enabled by high fares to pay a respectable dividend to its proprietors. (How long will this last?)

The St. Lawrence and Atlantic Railway is a much more important project to the inhabitants of Montreal, inasmuch as it will pass for upwards of 100 miles through an agricultural country naturally depending upon Montreal for its supplies. But it is much to be feared, nay almost certain, that before the respectable Rip Van Winkles of our Metropolis can be aroused, the several American lines leading from Boston will be pushed up to the head waters of the Connecticut, and that market offered to our Eastern Townships which we have so long and so criminally withheld from them. But this road cannot be brought *into the City*, and must be but an imperfect means of supplying its wants. Its hopes are more upon the 'through' trade and travel. As an outlet however for the agricultural productions of the districts through which it passes, and as a means of supplying the city with firewood, vegetables, fruits and articles which without a Railway would not reach the market, (*and as a means of promoting manufactures*) it will be successful beyond a doubt. This trade, the Railroad makes for itself – will always keep, and be the means of increasing.

But as a means of supplying the City, no route can be projected which will be able to compete with the extension of the Lachine Railroad toward Prescott. Thousands of pounds worth of firewood, butter, eggs, milk, vegetables, fruits, poultry and live stock of every kind, would reach the city daily, which will *never reach* it without a Railway. Instead of milk and water, bad butter and stale vegetables, we would have pure milk, taken from cows fifty miles in the country at five in the morning, delivered in the City for our breakfast – the price of fresh butter, vegetables and firewood reduced, and a constant supply received. We would not see, as in last December, three feet wood scarce at 30s. per cord, because nature was lazy in building her bridge over the waters which surround Montreal. The value of property (within the Island,) along the route would be increased fourfold, and farms fifty miles distant would be placed in a better position than those which are now ten miles off; while the increased activity given to business in the city by the Railway, would keep up rents, and business men, particularly in the present unhealthy season (July), could have their dwellings ten or twenty miles out of town, where the difference in rents, supplies and other advantages, would more than compensate them for the Railway fare in and out daily, and the half hour's time on the road.

This road could be located so as to do the business of the Ottawa River and Bytown, (destined to be the third or fourth city of Upper Canada.) The Ottawa steamboat navigation is imperfect and tedious. The lumber trade on that river, employing a capital of £500,000 annually, is of the highest importance; the constant through travelling of the lumberer would be a great source of profit to the road. If Montreal, the natural market of Bytown and the Ottawa, does not exert herself, the latter will make no great effort to avoid a connection with Ogdensburgh, which can be done in less than half the distance to Montreal. It may be that our Canadian aristocracy and capitalists think these Railway 'notions' vulgar considerations of coppers; – if so, they forget the connection between the trade and politics of a country, they forget that even now *the question of our continuance as a Colony* is to be decided by the solution of the problem, whether flour can be carried from Upper Canada to Liverpool cheaper by New York than by Montreal?

Since the above was written the Lachine Railway has turned out a partial failure; – the Champlain Railway has been rebuilt with heavy rail; – the St. Lawrence and Atlantic has been opened for thirty miles and its construction aided by the City of Montreal; – the Seat of Government has been removed; – and lastly the people of Montreal have seen with a vengeance 'the connection between the trade and politics of a country.'[11]

Perhaps the design of that article (which was to advocate a road from Montreal to Toronto) was considered too extensive, but the inference which it was hoped would be drawn was that it ought at once to *be commenced by the extension of the Lachine Road such a distance only as would be warranted for the supply of Montreal* without reference to Western trade or travel. We wished to shew that a city like Montreal with a population of 50,000 inhabitants, *required* as an indispensable addition a Railway in *some direction* of about fifty miles in length, penetrating a good agricultural country for the supply of the daily wants of her own citizens; and communicating *directly with the city at all seasons of the year.* That it was a disgrace to such a city (the Metropolis) to remain in her insular position where it could be avoided, (the bridge at St. Eustache was not then built), and that the Railways on the south shore would never be unsatisfactory, because their ferries were too long – at certain seasons of the year there would be no intercourse, and at all

11 [The allusion here, of course, is to the welling up of annexationist sentiment in Montreal during 1849. The collapse of the trans-Atlantic trading system drove many disappointed Montreal merchants to the conclusion that union with the United States alone would relieve the commercial depression. For details, see D.G. Creighton, *The Empire of the St. Lawrence* (Toronto, 1956 ed.), pp. 349-85, and Gilbert N. Tucker, *The Canadian Commercial Revolution, 1845-1851* (Toronto, 1964 ed.), pp. 129-47.]

seasons, delay, risk, and transhipments. That although the partial failure of the Lachine Road as projected was unavoidable, its construction was to be hailed as an earnest that one Corporation would be compelled in self defence to take the course so necessary to the well-being of the city.

We now repeat that if the Lachine Railroad be extended fifty miles through a good country toward Prescott it will soon pay more than legal interest upon the whole investment. With reference to the side of the Ottawa to be selected for the extension, this should be determined by thorough examinations; *cæteris paribus*, we should say that as part of the Main Western line 'grades' would have much to do with the decision. If these are found to be equally favourable, then the route which would comprehend most villages, water power, and agricultural products, would be the most productive.

With the power of extension we believe the Lachine Road will become one of the first Railway stocks in Canada. As the last link in the iron chain which must ere long connect the Great West with the seaboard at Montreal, this road would have borne over it the accumulated freight and travel of six hundred miles of a pathway from the St. Clair, through the very *vertebrae* of Canada to ship navigation; – while as a minister to the daily wants of an increasing population, and large foreign and coasting fleets, it would have never failing sources of wealth, if all foreign helps should fail. As Montreal is the largest city in the Province – so long as it continues so a Railroad terminating within the city limits must do the largest *local* business of any road in Canada. But the most important advantage which the first Corporation leading from Montreal westward will enjoy over the more remote ones, is that a large amount of the earnings of the road will be upon *freight of a local character, which will either not bear long transportation or pays a higher rate than products of the same description from the interior can afford;* – and lastly the Western trains will make up the load for this division so that the engines will be worked up to their full capacity, thus diminishing the cost of transport.

The following is an estimate from the best authorities, of the value of the annual consumption of articles of country produce *by the inhabitants* of the city of New York, for 1841:

Fresh beef	1,470,000
Fresh veal	365,000
Fresh mutton and lamb	335,000
Fresh pork	600,000
Poultry, game and eggs, &c.	1,000,000
Vegetables and fruits	1,200,000
Butter, cheese and lard	1,500,000
Flour, meal and other breadstuffs	3,000,000
Hay and oats	750,000
Firewood and coal (exclusive of steamboat fuel)	2,500,000
Salted beef, pork and hams	1,200,000
Milk	1,000,000
Not enumerated, &c.	580,000
	15,500,000

During the six months ending Sept. 30th, 1843, 2,991,161 – say 3,000,000 – quarts of milk were furnished to the city of New York, from the first fifty miles of the New York and Erie Railroad, when that work came into operation, at a price 33 per cent less than former rates: this of course reduced the price of the whole consumption of 16,000,000 of quarts, from six cents to four cents – thus effecting a saving to the city upon this article alone of £80,000 per annum.[12] The consumption of these articles of country produce amounts to about $50 (£12 10s.) per head of the population of New York.

Now we believe the inhabitants of Montreal eat and drink as much per head as their leaner brethren in the good city of Gotham. It has been charged against us by our rectangular cousins – that we have been too much inclined to waste our substance in riotous living; – that one evil arising from our Colonial position is our inclination to imitate our rich relations upon the other side of the Atlantic – in ostentatious hospitality – in lugging harlequin footmen around the streets for the amusement of children or the admiration of Iroquois, instead of 'footing it' ourselves – and in making our stomachs a disputed territory between wine and

12 The quantity supplied by this road in 1847 exceeded seven millions of quarts.

Caledonia water – pastry and blue pills – 'hot-stuff'' and soda. If however we consume more than we really require, it is to be hoped that prudence and patriotism will induce us to imitate the temperance and frugality of those New Englanders who live within their incomes and invest their surplus in Railways or manufactures, instead of supporting foreign vineyards – feeding extra horses, 'lions,' 'tigers,' 'bulls,' 'bears,' *et hoc genus omne* – animals which could be better employed in agriculture or would be fitter subjects for the chase.[13]

We think however, we will be safe in assuming the annual consumption of country produce for Montreal, as above described, to be £10 per head yearly, which is twenty per cent less than it is in New York: this will make the annual value of the city's consumption (assuming the population at 50,000) amount to £500,000.

Now, we have seen that upon one article alone, milk, the saving effected by fifty miles of Railway amounted to 33 per cent – and there is no good reason to doubt that a similar saving was effected in the other items of consumption. But we are rather chary of estimates, and think none will quarrel with us if we say that five per cent, at least, would be the reduction effected upon the cost of *all* these articles to the city of Montreal by the extension of a Railroad, from the St. Antoine suburbs fifty miles into a good agricultural region. This would amount to an annual saving of £25,000 – a sum which would pay the interest upon the cost of such a road!

Some sanguine persons would place the saving at two, three or four times this amount: we dare not say what we think, nor need we do so, for we feel confident that it only requires to be viewed in this light to force an universal acknowledgment of its importance. We may be accused of exaggeration in having said that *Canada* loses annually, by her want of Railroads and a winter market, enough to build fifty miles of Railway: no apology for this opinion will be necessary if it be admitted that *Montreal* alone could save annually enough to pay the interest upon so much road.

The earnings of the Boston and Worcester road for 1848, amounted to $4,600 per mile *more* than the Western Road. The first-mentioned road forms the last forty-five miles of the route from Albany to Boston. The earnings on the line from Utica to Albany are

13 See Appendix A.

more than double the amount per mile of those upon the Buffalo and Attica road, which is the first of the series between Buffalo and Albany. The same comparative superiority of the eastern sections over all others could be shewn upon all the outlets from the west; in fact it is as certain and unchangeable as the increase in the volume of streams as they approach their embouchure. This is the position of the Lachine road: 'It is always the darkest just before day.' We feel confident that however disheartened the Directors of the Lachine Railroad may feel at the unavoidable but to them unexpected result of their enterprize, they will very soon see their true policy and their great advantages over any other Canadian road, and will apply themselves with renewed vigour not only to the working out of their own interests but to the supply of that great want of their fellow-citizens, an uninterupted daily communication with the *main* land and the west. The eyes of Canada – of America, are upon them. If Montreal aspires to rival New York in the trade of the West she *must* offer equal facilities. The value of time is becoming daily more and more appreciated. A Western Canadian merchant can now reach New York from the Niagara frontier in thirty hours (and as soon as the Hudson river road is completed, in twenty hours,) in the month of March, and make his purchases to be shipped by the first opening of the navigation – or he can receive weekly supplies of the lighter or more valuable articles by Railroad from Boston or New York – when he would not risk his neck or his health, *staging it* for four days to Montreal at a season when it would be impossible to bring goods out of that beleagured city.

Railroads have changed the usual system of doing business. Many Western dry goods merchants have abandoned the old method of laying in spring and fall supplies. Weekly invoices of goods are brought in by the Railroad – quick returns are made – the newest patterns are secured – no dead stock is allowed to accumulate – and the saving in time, in interest, in depreciation and loss from too large or unsuitable a stock, more than compensates for any extra cost of transport by Railway – a mode which is known to be preferable for certain descriptions of merchandize.

In conclusion – as a people we may as well in the present age attempt to live without books or newspapers, as without Railroads. A continuous Railway from tide water to Huron upon the north side of the St. Lawrence, we *must* have, and as it will be the work of years we should lose no time in commencing it. It is instructive to view the grounds upon which these projects are undertaken in countries where their operation is understood. In projecting the Petersburg and Shirley Railroad, in Massachusetts, the 'friends of the enterprise' take up the townships through which the road would pass, and thus 'calculate':

Townsend has 7,000 acres of wood and timber land, averaging from forty to fifty cords per acre. After supplying fuel for home consumption, we estimate the actual growth to be equal to one cord for every three and a half acres, per annum, which will be 2,000 cords for market, exclusive of sawed lumber and ship timber.

The north easterly part of Shirley, the north part of Lunenburg and the west part of Pepperell, together with the towns of Brookline, Mason and Ashby, have an aggregate of wood and timber land, nearly or quite three times as large as that in Townsend, and quite as heavily covered.

The town of Sharon has now a steam mill that cuts one million feet of sawed lumber annually. This town and Temple, having large quantities of wood land, and being too far from a depôt at West Townsend for the transport of wood, will therefore do the coal business that is now done in the towns below them – and this branch of business will furnish at least three thousand tons of transport to the road annually.

It is a well known fact that the towns of New Ipswich, Temple, Mason, and Ashby, are rich in agricultural resources, and will supply much tonnage of produce to the road. It is not unfrequent for farms in Mason to grow 1000 bushels of potatoes each (weighing about 37½ tons), for the starch factory in Wilton, present average prices about twenty-two cents per bushel. This article could be transported to West Townsend much easier than to their present market, and the average price in Boston is such as to command this business.

The manufacturing interest in this section is also well known to be somewhat extensive. The present transport of casks of all kinds from Townsend to Boston is $6,750 annually. Brookline has this branch of business to nearly the same amount of freight, and both of these towns have much unimproved water power, and great facilities for brick making, much of which is in the immediate line of the contemplated road.

How much unimproved water power have we in Canada? Have we no farms which grow 1000 bushels of potatoes each? no saw-mills cutting 1,000,000 feet per annum? The writer knows one establishment in Canada which cuts more than 10,000,000 feet annually. There is a large growing trade along the whole extent of our Frontier in this article – which we can produce *ad libitum,* and the whole value of which is from labour applied here. Our exports of sawed lumber to the United States will probably double, in 1849, those of any former year, amounting to more than one hundred millions of feet: Railroads alone will bring out the distant reserves of this article.

Have we no facilities for brickmaking, or do we still continue to import bricks from England as we did a few years since? The truth is – men have starved upon the richest soils and in the finest climes, as in India, Ireland, or Mexico, while the children of the 'Pilgrim Fathers' have grown rich from their granite, their wood, and their ice: they see 'sermons in stones,' and wealth in shoepegs at two dollars a bushel. The chief elements of the extraordinary success of the Americans are such as we in a great measure possess, although we have obtained them too recently to have yet experienced their effects, viz., the control of our own trade – and *facility of association* – hitherto hampered by legislative requirements at every step.

It is true that we have been stimulated – by legislation in which we had no voice – to an over production of food for which we have no home market, and upon which we must submit to a discount, until we can make one.[14] We have also political incertitude, for the continuance of which we have no one to blame but ourselves. The habit of association in New England, (for there it has become a *habit,* as we trust it will soon be here), is the prominent instrument in their prosperity. In a mistaken love of sole proprietorship, (in imitation of the wealth of the Mother Country), we either do not move at all in a promising enterprise because the investment is beyond our reach, or we place our necks in the halter by borrowing to such an extent that the first 'pull up' invariably produces strangulation. If we would but contemplate the almost illimitable powers of

14 The construction of Railroads is the first step towards attaining this desirable object.

association for manufacturing or commercial purposes, compared with the largest individual efforts, we would be forced to acknowledge the existence within ourselves of a mine of wealth and power, unheeded now, but which, if relieved from the pressure of indifference and incredulity, will expand into useful activity. In a town of but moderate population the humble mechanic may have his house lighted with gas and supplied with water – luxuries which the seigneur in his lordly country mansion cannot aspire to.

Perhaps the most striking instance of great results from small contributions is the penny post; – but everywhere examples meet us – in the news-room – in public baths – and even in the factories of New England, many of which are owned by the operatives and small farmers.

A Railroad from Montreal to Hamilton would have half a million of customers exclusive of those beyond the termini, for it would exact tribute from the industry or consumption of every soul upon or adjoining the line. If it be 400 miles long, and can be built for £7,500 per mile, the cost will be £3,000,000; and if the net earnings be taken at ten shillings per head, (instead of twelve shillings and sixpence, the proportion of the agricultural counties on the line of the Erie Railroad), we have £250,000 – or eight and a half per cent. Before the road could be completed, the population and wealth will have increased, and the expenditure of such a sum upon the route will have added so much to the ability of that route to support the road.

Is it time then to move in this matter? Do we not want this road now? Will we not need it before it can be constructed? Will it not be indispensible as soon as the Montreal and Portland Road is opened? We lost millions of dollars in the winter of 1846-1847, because we could not get our produce to the seabord. If a demand springs up again in December upon the seaboard for our flour, butter, ashes, or lumber, must we again wait until May before we can move, and when the Mississippi will have flooded the markets?

If the liberal provisions of our Railroad law prove inefficient to produce association and corporate effort, shall we allow it to drop? Shall we not rather as *a people,* through our Government, take it up, *'coute qui coute.'* We cannot any longer *afford* to do without Railroads. Their want is an actual tax upon the industry and labour of the country. Men may talk, says an eminent New Englander, about the burden of taxes to build Railroads, but the tax which *the people pay* to be without them is an hundred fold more oppressive.

In 1836 Massachusetts became a Stockholder to the extent of $1,000,000 in the Western Road, and by three subsequent Acts issued State scrip for $4,000,000 more, for the same object. The city of Albany gave for the same purpose $890,425 – the amount subscribed by private Stockholders only being one-third of the cost of the road. Georgia, Michigan, Delaware, States all inferior to Canada, have been equally liberal. They could not wait for the overflowing of accumulated capital, to seek out these projects. They considered the State 'but one wide extended charity to aid, protect and benefit each other' – the patron of the public good. Massachusetts looked upon the Western road as a State work; and upon the interests of the people at large as paramount to any individual or corporate ones which might desire this work. Canada must so consider a Railway from her seaport to the heart of her Western territory. The towns and cities on the route contain sufficient commercial intelligence and wealth to lend their credit for a large portion of the stock, and if the agricultural interests hold back, their representatives should be further appealed to. An hundred thousand pounds may be obtained by pledging the honour and the industry of a corporate town, where five thousand could not be spared by the *individuals* composing that town; – because the interest only will be required – of the burden of which the road upon completion will relieve them, and at the same time undertake the extinguishment of the principal.

Upon the same principle with still less inconvenience, the Canadian people at large, through their Government, may with equal propriety and benefit, procure the means for constructing any eligible line of Railway, by paying, for two or three years, the deficient interest on its cost. But it is highly desirable that wealthy individuals and corporate towns and bodies should take the lead and management. The Government stand ready under the late Act to second their efforts – and we have no doubt would advance a step further to meet private action, rather than see a deserving project fall to the ground.

Our present financial difficulties should be no obstruction, for in a very few years our public canals will relieve us from all uneasiness upon this head, and if we only make the same determined provision for the future payment of our liabilities, as has been made by our more deeply indebted neighbour – the State of New York – our credit will at once, *for all judicious investments,* stand as high as hers. New York, Pennsylvania, Maryland, Ohio, Illinois, and Louisiana, are all more deeply in debt than we are – but in them public improvement has not been suspended.

Our unoccupied routes have in themselves a value – but until there are charters, organization, and a fitting spirit and appreciation of Railways shewn, there is nothing to attract the passing capitalist.

Mr. W. Harding, in his 'Facts bearing on the Progress of the Railway System,' read before the British Association in August, 1848, says:

No limit can be assigned to the number of travellers which cheapening and quickening the means of conveyance will create. The introduction of the Railway, even where Steamboats already afforded a most pleasant, rapid, and cheap communication, increased the number of travellers (between Glasgow and Greenock) from 110,000 to 2,000,000 – 2,000,000 being *five times* the population of the district. In 1814 the number of passengers per annum between Glasgow and Paisley was only 10,000. In 1842 the number was upwards of 900,000: the *population* during this period has only doubled itself, while the *traffic* has multiplied itself ninety-fold – that is to say, for every journey which an inhabitant of Glasgow or Paisley took in 1814, he took forty-five journeys in 1843 ... The Railway System has doubled itself in three years. The importance and value of the traffic in goods and *cattle,* relatively to the passenger traffic, have become more apparent ... Whatever falling off in dividends there may have been is to be attributed *to the capitalization* of loans and the creation of fictitious capital by the purchase of Railways at premiums and therefore at sums beyond what they cost.

Lastly – we are placed beside a restless, early-rising, 'go-a-head' people – a people who are following the sun Westward, as if to obtain a greater portion of daylight: *we* cannot hold back – we must tighten our own traces or be overrun – we must *use* what we have or *lose* what we already possess – capital, commerce, friends and children will abandon us for better furnished lands unless we *at once* arouse from our lethargy; we can no longer afford to loiter away our winter months, or slumber through the morning hours. Every year of delay but increases our inequality, and will prolong the time and aggravate the labour of what, through our inertness, has already become a sufficiently arduous rivalry: but when once the barriers of indifference, prejudice and ignorance are broken down – no physical or financial obstacle can withstand the determined perseverance of intelligent, self-controlled industry.

We submit the foregoing view of the RAILWAY SYSTEM and our position in relation to it, to the generous and patriotic consideration of every intelligent merchant, manufacturer, farmer, and mechanic – to every Canadian, native or adopted – and ask them:

Shall we have Railroads in Canada?

APPENDIX A

WHAT RAILROADS DO FOR THE LAND AND HOUSE OWNERS

From *Hunt's Merchants' Magazine,* December 1848

Almost monthly the avenues of trade are increasing, and facilitating the transportation of the rich produce of the interior to the Atlantic border. The demand for capital, for the prosecution of these great lines of traffic, has been a decided cause of the high rate of money on the Atlantic border. Massachusetts has been particularly active in the construction of these noble works. In the last three sessions there have been chartered the following roads:

		Capital
1846	18 roads and branches	$5,795,000
1847	16 roads and branches	4,822,000
1848	19 roads and branches	7,105,000
	Stock of roads in operation increased	3,945,000
	Total	$21,667,000

The total length of roads in New England is 1,126½ miles, and the cost over $37,000,000.[15] This large expenditure has been effected only by absorbing all the surplus earnings of almost all classes of society. The accumulating *dividends of capitalists of all grades have sought this direction,* and, as a consequence, a far less amount has been available for the ordinary employments of industry. Even the Savings Bank deposits have been applied in this direction. The direct investments of the Massachusetts' Savings Banks in these works were $44,389, and loans upon Railroad stock $300,698. The income of the roads increased from $1,961,323 in 1846, to $2,564,190 in 1847. The effect of these multiplied means of communication upon the trade and property of Boston is magical.

15 This does not include the debts of the Corporations. The expenditure exceeds $50,000,000. See Appendix H.

Table of the assessed valuation of property in Boston and New York:

	Boston Estate, real and personal	New York Estate, real and personal
1841	$ 98,006,600	$255,194,620
1842	105,723,700	237,806,901
1843	110,056,000	228,001,889
1844	118,450,300	335,960,047
1845	135,948,700	230,995,517
1846	148,839,600	244,952,404
1847	162,360,400	247,153,303
1848		254,192,027

It will be observed, that the different modes of valuation in the two cities are such, that the figures do not give a correct idea of the actual comparative wealth, but in a series of years they show the comparative progress, more particularly in respect of real estate, which, while that of New York has remained nearly stationary, that is to say, was nearly the same in 1847 as in 1841, that of Boston has increased 60 per cent in value. *This has been the direct result of the Railroad influence.* It will be observed, that notwithstanding the number of persons that have moved from Boston into neighbouring towns, the *increased value* of the property taxed is $74,000,000, nearly *double the whole cost of the Railroads.* That New York has taken a start during the past year, is to be ascribed to the general prosperity and the growing *influence of the Erie Railroad.* The Erie Railroad is now progressing through the lower tier of counties, the population of which was, in 1845, 362,103, or about the same as the upper tier when the canal was built. The whole area commanded by this road is 12,000,000 acres of the best land, and the population occupying it numbered 532,000 in 1844.

The Reading Road, running 100 miles from the mines to Philadelphia, has cost nearly $11,000,000, and brought down last year 1,256,567 tons coal, thus establishing the capacity of a Railroad even at enormous cost to carry coal in opposition to a Canal ...

We shall then realize the fact that the Erie will be the *longest and most important Railroad in the world,* and its income will be commensurate with its importance. It will be observed, that although it will on its completion drain an area of 12,000,000 acres, containing in 1844 a population of 532,000 persons, the section now in operation to Port Jervis communicates with only 40,000 persons, and an area of 428,890 acres. Yet its income is $1,000 per day, and its nett profits $150,000 per annum!

[This gives an average nett earning of eighteen shillings and ninepence per head on the population.]

Extract from *Hunt's Magazine,* August 1849

It is doubtless the case that, at this moment, capital, as we have slightly indicated, is accumulating throughout the country, with a rapidity never before known; that is to say, there is more wealth being produced, *and less consumed by extravagant living,* through the operation of false credits, than ever before; but the capital so increasing is being converted on an extensive scale *from floating to fixed capital;* that is to say, *railroads,* public works, buildings, and machinery, all of which, although ultimately they will be productive of a still more rapid development of wealth, for the moment cause a demand for floating capital beyond, perhaps, even its enhanced supply. In the New England States the rapid increase of Railroads has been productive, since their regular operation, *of a rise in the value of property, in Boston alone, to an amount greater than the whole cost of all the Railroads in New England;* and the profits of the enhanced trade they have created in that emporium, divided among the community, has probably been far greater than the aggregate sum of the dividends paid by all the Railroads to their Stockholders.

In some of the Western States, particularly Ohio, [and may we not say, Canada,] there is a far greater expenditure of capital, *through individual extravagance in living,* than in the New England States. The increase of Railroads and manufactories in the Southern and Western States is calculated to promote the accumulation of local capital, to cause a husbanding of sectional resources; and while capital is kept in the new States to reproduce itself in industrial occupations, the profits of the Eastern States will become less considerable.

Progress of railroads in New England in 1849 (miles):

Cape Cod Railroad	27½
South Shore Railroad	11½
Norfolk County Railroad	26
Milford Branch Railroad	12
Vermont and Massachusetts Railroad	35
Connecticut River Railroad	11
Cheshire Railroad	37
Sullivan Railroad	28
Vermont Central Railroad	65
Bristol Railroad	12
Northern Railroad	4
Boston, Concord, and Montreal Railroad	36
Passumpsic Railroad	40
Worcester and Nashua	45
Portland and Lewiston Railroad	27
New York and New Haven Railroad to Harlem Railroad	60
Section of Ogdensburg Railroad	12
Stoney Branch Railroad	14
Lowell and Lawrence Railroad	12
Total miles	515

[The above is the number of miles of Railroad *brought into operation,* in New England alone, in the year ending February, 1849; all but one lead directly into Boston, and nearly all are extensions of Massachusetts Railroads, built by her capital and enterprise.]

APPENDIX B

WHAT RAILROADS DO FOR CONSUMERS

The Erie Railroad last year (1847) running 53 miles, supplied the following articles to the city of New York:

		Quantity	Est. value
Milk	qts	7,090,430	$283,616
Butter	lbs	3,758,440	676,519
Fresh meat		3,007,890	150,490
Cattle (beef)	head	2,362	86,853
Calves	head	11,457	51,649
Hogs		5,548	38,366
Sheep or lambs		8,198	29,975
Strawberries	bskts	389,920	15,596

In addition to the above, large quantities of poultry, game, fruit, vegetables, &c., are brought to market. The freight received by the road for the transportation of milk alone, was $35,450.

APPENDIX C

WHAT THEY DO IN OHIO – A FARMING COUNTRY

Mansfield and Sandusky Railroad
The following tables shew the passengers and the principal articles of freight transported over this road, in 1846 and 1847:

		1846	1847
Passengers		9,873	20,737
Freight:			
Wheat	bushels	306,255	504,081
Corn, oats and barley	bushels	4,369	13,713
Flour	barrels	11,315	62,598
Highwines and whiskey	barrels	1,125	3,235
Cranberries	barrels	839	1,046
Eggs	barrels	56	not given
Salt	barrels	9,502	6,613
Wool	pounds	116,833	
Butter and lard	pounds	309,742	680,248
Ashes		230,535	396,560
Tobacco, in hhds		42,192	80,190
Pork, bacon, &c.		86,957	1,361,624
Seeds – clover, flax and timothy		442,206	1,012,972
Dried fruits		19,494	181,450
Merchandize and furniture		1,847	3,110
Potatoes	bushels		2,912
Shingles	M.		611
Oil cake	pounds		47,605
Wool and feathers	pounds		210,903

APPENDIX D

WHAT THEY DO IN A GRANITE, ICE, AND 'WOODEN NOTION' COUNTRY

Table of tonnage over the Fitchburgh Railroad (Mass.) for the years 1846 and 1847:

		1846	1847
Tons transported upward		47,752	73,219
Tons transported downwards		41,105	61,979
Total upward and downward		88,857	135,198

In the above statement *ice* and *bricks* are excluded, which amounted as follows:

Ice	tons	73,000	77,505
Bricks	tons	39,308	31,772
Total tons, including ice and bricks		201,165	244,475

Quantity of wooden ware, paper, and wood, transported over the road during the year 1847:

Chairs	425,702
Pails	1,033,958
Reams of paper	166,752
Tubs	220,993
Clothes pins	4,228,206
Wash boards	101,459
Barrels	88,573
Kegs	164,295
Cords of wood	9,174
Candle boxes	174,177
Number of passengers carried in the cars the past year	494,035
Number of passengers carried one mile	8,009,437

APPENDIX E

HOW THEY DO IN THE NORTH

The Western (Massachusetts) Railroad

Years	Passengers	Merchandise	Mails, &c	Total	Expenses	Bal. receipts
1842	$266,446	$226,674	$19,556	$512,688	$266,619	$246,068
1843	275,139	275,696	23,046	573,882	303,973	269,909
1844	358,694	371,131	23,926	753,752	314,074	439,688
1845	366,753	420,717	26,009	813,480	370,621	442,858
1846 (11 months)	389,861	459,365	29,191	878,417	412,679	463,738
1847	502,321	785,345	37,668	1,325,336	676,689	648,646
1848	551,038	745,909	35,120	1,332,068	652,357	679,711
1849	561,575	745,394	36,841	1,343,810	588,322	755,488

Number of through and local passengers for each year since the road was opened:

Year	Through passengers	Way passengers	Total
1842	18,571	171,866	190,437
1843	26,595	174,370	200,965
1844	24,330	195,927	220,257
1845	19,192	204,442	223,634
1846 (11 months)	29,883	235,831	265,714
1847	34,299	354,011	388,310
1848	33,731	371,883	405,614
1849	33,751	402,053	435,804
	220,352	2,110,383	2,330,735

APPENDIX F

HOW THEY DO IN THE SOUTH

Georgia Railroad

	1848	1849	Increase
Passengers	$157,694 67	$166,484 04	$ 8,789 37
Freight	280,486 27	376,957 07	96,470 80
United States mails and rents	38,871 74	38,573 48	–298 26
Total	$477,052 68	$582,014 59	$104,961 91
Expenses	175,552 84	195,782 88	20,230 04
Nett profits	$301,499 84	$386,231 71	$ 84,731 87

APPENDIX G

HOW THEY BEAT CANALS

Coal brought from the Schuylkill Mines by railroad and canal (tons):

	Railroad	Canal	Total
1841	850	584,692	585,542
1842	49,902	491,602	541,504
1843	230,255	447,058	677,313
1844	241,492	598,887	840,379
1845	822,481	263,587	1,086,068
1846	1,233,141	3,440[16]	1,236,581
1847	1,350,151	222,643	1,572,794
1848	1,216,232	436,602	1,652,834

The Railroad was first opened in the year 1841. The amount of coal previously brought down by the Canal averaged about 450,000 tons per annum for the six years previous to the building of the Railroad, and never in any one year reached 524,000 tons.

16 Great freshet which injured the Canal.

APPENDIX H

HOW THEY PAY IN MASSACHUSETTS

In Senate, March 15, 1849
The Joint Standing Committee on Railways and Canals, to which was referred the Annual Returns of the several Railroad Corporations in operation within the Commonwealth, Report: That returns have been made by thirty-seven corporations.

The cost of the several Railroads, as appears by the returns, is		$46,886,991 93
The debt of the several corporations, as per returns, is	12,420,201 19	
The aggregate surplus fund is	1,349,230 08	
Difference		11,070,971 11
Total cost		57,957,963 04[17]
The earnings of the several corporations were	6,067,154 02	
The expense of working the several roads was	3,284,933 38	
The net earnings of the same		$2,716,920 30[18]
The length of the main road is	954.346 miles	
The length of branches is	88.810 miles	
Total	1,043.156 miles	
The length of double track	220.212 miles	

During the past year about 300 miles of Railroad have been put in operation on the various lines leading to Boston, many of which are far from being completed

17 A great portion lately expended, and as yet, unproductive – see next page.

18 This is about $3 40c. (17/0) per head on the population.

The miles of Railroad finished in New York, it is believed, do not exceed 750.

The whole number of miles in the United States is stated at 6,421¼, of which nearly one-sixth part is in Massachusetts.

The extent of Railroad finished in England, at the end of the year 1848, and in operation, was 4,420 miles, constructed at a cost of £131,000,000 sterling, or $628,000,000.

The average cost per mile is about $142,000.

These roads are thoroughly built, generally with two or more tracks.

There is no road in this country which cost the average of the English lines, excepting, perhaps, the Reading Railroad in Pennsylvania.

The traffic on the English roads, in 1848, amounted to £10,092,000, or more than $47,000,000.

The net returns were about 4¼ per cent on the outlay.

The expense of working the English Roads is less than fifty per cent of the gross earnings.

The expense of working the Massachusetts roads is a fraction over fifty-four per cent.

The committee have taken thirteen roads, (upon whose returns reliance can be placed, and none of which commenced operations within the year,) and averaged the dividends upon the cost of the roads.

	Cost	Dividends
Berkshire	$ 600,000 00	$ 42,000 00
Boston and Lowell	1,800,000 00	144,000 00
Boston and Maine	3,249,804 52	252,798 50
Boston and Providence	2,893,300 00	175,349 00
Boston and Worcester	4,245,175 00	325,500 00
Connecticut River	1,234,970 00	69,960 00
Eastern	2,655,700 00	239,628 00
Fall River	1,050,000 00	68,250 00
Fitchburg	2,735,910 00	201,029 50
Nashua and Lowell	525,000 00	50,000 00
New Bedford and Taunton	400,000 00	24,000 00
Old Colony	1,601,415 00	91,362 50
Stoughton Branch	85,400 00	4,270 00
Taunton Branch	250,000 00	20,000 00
Western	5,150,000 00	366,000 00
	$28,476,674 52	$2,074,147 50

Mean rate per cent upon money paid in, 7.283. The above is an approximation to correctness, though not entirely accurate. The Western Road, for instance, paid 8 per cent; by the table, it is less. The discrepancy is caused by the fact, that new stock has been created in the present year, and has been expended in construction, thus adding both to capital and cost of road during the year, while one of the semi-annual dividends was declared upon the last year's capital. The dividends are declared upon the capital paid in, and not always upon the cost, and this will show a difference between the table and the actual dividend, in cases where the cost of road varies from the amount of capital paid in. It should be added, that, in all statements relative to the Western Railroad, the dividends are reckoned upon its chartered capital which now stands at $5,150,000. In addition to which, there has been provided for its construction, and received by the corporation £899,900 sterling bonds, payable with interest at five per cent, sold at an advance of not less than 8 per cent – $4,319,520; Albany city bonds $1,000,000, interest 6 per cent, making the total means provided for its construction, $10,469,650, from which there has been paid, into the several sinking funds, $459,578 62, leaving, for construction and equipment of road, $10,009,941 38. The cost of the road to the date of the return is $9,900,153 76, leaving in possession of the corporation a balance of construction funds amounting to $109,787 52. The balance of interest paid by the corporation the past year is $266,380 77. The first dividend was declared upon forty thousand shares, the second upon fifty-one thousand and five hundred, and were each four per cent. Of the surplus of $47,330 41, $45,883 34 must be paid into the general sinking fund, which will leave the sum of $1,498 07 to be added to surplus fund of former years.

APPENDIX L

HOW THEY PAY IN ENGLAND

British Railway statistics

From the *Civil Engineer and Architects' Journal*

	Passengers	Receipts	Goods – tons	Total receipts
1844	27,763,602	£3,439,294	9,823,536	£5,584,982
1845	33,791,253	3,976,341	12,522,973	6,649,224
1846	43,790,983	4,725,215	15,871,179	7,664,874
1847	51,352,163	5,148,002	16,699,362	8,949,681[19]

The capital expended on Railways has been likewise given by Mr. Hackett, from which we can learn the amount expended in each year:

	Whole capital	Expended	Miles opened	Total miles
1842	£ 52,380,100	–	–	1,532
1843	57,635,100	£ 5,255,000	59	1,586
1844	63,489,100	6,844,000	194	1,780
1845	71,646,100	8,157,000	263	2,043
1846	83,165,100	12,579,000	503	2,610
1847	109,528,800	26,363,700	839	3,449

The total amount of Railway expenditure from 1842 to the end of 1847 was £57,548,700. The total amount of Railway income in these years has been £38,884,181.

Of course, the whole of this income cannot be treated as real capital, no more than can be the whole of the expenditure; but it is a significant fact, that while the *whole expenditure* has been £57,548,700 in five years, from 1842 to 1847, the *receipts* have been £38,884,181, or *more than two-thirds* of that amount. This is

19 1848 £10,059,006 1849 £11,013,817
There has been invested in British Railways, up to January, 1850, £200,000,000 ($1,000,000,000). There are completed 5218 miles, at the cost of £180,000,000.

deserving the attention of those who direct their attention toward the subject of Railway capital.

From Mr. W. Harding's *Progress of the Railway System*

The length of Railways sanctioned by Parliament at the commencement of 1848, but not then open, was 7,150 miles. These new Railways are principally designed for the *accommodation of the agricultural parts of the country.*

When the Railways now in contemplation are completed we shall have 10,000 miles, on which 140,000 persons will be permanently employed at good wages – representing at five to a family – three quarters of a million of the gross population.

Mr. Hyde Clarke shows the increase of travel caused by Railroads:

	Travellers from old coaches, &c.	New travellers
1844	10,300,000	17,400,000
1845	12,900,000	20,800,000
1846	16,000,000	27,000,000
1847	21,000,000	30,000,000

Reckoning that each passenger is on the average carried twenty miles, each male adult in this country will be carried that distance six times in the year – an extent of accommodation which must have a great effect on trade and on the distribution of labour.

An 'Observer' in the *London Morning Herald* states that it has been estimated that Railways have effected a saving of £12,000,000 annually on the traffic of the country, although they comprehend as yet but a fraction relatively of the whole traffic of trade.

APPENDIX M

HOW RAILROADS CATCH FISH

From Hyde Clarke's *Contributions to Railway Statistics*

This traffic is of the greater importance, as it gives a positive addition to the supply of food in the country, and is therefore of great national benefit. Railways stimulate the production, or economise the cost of production, of grain, meat, and other articles of food; *but all fish that can be carried inland, is so much added to the resources of the country* – In this respect, Railways have done much and can do more, both for the supply of food to the country, and for the promotion of the fisheries.

This traffic is very remunerative and does not bring less than 10s. per ton. The gross tonnage of fish carried on the English Railways may be reckoned as 70,000 tons; or, on the lowest computation, the food of as many individuals. Fresh fish, meat, butter, fruit, &c., cannot be brought from great distances except by Railway. Milk is now largely carried on the Eastern Counties and other Railways, under arrangements by which the companies can bring back the empty cans.

[Codfish, oysters, and lobsters, brought daily by Railway from Halifax or Portland, would be an agreeable change of diet for inland Canadians – and would lighten the *maigre* days.]

APPENDIX N

WHAT THE WORLD THINKS OF RAILROADS

Table of railroads in operation, January 1, 1849, and of their cost, including equipments – carefully estimated from official returns, &c.:

	Miles	Average cost per mile	Total
New England and New York	3,952	$ 27,500	$ 108,186,237
Other parts of the United States	4,192	25,000	104,922,179
Canada	54	32,000	1,731,000
Cuba	273	–	9,473,000
Total in America	8,471	26,500	224,312,416
Great Britain	4,721	170,000	802,571,500
France	1,256	110,000	138,500,000
Germany	3,371	50,000	168,500,000
Belgium	497	80,000	39,640,000
Holland	163	25,000	4,062,000
Denmark and Holstein	284	40,000	11,281,000
Switzerland	79	50,000	3,650,000
Italy	164	90,000	14,625,000
Russia	113	60,000	6,781,000
Poland	188	50,000	9,375,000
Hungary	157	50,000	7,850,000
Total in Europe	10,993	$110,000	$1,216,875,500
Total	19,464	$ 74,000	$1,441,187,500

At the close of 1848, the Railroads built and in progress in the United Kingdom and Ireland were 12,481 miles in length, and their estimated cost $1,567,887,013; in France, 3,841 miles, at a cost of $416,000,000; and in Russia, 1,600 miles, at a cost of $170,000,000.

APPENDIX O

THE FOLLY OF CHEAP ENGINEERING

The following is a list of the Railroads which have been engaged in relaying their tracks with heavy rails during the past year (1848), together with the quantity of iron which has been contracted for, in England, for that purpose (tons):

Syracuse and Utica	2,500
New York and New Haven	6,000
Eastern	2,000
Boston and Worcester	4,000
Western	5,000
Vermont Central	8,000
Vermont and Massachusetts	4,000
Rutland	8,000
Old Colony	2,000
Boston and Providence	1,000
Stonington	1,000
New Haven and Hartford	3,000
Concord and Portsmouth	4,000
Lawrence	2,500
Boston and Lowell	1,000
Utica and Schenectady	2,000
Tonawanda	2,000
Buffalo and Attica	4,000
Ramapo	2,000
Somerville (about)	2,000
Total	66,000

APPENDIX P

HOW THEY PAY IN NEW YORK

Shewing the business done on the railroads between Albany and Buffalo, and on the New York and Erie line, in the year 1848 (from official returns)

Name of road	Number of miles of road in operation	Cost of construction	Number of through passengers	Number of way passengers	Total income from passengers	Income from freight and other sources	Dividends
Syracuse and Utica	53	$1,968,036 42	114,151	102,659½	$296,831 98	$380,839 46	$100,000 00
New York and Erie	74	3,276,618 76	28,324½	259,744½	125,722 32	185,190 43	133,437 32
Auburn and Syracuse	26	1,125,886 77	140,084	14,131	132,667 65	39,517 36	32,000 00
Attica and Buffalo	31	821,313 87	127,004	19,231	119,446 47	31,513 27	35,000 00
Utica and Schenectady	78	3,161,688 15	163,977½	106,435½	556,884 81	239,354 56	528,200 00
Tonawanda	43½	974,865 66	109,234½	39,209	160,963 27	57,338 46	49,427 00
Auburn and Rochester	78	2,644,520 35	100,782	108,477½	358,471 30	96,250 57	8 per cent[20]
Albany and Schenectady	17	1,606,196 70	236,889	–	113,741 88	62,180 55	70,000 00

Total cost, $15,579,168 68c. Total income, $2,956,914 34c., of which $1,092,184 66c. is from *freight*. Dividends, $1,159,625 63c. – or nearly 7½ per cent.

20 $211,561 63c.

APPENDIX Q

WHAT THEY DO FOR THE GRAZIERS AND DROVERS

The following are the proportions of cattle, &c., carried on British Railways:

	Cattle	Sheep	Swine	Receipts
1845	236,000	1,200,000	550,000	£102,000
1846	370,000	1,250,000	850,000	167,200
1847	500,000	2,000,000	390,000[21]	183,400

The total number of horses carried in 1847 was 99,405 and the receipts £80,216.

Taking the saving by conveyance of cattle on Railways at 40 lbs. per beast, 8 lbs. for sheep, and 20 lbs. for swine, the gross saving in 1847 will be 43,800,000 lbs. of animal food.

Large quantities of dead meat reach the London market by Railway from the country: it comes in excellent condition from *Scotland.* By means of railways, great quantities of hind quarters of mutton are sent up from the country – as the butchers there kill large quantities of sheep and sell the fore quarters at home amongst their own population – sending the hind quarters by Railway to London. It is the general opinion of butchers that country killed meat is better than town killed meat. It is ordered and sold by telegraph, and is not damaged by the journey, even in hot weather.
Evidence given in late Report on Smithfield Market.

21 Falling off caused by Irish famine.

APPENDIX R

HOW THEY DO IN THE WEST

The following are the articles brought to Detroit by the Michigan Central Railroad *during the month of November,* 1849:

Flour	bbls.	61,962	Whiskey	lbs.	202,387
Wheat	lbs.	11,155,805	Pig iron		40,933
Corn meal		331,647	Timber		202,704
Ashes		94,118	Carriages		1,000
Wool		5,751	Cattle		4,000
Barley		259,151	Horses		5,000
Cranberries		38,097	Sheep and hogs		40
Beans		26,124	Other 1st class freights		154,779
Grass seed		16,466	Other 2d class freights		46,341
Beef and pork		166,639	Other 3d class freights		9,922

	Through pass.	Way pass.	Total pass.	Receipts pass.	Rec. freight	Total rec.
1849	46,053	91,848	137,901	$321,114	$279,872	$600,986
1848	13,409	69,778	83,187	155,771	218,210	373,981
Incrs.	32,644	22,070	54,714	$165,343	$ 61,663	$227,005

Passengers West 78,187; Receipts $175,895.
Passengers East 59,714; Receipts $145,219.
Total Receipts 1849, $600,986; Expenses, $296,080;
Net earnings, $304,906.

From the above figures it will be seen that the business of this road has been rapidly increasing notwithstanding the prevalence of the Cholera in the last season; and that on this decidedly 'through' route – the *way* passengers *double* those going *through.*

Conclusion of the fourth edition,
Philosophie des chemins de fer, 1853

La bonne volonté avec laquelle les municipalités du Haut Canada se sont taxées elles-mêmes, depuis ces dernières années, fait beaucoup d'honneur à leur intelligence, et est une preuve que se taxer soi-même pour des améliorations locales n'est pas une chose regardée comme un fardeau. Port-Hope, dont la population n'est que de 2,500 habitans, a souscrit £ 50,000 pour son chemin de fer, s'imposant une taxe de plus de $ 6 annuellement par tête. Toronto a donné £ 100,000 au chemin de Guelph, et £ 50,000 à la ligne de Simcoe et du Huron. Il doit y avoir quelque chose dans un système pour porter des villes et des comtés à de tels sacrifices *apparents* ; mais le fait est que la taxation en faveur de chemins de fer est, sous tous les rapports, un placement très profitable. Un comté souscrit £ 1000 ou £ 1,500 pour chaque mille du chemin qui se trouve dans ses limites ; par ce moyen, il s'assure l'importation du double de cette somme, qui *sera dépensée* en-dedans de ses bornes. Chacun s'appercevra bientôt qu'une portion de la grande dépense d'argent occasionnée par le chemin de fer entrera dans sa poche; portion plus considérable que la taxe pour le chemin de fer qu'il consent à payer. La plus grande partie de l'argent comptant à dépenser *ici* pour chemins de fer doit être importée, et en obtenant les chartes, en organisant les compagnies, et en prenant des actions autant que nos moyens nous le permettent, nous posons les fondemens d'une propriété destinée à augmenter de valeur annuellement, et une valeur qui, en même temps qu'elle est pour nous, de mille manières, directement ou indirectement, d'un avantage inappréciable, est aussi une propriété que les capitalistes s'empressent de se procurer et de compléter.

Enfin, nous sommes placés à côté d'un peuple inquiet, matineux, marchant en avant, d'un peuple qui suit le soleil vers l'ouest, comme pour jouir d'une plus grande portion de la clarté du jour : *nous* ne pouvons pas nous tenir en arrière ; nous devons marcher vite, si nous ne voulons pas être dévancés ; nous devons faire usage de ce que nous avons, ou perdre ce que nous possédons déja ; capitaux, commerce, amis, enfans nous abandonneront pour des terres mieux fournies, si nous ne sortons *d'un coup* de notre léthargie ; il ne nous est plus loisible de fainéanter durant les mois d'hiver, ou de passer les heures de la matinée à sommeiller. Chaque année de retard ne fait qu'accroître notre inégalité : elle prolongera le temps et aggravera le travail de ce qui, par notre négligence, est déjà devenu une rivalité assez pénible; mais quand une fois les barrières de l'indifférence, du préjugé et de l'ignorance auront été abattues, nul obstacle physique ou financiel ne pourra résister à la persévérance déterminée d'une industrie maîtresse d'elle-même.

2 MONTREAL

A lecture on Montreal from the pamphlet,
Montreal and the Ottawa,
Montreal, np, 1854, pp.1-32

LADIES AND GENTLEMEN,
In selecting the name of your beautiful City for the subject of my remarks to you this evening, I feel some explanation is due respecting the intended scope of this Lecture. By assuming so comprehensive a title, I by no means profess ability to do justice to the subject, nor is it possible, within the limits of an evening's Lecture, to discuss a tithe of the subjects which affect Montreal.

For the sake of the many fair faces who have honored us by their presence this evening, I regret that we are compelled to consider almost exclusively, the weightier matters which concern this goodly City. Not that I would by any means intimate that such topics have no interest for ladies – that they are unconcerned about the welfare of their City – in other words, the prosperity of their husbands, their fathers and brothers. However vulgar the observation, none know better than the ladies that it is the annual balance sheet which determines the concerts and pianos – the summer jaunts and the sea-side bath – the furs and the velvets – the silks and the satins – the parasols and the scent bottles, and all the innumerable and incomprehensible elements which form a material basis for what is called domestic bliss.

The subject is familiar to you, and you may perhaps say to me, 'tell us something that we do not know'; what have you, a comparative stranger, got to say about our City? we know all about Montreal.

'Know thyself' is a maxim as applicable to communities as to individuals, and if I am guilty of presuming that you have overlooked something deeply concerning you, if I insinuate that you do not exactly embrace your full and true position – it is not that I arrogate a superior discernment, but perhaps offer views suggested by a somewhat greater indifference, as a looker on can sometimes determine the best move at chess more safely than the players. Life has oftentimes been compared to a game at chess, and in our day so keen is competition, so well understood are the causes of success or failure, that cities must struggle in their corporate capacity as well as families for their subsistence, and play out their part with the same patience and shrewdness, the same energy and decision which are everywhere and in every cause the essentials to success.

It is an undoubted fact that we all overrate what is remote, underrate what is familiar to us. The knowledge which concerns us most is generally the last acquired. The saying, 'far off cows have long horns,' is but a vulgar rendering of the divine proverb, 'a prophet is not without honour save in his own country.' Distance lends enchantment to our view of other things besides scenery. No man, it is said, can be a hero to his own valet, because there is nothing heroic in flannel drawers and a nightcap, and yet a man's a man for a' that – for George Stephenson, the father of the Locomotive Engine, after having remarked that he had dined with princes, peers, and commoners, and also that he had dined off a red-herring and gone through the meanest drudgery, summed up as follows: 'I have seen mankind in all its phases, and the conclusion I have arrived at is this – that if we were all stripped there is not much difference.' Our neighbours and commercial rivals seldom rate themselves below par, but a lingering remnant of colonial tutelage must, I suppose, be assigned as an explanation of the fact that there exists in this section of the Province a want of confidence in something or in somebody, and it must be either in our resources or in ourselves!

Perhaps a too great familiarity, as the copy book says, excites contempt. I had the fortune or misfortune to be born within hearing of the roar of Niagara; I saw that great cataract when so young that I do not remember any first impressions. I supposed the world was full of such places and, as a boy, passed on until my attention was attracted by the praises of strangers. Our children will weary with forty miles an hour on our Railroads, having had no experience of the bark canoe and the corduroy road, and they will daily gaze on the St. Lawrence, without being impressed with its surpassing volume.

To appreciate correctly our own position we should raise ourselves, if possible, beyond the influence of the smoke of our own City, survey impartially the operations which are going on round about us, and then determine whether we will set to work in earnest to improve our home, or at once change it and make room for more congenial spirits. One of the great causes of the rapid development of this continent is the fact that every man has had it in his power (from the cheapness of land and facilities of water communication) to gratify his whims as well as his necessities, and to pitch his tent in that precise spot where he desired to dwell. This deliberate choice of habitation is almost as much a duty as a privilege, for, if a man finds himself in the wrong place he becomes discontented, and with true human perverseness too often determines that that place shall not have the best of the bargain.

The next best thing to finding a ready-made paradise here on earth, is to make one out of such materials as present themselves, as the good wife does out of the humblest home. A man should not only be contented with his lot, but he should also make the most of it: and it is incumbent upon every one to investigate the resources of his homestead before he covets his neighbour's patrimony, else, like many over nice people, he may go through the bush and cut the crooked stick at last.

It may be objected that these are not the most appropriate subjects for a Mechanics Institute. It is usual, I know, on these occasions to make the subject a scientific one, to take up some of the -isms or the -ologies, and expound them. If I am guilty of any innovation in meddling with the domestic affairs of this City, my apology is that having been honored with a request to address you, I am more anxious to benefit than to amuse you. We are a practical people, and we live in an eminently practical age, and what more edifying, what more profitable subject can the Mechanics of this City discuss, than the causes which favor or which threaten the prosperity of Montreal. The prosperity or adversity of a city is immediately felt by every interest in it. The capitalist may survive 'hard times,' but the first symptoms of depressions are felt by the working classes – and by the working classes I mean all of us who labor for our subsistence. Wages go down – the brakes are at once put on – wives and children are denied former comforts and the limited enjoyment of the present is embittered by anxious forebodings for the future. If then the working classes, who form a decided majority of the body politic, are the most seriously inconvenienced by a stagnation or reaction in business – an inquiry into the causes which induce or avert the public adversity is surely most appropriate on their part, not only because they are the earliest and greatest sufferers, but because in their hands rests a remedy. We live in a country, thank God! where almost every man has some influence, and if he does not exercise it to his own advantage, it must be because he does not understand his own interest.

We too frequently wait to be led – perhaps in the end by the nose! – forgetting that if we only form a strong battalion politicians innumerable will volunteer to lead us on to victory and its spoils.

Now those enterprises are always the most irresistible which spring up from the people – those the most doubtful which come down from the public bureaux. When, therefore, the mechanics in a city, or the farmers in the country, become protectionists or free traders, temperance men or railroad men, it is amazing with what agility the leading politicians become convinced and place themselves at the head of movements which they can no longer withstand.

The moral of this is, that if the working classes study the resources and wants of their districts and devise any enterprise for its welfare, they can carry it because they have the votes.

The credit of a city or country is the great engine through which she is to recover or maintain her position, and the control of that credit is in the hands of the majority. It is unfair – nay, more, it is dishonest – that any portion of a community should evade their quota of contribution to enterprises in which all are interested, and from which all will derive proportionate benefit. The free horses should not be ridden to death. Montreal should therefore do as every city, county, town and township in the United States and Western Canada are doing – tax all for the benefit of all.

I propose, with your indulgence, to advert to some of the principal wants of this City – to take a rapid survey of its position, and the causes which have operated, and will operate for or against her, and trust the explanations made, will satisfy you that I could in no way be more useful than by drawing your attention to questions which must sooner or later be discussed; and, however mistaken my own views may be, succeed in enlisting your interests in some course of action, for action is the watchword of the day.[1]

Time was when a premium upon exports by the St. Lawrence, caused by a protected demand for our products in Britain, gave Montreal a monopoly of the export trade, not only of Upper Canada, but also of the Western States; while, at the same time, differential duties forced nearly all transatlantic imports through your warehouses. Now, not only has American export by the St.

1 [For a more detailed, modern study of the situation of Montreal in 1853 and after, see Jean Hamelin and Yves Roby, *Histoire économique du Québec, 1851-1896* (Montreal, 1971), especially pp. 101-40, 343-66; and Jacques Letarte, *Atlas d'histoire économique et social du Québec, 1851-1901* (Montreal, 1971), parts II and V.]

Lawrence ceased altogether, but transit privileges have been afforded over American routes to Upper Canada, so that she is exporting and importing through her inland ports at such a rate as threatens to reduce your City to the position of a country town, a mere trading point for a few miles of surrounding territory.

Again, it is but yesterday that the Green Mountains were an impassable barrier to the southern valley of the St. Lawrence, and the products of the industry of this thickly settled district were concentrated in Montreal. Now, faith in science has removed mountains, and numerous Railroads made and making are gathering where they did not sow, and probably another winter will see the whole surplus of the South shore carried off to Portland, Boston and New York, leaving nothing for shipment on the opening of the navigation.

The mere superiority of New York, as a seaport, over Montreal and Quebec, immediately upon the cessation of all protection in favor of the latter, was sufficient to turn the western tide through the diminutive channels of the New York Canals, in preference to the more capacious St. Lawrence. This result took place whilst you were competing upon equal terms, *i. e.* when transport by both routes was confined to water communications, equally influenced by frost, commencing and suspending navigation at the same time: but now a more formidable rival has appeared, one whose operation is not impeded by frost, whose path is not restricted to vallies of rivers where water navigation may be made, and who for nearly five months in the year has no competitor. The Ogdensburgh Railroad has run past you on the St. Lawrence, has turned your flank, and intercepted your supplies. This road passes disdainfully by us, preferring to climb over 1000 feet of elevation, in order to reach a village west of Montreal. It was natural to suppose that New York would seek the Western States without calling here, but when Boston also prefers a western point to this, when she attaches so little importance to us, and so much to Western trade, is it not time for us to value that Western trade, and revise our estimate of ourselves. While Boston offers a continuous Railway to nearly all that is valuable west of us, New York, by a line from Rome to Cape Vincent, gives a winter market to Upper Canada through Kingston. Three or four roads are congregating on the Niagara River and will penetrate to the most valuable parts of Western Canada. Similar lines will be multiplied, and when the demand arises during the winter, these roads will sweep the Western Province of its surplus before the ice leaves our wharves. If the country is emptied while we are curling in the Canal basin, what have we to export? If Upper Canada exports in winter, will she not import proportionally during the same season?

But you may say – we have our canals, and will be content with the business which they must bring us; – but let us look at this.

Quebec exports our timber, because rafts can go there cheaper than vessels can come after them, and because tide water assists the loading. Montreal has hitherto exported most of the agricultural produce, and imported nearly all the supplies from sea, because the batteau and durham boat, and the barge of the Rideau route could not profitably proceed to Quebec, and transhipment was therefore made here. But this is changed – the boats which now come down from the West will not continue to stop here unless you make it their interest to do so. You cannot yet bring up a ship drawing twenty feet of water, but hundreds of such can ride in the stream at Quebec, and there most assuredly Western propellers will meet them and exchange pork and flour for iron and salt, unless you make that exchange more profitable here. The possession of our large canals is the only thing which, since the loss of protection – the abolition of the differential duties and the opening of the Inland transit trade between New York and Western Canada can preserve Montreal. Quebec, come what may, can stand upon her timber toes. But at the same time, these canals are instruments which can be wielded with equal force against as well as for you. It is extremely fortunate that the completion of the canal was secured before the repeal of the Corn Laws. It is scarcely probable they would have been undertaken after that event, and it is pretty certain that if the St. Lawrence navigation had been in the state it was prior to the Union, all agricultural exports from Upper Canada, by the route of the St. Lawrence, would have ceased. The canals have placed the inexhaustible West within your reach, and you are nearer to the lakes and can carry between them and tide-water cheaper and quicker than any other city in America. But these are advantages which we must not merely talk about, but prove.

No sooner have we completed the Herculean task of our magnificent canals, than like all other builders we find we are not half done. Our competitors on the other side of the line have not only canals but railroads alongside of them. The canal is the street and the railway is the side-walk. Trade and travel can thus keep company. We have provided for the trade only, and made no provision for the travel. For nothing is more certain than that travel follows trade, because on those routes where the most business is done (as for instance the route from Albany to Buffalo) there there is the greatest travel. Now, if trade and travel are inseparable, we cannot expect to enjoy much of either until our travelling facilities are improved. This City has been by no means backward in railway enterprises – she has been forward, too forward literally. It would perhaps have been better for her in this respect, if she had looked backward – to the West and North behind her – rather than so much forward toward Portland and New England. I doubt whether we have made a good selection in amalgamating with Portland on a 'differential' gauge. We have, perhaps, thus thrown the greater capital and influence of Boston in favor of the Ogdensburgh road, and aided its completion. But it is natural that Montreal should first attempt the comparatively shorter connections with long American lines, than grapple with the magnificent distances towards the West; and the truth must be told, ours is rather an expensive country to furnish with commercial facilities, particularly with railways. We only require canals where we have rapids, but we must have railroads along the whole frontier, which is of a disproportionate length to the depth of country behind it. The Province, by a public guarantee and a trunk line, has undertaken to put a good face on matters: but we must look after the backing, otherwise the benefits will be too superficial – we will be all front, without the proper depth and solidity.

The Trunk Line, though of great public importance, will probably be so located as to be of but secondary utility to Montreal. The Western stream will be tapped at Kingston and Prescott by the Cape Vincent and Ogdensburgh Railways. Lastly, one of your best and hitherto surest customers, Bytown, is slowly but steadily working her way to Ogdensburgh, and will carry with her the trade of the Ottawa valley.

Thus, from having been in 1845 one of the most fortunate of cities, possessing almost a monopoly of the imports of Upper Canada, and having a premium on the exports of breadstuffs, American as well as Canadian, you are now assailed on all sides. New

York is not only fast taking your place as the outport of Upper Canada, but for the trade which still belongs to the St. Lawrence, Quebec will be assuming the position of a rival; while the railways of New England and New York are cleaning out the country before and behind you.

It is a fitting time, therefore, to 'take stock' and see where we stand. Our liabilities to ourselves, to our children, to the times we cannot evade; we should, therefore, look into our assets, take a careful and comprehensive survey of our position, and determine upon a course of policy and united action for the future. This result can only be accomplished by the formation of a strong and extended public opinion, based upon a thorough investigation. Nearly all great public works, here and elsewhere, are to be ascribed to the efforts of a few individuals generally deemed visionaries, humbugs, or rogues, by their contemporaries; but, in these latter days, our wants accumulate so rapidly that we should no longer wait for the appearance of apostles or champions of progress to lead us on; this was the feudal, the despotic system, but if we are capable of governing ourselves, we ought to be able to prescribe for ourselves and order what we want.

I will now briefly allude to the more important duties which are before us, each of which would be a fitting subject for an evening's discussion.

First in importance are our Navigation interests. It is her seaport which Montreal should most highly prize and most sedulously nourish, and as she labours under some disadvantages from natural causes, these must be noticed.

1st. The existence of some obstructions in the channel in and above Lake St. Peter, prevents the arrival of the largest class vessels from sea. These obstructions are fortunately not insuperable, and when we remember that Glasgow, which at one time was only approachable by fishing smacks drawing six feet water, now displays in the Broomielaw some of the finest craft afloat, we have every encouragement to persevere until Montreal shall be to Quebec what Glasgow is to Greenock.

2nd. In consequence of the limited frontage between the shoals under Point St. Charles opposite the Canal, and the Current St. Mary, there is an insufficient amount of harbour accommodation, and the value of that we have is reduced by local phenomena. The rise of water in winter and the shoving of the ice, prevent the erection of warehouses on the wharves, and of permanent machinery for discharging cargoes, so that the commerce of the port, particularly its business as an *entrepôt* is burdened with a heavy charge for drayage. The same local phenomena prevent us from laying up craft for the winter in the harbour, thus driving to other ports the population and outlay required for the winter repairs, and checking the descent of upper lake vessels as soon as the first frost sets in. Fortunately, indeed for this City, there is within reach of it a remedy for this objection. We are in the same position as at a tide-water port (in consequence of this winter rise of water) – and have the same need of docks, but we have not the flux and reflux of the tide to work them with; but we have an abundant supply of water close at hand, at a sufficiently high level for this purpose. The Canal basins are docks precisely similar to the kind which must be resorted to, but, although these are a great relief to the harbour they will not be accessible, on account of the shortness of the locks, to screw-steamers and the largest class of craft which may be expected at Montreal, and they are moreover no more than sufficient for the trade of the Canal itself.

We must, therefore, 'fence in,' from time to time, as many acres of the Point St. Charles shoals as may be required, and fill up the enclosure with water from the Canal, or from the river above the rapids. No excavation is required, and these basins may be approached through the Canal until the arrival of longer or wider craft calls for the construction of larger locks.

Point St. Charles is the proper point for the Railway Freight Termini, and for the Railway Bridge: the docks in the river at this point would therefore be accessible to railway tracks, so that the vessels and the railroad cars can, when necessary, be brought side by side, and elevators worked by water-power be employed to discharge grain. These facilities should not be confined to any one railway; it is the best arrangement for all railroads, terminating on either side of the river below the Lachine rapids. The natural causes we have alluded to, will always operate largely against both the Champlain and St. Lawrence and the St. Lawrence and Atlantic Railroads, in any attempts which they may make to do an extensive business in connection with the river. Shallow water, strong currents and the winter rise of the river, make the system of docks or basins such as those at the Canal, almost indispensible at St. Lambert and Longueuil, but the high head of water is wanting there. The Portland road looks to the St. Lawrence for its principal business: but to conduct this business – particularly the transport of wheat, corn, barley, &c., profitably, and on terms of equal competition with rival roads, it is indispensible that it should be able to have warehouses and elevators alongside of the craft coming down from the western lakes. Moreover if these South shore railroads make their termini in Montreal, they will get rid of the steam towage of deeply laden western craft from the Canal, over and up to Longueuil and St. Lambert.

Before these roads undertake any extensive expenditure in the river opposite Montreal, it behoves them to investigate the Bridge question and see whether the expenditure which they propose to make, if invested in a bridge would not be more profitably applied than elsewhere.

The City of Montreal should meet the Bridge question heartily and liberally, as a matter of self-interest. If the Railway termini are permanently established on the opposite shore, and no provision be made for a bridge, the imperfect mode of communication will create an interest there, which, instead of being auxiliary, as Brooklyn and Jersey City are to New York, will be rivals, and from their perfect communication with the most important parts of America, South, West, and East, will possess all the elements of absolute independence. Fortunately for the interests of this City the local unfitness of the South shore for a good connection with the St. Lawrence, in addition to the necessity for an unbroken communication with the line of Western Railroads terminating in Montreal, bring not only a powerful but a mutual interest to this Bridge question which guarantees its early achievement.

The good old City of Quebec has taken alarm at the railway operations at Point Levi, and has sought for a bridge, but the fates are against her; and there seems nothing for the ancient and modern capital, but emigration to the South shore, unless indeed she is content with the North shore timber coves, her citadel, a political menagerie every alternate four years, and the dining of American tourists. As the chances for any bridge across the St. Lawrence, below Montreal, are most remote, and no more favourable point for crossing exists above us, a bridge at this place will have the widest support provided Montreal takes steps to bring that support to it.

Now, the difficulties of crossing the St. Lawrence below Montreal, the distance of the railway from the South shore between Quebec and Montreal, even supposing the crossing were good, and the great length of time, five months of the year, during which the large population of the North shore are closed in, gives Montreal a monopoly, if she is wise enough to avail herself of it, of the business of this whole population, including that of the ancient and honorable City of Quebec herself. The impassable state of the St. Lawrence at Quebec, will cause all travel and imports for that city, for five months in the year, to be made through Montreal, and it will be your own fault if it is not done through here for the remainder of the season. The route from Quebec to New York will be as short by the North shore through Montreal, as that through Richmond and Sherbrooke, and to the whole West, still shorter. The North Shore Railroad, when reversed, becomes not only practicable but highly desirable. As a part of the Trunk Line, or as a means of giving an outlet to the intermediate country through Quebec, it could not be sustained, because Quebec is no market, and from the state of the river in winter, cannot be put in communication with a market. But reverse the proposition and start a road from Montreal, as an extension of the three roads going South, and of those to be built going West, and every section of it twenty miles in length as soon as opened can be properly worked and extended, as circumstances warrant, or be at once taken up as a whole. There is great encouragement for Montreal to embark in this enterprize, because she need fear no rivalry, the North shore is a regular *cul de sac,* and can never get an outlet or inlet as advantageous as that through Montreal.

I have said that no more favorable site for a bridge presents itself above us than can be found here. But I do not mean to say that the country cannot be permanently invaded, at Prescott for instance. By extending piers from the South shore to the edge of the channel, steamers with railroad tracks upon them can ferry loaded cars between Ogdensburgh and Prescott throughout the year, whenever necessity arises. The whole St. Lawrence valley west of us is so exposed to inroads from the United States, and so contiguous to a highly populous district on the other side of the boundary, that Montreal must not anticipate too much from the Trunk Line. But there is a region west of her, for the trade of which she can put forth her energies under encouraging auspices. The valley of the Ottawa above Bytown and Perth, is a *cul de sac,* with no outlet above these two towns. It is well settled, and a good agricultural country for nearly one hundred miles above Bytown and the most valuable timber region perhaps in the world. It abounds in minerals, fertile soil, and water power unlimited. The import trade of this region is greater, for the population, than perhaps any other part of America; because, not only must the greater portion of their consumption be imported, but as the lumbering business is conducted on the cash principle, and wages are highly remunerative, the population are more able, and do consume more and live better than any country population I am acquainted with. I speak from experience when I say that I never saw elsewhere money more plenty, and the means of comfort more universally diffused than on the upper Ottawa. The reason is, that the population instead of being idle during the winter, and consuming their substances like bears in a hollow tree, are steadily employed on cash wages.

We have said that this valley is a *cul de sac.* None but the Voyageurs go through it. But it is a *cul de sac* unlike the North shore below, for there the farther you go after you pass Quebec, the worse you are off. Not so with the Ottawa; if you only burst the narrow belt between the upper Ottawa settlements and the broad expanse of Lake Huron, you are at once on the track of the Chicago, Wisconsin and Superior trade. Western produce from Chicago to Michigan and Superior can be delivered on the Georgian Bay, at a point nearer to Montreal than Hamilton is, as cheaply as it can be carried to Sarnia or Detroit.

This project may be deemed premature and too extensive, but it is not necessary that it should now be undertaken as a whole. Over one hundred and fifty miles from Montreal westward may now be safely undertaken as a local road; and as far as Montreal is concerned as a matter of necessity and self-preservation. The Bytown and Prescott road now far advanced will carry out the Ottawa trade to Prescott where it meets the Trunk Line, but, as there must be transhipment at this point in order to come on the Trunk Line which is of a different guage, the Ogdensburgh route will be more advantageous.

Again, it has been shown that the Railroads on the South shore, opposite us, will not bring produce into market, because this produce will find a better market to the South. The Trunk Line skirting the bank of the St. Lawrence between Prescott and Montreal draws from one side only; and as the farmers in the rear must come out to the front, in order to get the Railroad, they will be brought so near the Ogdensburgh road, that they may be induced, particularly during the winter when they have their best roads, to cross Lake St. Francis on the ice to the Ogdensburgh line, as they are now doing. That the business which is brought from above Prescott may be stopped there or at Kingston, has already been mentioned. Again, as the farmers of the interior, between the Ottawa and St. Lawrence, must now come to the latter for a market and an outlet, their position will not be improved by a Railroad also on the river; it will not shorten their teaming, and, therefore, the influence of the Grand Trunk in developing this portion of the Province near Montreal will be feeble. Now, it is of great importance to Montreal that she should have a road which will traverse an agricultural district, because the consumption of a large city will pay the Railway transport on every article, even of the coarsest description of agriculture, or of the forest, which can be found within one hundred miles of it. Thus we can bring firewood, hay, milk, potatoes, lumber, &c., from Two Mountains, or Glengarry, and the Counties west of there, when we cannot afford to bring these articles from points west of Kingston.

The location of the Trunk Line on the front, as a provincial work for through travel and the mails, therefore not only justifies but creates a necessity for another line in the rear, which can neither be called a parallel nor a competing one: for it will do a business, and create a business which cannot and will not be done by the Trunk Road. Such a route is now absolutely essential for the protection of the interests of this City as a means of preventing the tide of the Ottawa trade from flowing toward the St. Lawrence and thus placing it in dangerous proximity to the Ogdensburgh road.

If I have succeeded in making myself clear on a subject so trying to your patience – it will be conceded that the great Ottawa railroad should forthwith be commenced. Whether or not, the present favorable position of the money markets, and the eagerness for investments in all promising Railroads should be taken advantage of, to place the whole route to Lake Huron in the market – does not affect the question. A Railroad from Montreal up the Ottawa can now be profitably sustained as far as the counties of Lanark and

Carleton. The extension to Lake Huron must follow sooner or later, nor will it stop there.

The four great Lakes – Ontario, Erie, Huron, and Superior are separated by three peninsulas – at Niagara – Detroit – and Sault Ste. Marie – to these points must all surrounding Railways converge – for at these points connections and crossings may be constantly maintained. A railroad terminating on the Georgian Bay would be confined to its local business, for four or five months in the year, as is the case now with the Ogdensburgh road; but if extended to Sault Ste. Marie and carried over into the peninsula of Michigan, it could thus penetrate Wisconsin, Minnesota, and the Upper Mississippi, to all of which it would be the shortest route to the east, and draw over it a stream of traffic which can hardly be overrated.

This route, when made, must become one of the great lines of this continent. It is a route worthy of this City. If Portland could project and successfully urge forward a route through the Mountains to Montreal – the latter with double her population may with confidence cope with an undertaking not more than double the extent. The particular and indeed supreme importance of this route when opened to the Western trade is that it would place Montreal on the route of the great American trade from West to East and vice versa. Wherever a town is by canal or railway wheeled into the line of this trade, the effects, as at Buffalo, Oswego, and Ogdensburgh, are immediately perceptible. Montreal would then have the double advantage of an inland transit as well as a sea trade.

But it is not pretended that such a railway – which would secure the travel and a portion of the trade of the North West – would be sufficient to enable us to compete with Buffalo, Oswego, and Ogdensburgh, for the carrying trade between the East and the West. Those points have the benefit of our unequalled Inland Navigation, which supplies such an extraordinary amount of freight that the quantity which any city which is on this track may aspire to, is only limited by her enterprise and means. Whatever vicissitudes or temporary checks may befall our sea trade, this inland traffic is ever to be depended on – and if there be any possible means whereby Montreal can be placed upon the carrying route between the manufactures of the East and the consumers of the West – and between the food producers of the West and the food consumers of the East, no effort should be spared to attain this enviable position, in order that whenever the sea trade is unpropitious we may have the second string to our bow. Now there is one million of tons to be sent from the West to the East every year, and there is one-fifth of a million of tons to be sent from the East to the West. This commerce does not belong by right to any one route, the whole of it is open to the competition of Dunkirk, Buffalo, Oswego, Ogdensburgh, and Montreal, and the last comers appear to be the favourites.

It would seem at first view that Montreal was too much out of the way to indulge in any expectations of benefitting by this water-borne traffic between the Eastern and Western States. In point of distance, it is true, that starting from Cleveland or Hamilton, the route to New York is much more direct through Buffalo and Oswego than via Lake Champlain, but experience is more valuable than opinion, and the facts that the great majority of the business done over the Ogdensburgh road is with New York proves the truth of the old saying, 'that the longest way round is sometimes the shortest way home.' The reason is that a cargo of flour from the Lakes can reach New York quicker through Ogdensburgh and Lake Champlain, with but 66 miles of canal, than through Buffalo and Oswego with 363 and 209 miles of canal respectively, because a propeller from Cleveland to Ogdensburgh will carry – at eight miles the hour – the load of five canal boats, which move only about 2½ miles the hour.

Now, it is in our power by constructing a canal, to enable that propeller to proceed directly into Lake Champlain instead of stopping at Ogdensburgh, and thus save two transhipments and their accompanying damage and detention – and in so doing, to raise the stock of our St. Lawrence Canals to fully double their present value, and bring one of the greatest currents of commerce within our reach. As an instance of the effect of having and of not having an interest in this Western trade – it is sufficient to refer to the fact – that the tolls received on the Welland Canal are nearly three times greater than those received on the St. Lawrence Canals.

It cannot be denied that there has been some prejudice, or at least some indifference displayed in relation to this Canal, in consequence of the proposed point of departure, Caughnawaga. The entrance of a Canal at Caughnawaga would not benefit that point unless there were transhipment – and now that a Railroad is there, which will cause transhipment, any attempt to arrest the destinies of

Caughnawaga will be as vain as it would be, on our part, suicidal. The Canal is now necessary to enable Montreal to compete with Caughnawaga – to make this City the depot and entrepot and enable vessels to load here for Lake Champlain instead of forcing this business to be done at Caughnawaga.

The great portion of the business of this Canal would be through trade, which if not invited down here would remain at and above Ogdensburgh. The benefit to be reaped by Montreal from the work is chiefly incidental – and the larger the trade of the Canal the greater will be these incidental advantages. With such a stream of shipping, as this Canal properly located would induce, a large portion of which would be partially laden or in ballast, you could send up freights to the Western Lakes at the lowest rates – and at any moment by the aid of the telegraph, arrest a cargo destined for New York, if required to complete a contract here. This Canal would complete your position as a depot or produce market, so that you could store here either for the Gulf trade and the Lower Provinces by sea navigation – or for New York and New England by Inland waters. When once Montreal is placed upon the route between New York and Chicago, steamers ascending or descending could fill out or exchange a part of their cargoes here, and this facility of trading inland in all directions on the best terms must exercise a powerful influence over our sea trade and tend greatly to increase the number of vessels arriving here. The trade between the Western Lakes, and New York and New England, together with the Ottawa lumber trade, must comprise the great bulk of the future commerce of this Canal. If Montreal desires to reap the greatest benefit from this work, she should place it where it would be most efficient, and to be most efficient it should be located where it will be most convenient to this Western and Ottawa trade – neither of which should be burthened with the additional lockage of the Lachine Canal doubled – when they have no business to do here. So far from 'diverting trade' from Montreal, this Canal would simply restore to the St. Lawrence Canals, trade which has been diverted from them by the Ogdensburgh Railway. The trade of Upper Canada and the Western States now finds its way to New York through cheaper routes than by Montreal. If Caughnawaga can attract it from Ogdensburgh, and Longueuil cannot do so, surely it is better for Montreal to get it any where within reach than to see nothing of it whatever. Even if you were to reap no incidental advantages it could do you no harm, and inasmuch as it must give increased impulse to the Ottawa lumber trade it would enrich the country behind you – enrich your customers and thereby enrich you.

Caughnawaga should be treated as one of the future suburbs of this City. From the St. Gabriel Lock, which will ere long, be a central point of departure, Caughnawaga can be reached in about the same time and cost as Longueuil. There would be no more lockage between the Sea and Lake Champlain via Caughnawaga, than by any other route, and in this case, the up trade of iron, salt, coal, fish, &c., must pass through Montreal, whereas in the other, it would stop at Longueuil, making that point quite as efficient a rival as Caughnawaga. So also with the down trade, I mean that intended for Lake Champlain – supposing that you could induce it to undergo 90 feet of unnecessary lockage – it would either descend by the rapids direct to Longueuil, or if it passed down the Canal, it would do you no more good, than it would do to Beauharnois or Cornwall.

The same arguments which are used for the Champlain Canal will apply to the improvement of the rapids, between Coteau du Lac and Montreal – with this additional consideration, that the whole benefits of this expenditure would tell upon both the Sea and the inland trade of this City. When we reflect that our largest Mail Steamers every day descend from Prescott to tide water without passing through a Canal or Lock, it is wonderful that we should not sooner have inquired into the causes which prevent all boats, freight as well as passenger craft, descending by the river, and thus reduce the time and cost of bringing cargoes to the seaports. I can speak from personal knowledge when I say that the impediments to this unrestricted navigation of the rapids, by all boats which may reascend the Canals, are utterly insignificant when compared with the effect to be produced by their removal. The improvement of the rapids and the construction of the Ship Canal to Lake Champlain are works of the very first importance, and would produce greater results from the expenditure required, than any other works in the country, perhaps upon the Continent, and certainly are more worthy of the consideration of the Legislature than such speculations as the Sault Ste. Marie Canal.

We have now taken a cursory view of some of the leading enterprises which Montreal should promote in order that she may build up her commerce upon a more solid and enduring foundation than one based upon commercial legislation. Legislative measures are certainly the cheapest modes of relief, but when they are contested so as to partake of the character of class legislation, they are ropes of sand. Nothing can be more dangerous – nothing more hostible to the best interests of this City can be devised – than the attempt to confer by temporary Acts of Parliament commercial advantages upon the seaports at the expense of the inland ones. To engage in a war with Upper Canada upon these points would be to alienate your best customer. You cannot fail to be as unsuccessful in result as you would be unjust in position.

The constitution of the United States prohibits the levying of greater duties at one port in the Union than at another. Goods entered at Chicago via Montreal, are liable to no more duty than those entered at New York. Instead, therefore, of attempting to force the trade of Upper Canada by Legislation, through the St. Lawrence, invite, coax, not only this trade but that of the whole North West through this river, by making it as free as the Ocean. Then you will make Oswego, Cleveland and Chicago, Hamilton, Kingston and Toronto, Inland Seaports, if I may use the term, and unite them with you in one common bond of interest.

This indifference upon the subject of the free navigation of the St. Lawrence is in the Lower Provinces, at least, almost criminal. Upper Canada, with the power of selecting New York or Montreal, can afford to neglect this question. The Lower Province, which will be the greatest gainer by the measure, appears to attach a value to the monopoly she possesses, whereas it is a positive curse to her. Sam Slick tells us of a bear which having seated himself upon the moving log in a saw-mill, and becoming annoyed with the encroachments of the saw, embraced it with a characteristic hug until it cut him through, tumbling a hairy slab of bear's meat on either side of the saw log. Now all parties must admit that the commercial position of the Lower Provinces is chiefly to be maintained by an increase of Shipping. Is it wise then to 'hug' a system which discourages an increase of Shipping, and which is cutting us in two? Have you any thing to fear from a crowd of American merchantmen in the St. Lawrence? Why not exclude the travellers of that country from our Hotels and Steamers? There is as much reason in the one course as in the other. Canada East is Commercial, Canada West is Agricultural; if like the Northern and Southern States they clash – the Union Act may like the U.S. Senate maintain equality of representation in the face of inequality of population, but this will only be submitted to upon the basis of perfect commercial equality. Upper Canada will, ere long, possess double the population of the Lower Province, and will certainly claim equal rights.

But there is an interest growing up in this country which will inevitably overpower all others, and overturn any unequal legislation bearing upon the Inland trade. The Railways cannot go to sea. The surplus of this country has for more than one-third of the year no other market, nor any other outlet to a market, than that to be found in or through New York and New England; and it cannot be supposed that this great interest will consent to be debarred from the international trade inland, even if the people who were supplied by it were content to submit to so short-sighted a policy.

I have alluded to a question of public policy because it is one which most deeply concerns your welfare. Montreal, while she should never forget her interests as a seaport, should also recollect that these interests depend on her ability likewise to maintain an inland trade. If you are enabled to overcome the deep tide water advantages of Quebec, for transhipment between the Ocean and the Lakes, it will be because you possess other advantages which Quebec does not which will enable you to compete successfully with her. The ability to bridge the River, the large surrounding area of fertile and populous country, the junction of the Ottawa with the St. Lawrence, the proximity of New England with her millions of consumers, and of the West with its rapidly increasing millions of producers for whom you may become the successful caterers – these conditions will enable you, by the aid of Railways, to bring about a concentration of trade and travel here which is impossible at Quebec. But if by a mistaken policy you spurn the inland trade, which is always here always increasing, and fall back solely upon the fluctuating and uncertain trade by sea, prospering chiefly from the negative fact that ships come here when they can find nothing better to do elsewhere, you will, like Ephraim, be 'let alone.' Before we ask Upper Canada to import through our warehouses, we should satisfy her of our ability to discharge the responsibilities we would assume. How would you supply from the Ocean your Western nursery in winter? Not through the United States, for of course Uncle Sam would not be long in bottling us up in the route for which we had evinced so strong a predilection; nor could we complain, after discriminating against him, if he should withdraw the bonding and warehousing privileges by which we make use of his seaports when our own are useless. How then is Montreal to provide an outlet for her young and rising family in Western Canada during the five mortal months of winter? Echo answers – HALIFAX AND QUEBEC RAILROAD!

It is a wiser as well as a more honorable policy to endeavour to better ourselves by legitimate means rather than at the expense of others, and experience has shewn that in free countries no other course can be depended on. I do not pretend to say that differential duties in favor of the St. Lawrence will not grant advantages to Montreal which she does not now possess, but I do believe they will bring with them disadvantages more serious; that while we grasp at the shadow we will lose the substance. I would prefer directing your attention to enterprises the beneficial effect of which can neither be conferred upon you nor taken from you by legislation, and which, if they do not make you friends, will at least not add to your enemies, and will be equally useful and indispensible to you under any system of commercial legislation. Of what use would differential duties and increased trade be to you unless your Harbour be enlarged – unless vessels of deeper draught can come to your wharves? It is more profitable, therefore, to direct our attention to objects which we cannot dispense with, and which will be far more efficient means of attracing and securing the trade and sympathies of Upper Canada and the West than engaging in a struggle in which we can obtain nothing permanent but the ill-will of those whom it is our interest to conciliate. The very agitation of schemes which, however mistakenly you may consider it, are yet sincerely looked upon in Upper Canada as an attempt at a sort of commercial robbery, will drive Western Canadian merchants in disgust to New York. This is not a question between Free Trade and Protection – neither of which systems as a whole are suitable for us any more than that the same food would assimilate in the digestive organs of the infant and the full-grown man. This is a question between the inland and the seaports – the former *seventy* in number, the latter only *two* – a question which it is proposed to settle not by fair and honourable commercial rivalry but by coercive legislation.

There are other subjects of interest which time will not allow me to enter upon, significant of the future that is in store for Montreal. The water power of the St. Lawrence capable of driving its millions of spindles will sooner or later be called into activity. Our magnificent rapids cannot much longer be allowed to flow uselessly to the sea – the admiration of travellers – the toys and playthings of romantic maidens – the gigantic rocking horses of annual flocks of tourists who come and go as regularly as the wild geese.

There are also minor wants but not less important, to be noted. The health of the City calls for an efficient system of drainage and sewage, for which the topography is favorable. You have perhaps escaped the cholera at the expense of one-third of the City in ashes. Fire is the only thorough scavenger for a city badly drained: and it is perhaps fortunate that the same poverty which causes our early towns to neglect their drainage also builds of combustible materials, thus providing the future fuel for the purifying process.

Your physical wants provided for, the moral ones come next, although some philosophers – forgetting that the gospel was not preached to the poor until the lepers were cleansed, the dead were raised, the blind received their sight, the lame walked, and the deaf heard, – would reverse this proposition.

You need a Public Library. This City is certainly deficient in this important respect. You also need an Alms House – a public receptacle for beggars – where the idle may be made to work and the impotent be cared for. Our door bells are ever on the ring – our housemaids ever on the run to answer the calls of shivering wretches – and who shall discriminate between the worthy and the unworthy; – we can refuse none, for we may 'entertain angels unawares.'

And having done our duty may we not also enjoy ourselves – may we not combine the useful with the ornamental, and while the City is young, before it numbers its hundreds of thousands, set aside public lungs to let in the light and air of heaven among our thickening streets – lay off Parks and Gardens to give new attractions to the stranger – new recreations to the toil-worn citizen.

Cannot Nuns' Island be secured as a Water Park for the future use of the City? Should not the vacant fields on either side of St. Catherine Street between Philip's Square and the Protestant Orphan

Asylum, be laid out as a park before they are built over – where the pure air and the constant breeze drawn around the head of the Mountain may be enjoyed by a few minutes' walk from the busy haunts on either side of McGill Street. And the long-talked-of Boulevard? Will not Montreal avail herself of the magnificent features of the Mountain to have a drive where the tired mechanic may sport his cab or sleigh with wife and baby alongside the gay turnout of the merchant prince, or the high official? Will she not covet an attraction which few cities in America can and none have availed themselves of. Would it not arrest for a day the tribe of pleasure-seekers who seem to be the legitimate descendants of the famous –

Mynherr von Slam,
The richest merchant in Rotterdam,

– and who seem to have inherited his cork leg. May it not be even possible that the facilities afforded by Railways will induce many of the wealthy idlers who congregate in New York and Boston to visit us during the winter, to wrap themselves in our furs and enjoy that abundance of snow, that keen exhilirating atmosphere which they so much prize 'down south,' and of which we have perhaps a surplus.

In conclusion, permit me again to vindicate the propriety of the topics brought under your notice this evening. Is there not a marked change in the general appreciation of what are called public improvements? Is not the English tongue rapidly girdling the earth? California and Australia – and who is not interested in them – who has not friends there – having in the duly appointed time revealed their hidden treasures, America has opened up the Isthmus of Darien while England is breaking through that of Suez. America is agitating a Railway from the Atlantic to the Pacific – England one from the British Channel to the Ganges, from Calais to Calcutta, passing through Constantinople and the valley of the Euphrates, with a station at Antioch and a junction to Jerusalem. In the Ohio basin, in the Mississippi valley, on the Atlantic slope of the Alleghanies, throughout Western Canada, from the Saguenay to Panama, from Halifax to San Francisco – everywhere one subject, the making of Railways, rules the public mind. Shall we alone fold our arms until the question is put, why stand ye here all the day idle? What other city of this population has not made, or is not now undertaking all the practicable routes within her reach?

Practical mechanics is the hand-maid of Science. The Printing Press has distributed the hoarded lore of Time. The civilization of a country is but another term for the Arts and Sciences of that country. The Ancients were the fathers of Astronomy, of Mathematics and Sculpture: in Euclid, in Archimedes, they had their Bacons and Newtons but they had not their Watts and their Arkwrights – nor was the world then ready for them.

One great civilizing engine the Romans understood and employed – perfect roads. The spread of Christianity, the first great moral revolution applied to the earth, devolved upon that age and that empire which alone of all previous ages and empires possessed the capabilities for giving effect to the Divine injunction – 'Go ye into all lands preach the Gospel to every creature.' The broad, hard inimitable highways which radiated from ancient Rome into every conquered Province between the Pillars of Hercules and the banks of the Euphrates were garrisoned up to the very borders of that barbarian cloud which hung for centuries over the Roman frontier. These great arteries worked by the heart of the then mistress of the world pent up the flood of barbarism until Christianity had taken root, until it alone survived the wreck and triumphed over those fierce intruders who had just broken the secular power of hitherto invincible Rome.

Constructed to convey the mail clad cohorts, the relentless Eagles, and the swift vengeance of the Roman Senate into revolting provinces, these noble roads were in the providence of God made the efficient and indeed the indispensable means of waging a spiritual warfare, and bore with jealous care the swift footed messenger of the Gospel of peace beyond the lofty Alps and the far distant Pyrenees. And may not we be entering upon those latter times, when many shall run to and fro and knowledge shall increase? and may not the vast, the almost incredible extension of the Railway system, the Electric Telegraph, and the Ocean Steamer over all the Christian Earth, be a forerunner – a necessary and an indispensable forerunner – to that second great moral revolution, the Millenium – 'When the sword shall be beaten into a ploughshare and the spear into a pruning hood; – when nation shall not rise up against nation, neither shall there be war any more.' It may be a heresy – but is there not reason for a belief that the regeneration of the dark corners of the earth is to be accomplished, not through the pulpit alone, nor by sectarian schools – nor yet the philosophy of cheap literature – nor by miracles – but by a practical elevation of the people, to be brought about by a rapid development of Commerce and the Arts. Ignorance and prejudice will flee before advancing prosperity. Wherever a railway breaks in upon the gloom of a depressed and secluded district, new life and vigour are infused into the native torpor – the long desired market is obtained – labour now reaps her own reward – the hitherto useless waterfall now turns the laboring wheel, now drives the merrier spindle, the cold and hungry are now clothed and nourished; and thus are made susceptible converts to a system the value of which they are not slow to appreciate. The pulpit will have then its grateful listeners, the school its well filled benches – the stubborn opponents of wordy philosophy will then surrender to a practical one the truth of which they have experienced.

Let then the bigot, the theorist, and the agitator ply their unprofitable trade – let them lay the flattering unction to their souls that they alone are engaged in the high and holy cause of moral elevation. Let them commisserate the apparently low aims, the ceaseless toil and drudgery of the practical mechanic; – but know for a certainty that bigotry and intolerance, agitation, and the highest order of speculative philosophy have existed in the midst of starving and uneducated masses; – that it is the Steamboat and the Railroad which has peopled the recent wilderness of the North West – and by granting facility of access and by securing a reward to labor, have diffused a degree of comfort and prosperity, unprecedented in history. Every new manufacture, every new machine, every mile of railway built is not only of more practical benefit, but is a more efficient civilizer, a more speedy and certain reformer, than years of declamation, agitation, or moral legislation. And shall not the mechanic, ever the pioneer of progress, lift up his eyes from the work bench and look ahead? Has he, the humble instrument in a mighty revolution, no right to think on such things? 'Thou shalt not muzzle the ox that treadeth out the corn!'

I venture to believe that, as mechanics we may devote some moments to a consideration of the tendencies, the prospects, and the utility of the great enterprises, which give character to the age, and in the execution of which we are in a greater or less degree the agents – that this feeling of being useful in our day and generation will while away with a diminished degree of weariness the many hours of labor – that as you ply the busy hammer or wield the heavier sledge some of you may dream that you are fast driving nails into the coffin of prejudice, of ignorance, of superstition and national animosities; that as you turn down the bearings or guide the unerring steel over all the 500 parts of a locomotive engine, fancy will picture you cutting deep, and smooth, and true, into obstacles which have so long separated one district, one family, one people from another – and that you may exult in the reflection that those huge drivers will yet tread out the last smouldering embers of discord, that those swift revolving wheels – by practically annihilating time and space and by re-uniting the scattered members of many a happy family – will smooth the hitherto rugged path, fill up the dividing gulf, break through the intervening ridge, overcome or elude the ups and downs of life's chequered journey, and speed the unwearied traveller upon his now rejoicing way.

MONTREAL, January 1853

3 A SEQUEL TO THE PHILOSOPHY OF RAILROADS

A sequel to the Philosophy of Railroads
by Thomas C. Keefer, CE

Extracts from lectures on civil engineering, delivered at McGill University, 1855-6

T.C. Keefer's petition to the legislative assembly, April 1856

Statement of the Honourable John Ross before the legislative council, Friday, 25 April 1856

Letters of explanation to the Montreal *Herald*, May 1856

Editorial from the Toronto *Leader*, Thursday, 13 May 1856

T.C. Keefer's statement in reply and letter in defence published by the *Globe*, 14 May 1856

Editorial from the Toronto *Leader*, Saturday, 17 May 1856

[The contents of this somewhat confused pamphlet have been reorganized into chronological sequence and the statement by the Honourable John Ross and the editorials from the *Leader*, which state the other side of the argument and to which Keefer addressed his pamphlet, have been interleaved. The *Sequel* was printed originally by Lovell and Gibson, Toronto, in 1856.]

Extracts from lectures on civil engineering, delivered at McGill University, 1855-6

It may be argued that, after our public works are completed, the number of Engineers will be limited, and insufficient to sustain a special school of instruction. The first is to a certain extent true; it is not probable that there will be anything like a proportionate progress with regard to public works for the future; and it is pretty certain that, though we may have the will, we will not have the power to expend money at the rate we have been doing in the last four years. But this by no means is an argument that we will have less need, on the whole, of practical and scientific information on Engineering subjects. For, as many persons are more able to make money than to keep it – so it is easier to construct public works than to take care of them – particularly under corporations or public governments.

With corporate bodies a 'concern,' as it is called, is sometimes made a losing one by ignorance or design, whereupon it falls into hands which, despairing of dividends, manage it for the sake of the incidentals. A Railway which never pays a dividend, may yet pay a commission and, so long as its receipts or credit are sufficient to pay working expenses, public spirited individuals will be found, who will give their energies to retrieve a sinking property, in consideration of moderate salaries, and the usual commission on the rolling stock annually purchased, the iron for the repair shops, the rails for renewal, the purchase of fuel, oil, &c. If the property be promising or productive, any tendency to plethora is carefully kept down by resort to similar contrivances – at least until, by judicious management, the despairing stockholders can be bought out.

This is an unfavourable view of human nature, but it is believed to be true, to a greater or less degree, as to some of the most, as well as to some of the least, productive railways; and it is chiefly the result of ignorance on the part of the shareholders at large as to the nature, wants and value of their property. 'Knowledge is power,' and the strong in railway knowledge prey upon the weak.

With popular governments the case is much worse, as no other qualification than political interest is needed, at least none is so effective, and the result of this system is, that Michigan sold her railway long ago; Pennsylvania, in despair, has advertised all her public works for sale, while the last State Engineer of New York recommended the sale of the Erie Canal, a work capable of yielding a nett revenue of millions, as the only means of protecting it from the plunder of State officials. In a fit of despondency we, a few years since, sold all our public works except the canals, and unless these can be better managed than they have been, they will also be brought to the hammer. Indeed, I believe a proposition for their purchase or lease has lately been made. The Lachine Canal has been converted into a mill race, and in its present state is incapable of a large trade – the only remedy having been delayed and suspended while the railways have been pushed on. The navigation of the Ottawa at St. Anns has been trampled down by the same iron heel.

The best antidote to this incompetency in politicians and their proteges, with respect to engineering subjects, is to supply each political party with a sufficient amount of engineering ability, so that when they have no higher motive than the credit of their party, they may at least have the means of making a good appointment; in short, to make some knowledge of engineering as essential to the embryo Commissioners of Public Works, Railway Commissioners, Canal Superintendents, &c., as is that of the law to the expectant Solicitor or Attorney General, County Judge, or Queen's Counsel. No man can be considered well-educated without some knowledge of Mathematics and Mechanics, although he may make a considerable figure in public life without them – and as a gentleman may study both without being necessarily a Newton or a Descartes, a Watt or an Arkwright, so a popular knowledge of Civil Engineering may be imparted without the necessity of making Smeatons, Telfords, Brunels, or Stephensons.

It is time, therefore, that Civil Engineering became a branch of popular education in our Seminaries of learning, and when this has borne its fruits we shall not feel the want of it in our Legislature as much as is now done. Had there been even a few Engineers in our Parliament (as is the case in the British) there might have been a little less of folly – and something more than folly – perpetrated there. It may be asked, why do not our Engineers go into Parliament? It is to be presumed that some of them could get there as well as Lawyers, Doctors, etc. Most M.P.P.'s are volunteers; few are dragged like Cincinnatus from retirement; and an Engineer has the same right, as he has the same opportunity, to canvass a constituency, make non-committal speeches, be obsequious to the father, flatter the mother, and kiss the child, as any other man. The probable reason is that, like many other respectable men who keep out of Parliament, they are now better employed; but make them by your colleges as numerous as Lawyers, Doctors, etc., and some of them will be driven there – by necessity.

But it is in the future management of our Railways that the wisest field will be opened for the application of an Engineering education. There is scarcely one of the thousand employées required, who would not be the better qualified for his post, and what is more important to him, be eligible for promotion, if he had the advantage of attending a class in Engineering. Lastly, the necessary growth of the manufacturing interest, and the application of steam and water-power must call for increased Mechanical and Engineering knowledge, and this, with our Canals, Harbours, Railways, Gas and Water Works, the sewerage of our towns, drainage, &c., open a field more extensive than that of the legal and medical profession combined; and in which, if all the employées have not some Engineering education, all that can be said is, they ought to have it; and, if given the opportunity they will most probably seek it.

Although Engineering is a pursuit eminently calculated for the display of genius (and I have already adduced this as a reason for not hampering the practice with any protective restrictions) I do not wish to be considered as maintaining that, to be an Engineer, a man must possess extraordinary endowments; there are many grades in the profession, as in the army; but I wish to guard parents and guardians from supposing that in this profession a man may rise to eminence by mere routine. In every profession the men of mark are limited in number; but, as the most general object in selecting a profession is to obtain a respectable livelihood, ordinary qualifications, allied to industry and integrity, will be sufficient for this purpose *so long as the supply does not exceed the demand.* And here I would draw the great distinction between Engineering and the other professions. Almost every man (as well as woman) requires the services of a doctor at some period of his or her life; without any fault of your own you may be driven to a lawyer; and if you attain even moderate means you will, probably, employ an architect; but few individuals require engineers. Their patrons are extremely limited, and are almost exclusively confined to corporations or governments. Latterly the practice has obtained of including the engineering in large contracts, in which case the contractor becomes the patron or employer of the men whom he formerly took his orders from. This does not increase the number of the employers (as it merely substitutes the contractor for the government or the corporation) while it lowers the position of the engineer from that of an arbiter between both parties to that of an agent of 'the party of the second part.' This system is only applied to projects which are dependent upon stock operations, and where Governments or Corporations admit their inability to be their own financiers, by giving an influential contractor his own prices and his own engineers, in consideration of his taking such securities as they have to offer, and which he undertakes to float off by means of his superior connections. Wherever parties possess the power to pay in cash or to negotiate their own securities, they will always give out their work by competition, in which case they secure a working class of contractors – the same, indeed, as are necessary to the speculative middle man, who takes his pay in stock, or bonds – and get their work done as it ought to be done, under a *bona fide* supervision and for moderate prices.

The only occupation for which a practical Engineer is qualified when employment is denied him in the line of his profession, is that of a contractor, and this is a more legitimate and honorable course for him to adopt than that of dabbling in contracts *sub rosa.* In fact when he becomes a party to contracts he should cease to practice as an Engineer, for his legitimate position is similar to that of a broker, who is not allowed to traffic in matters where he is professedly a confidential agent.

There is no reason why the important business of contracting for large works should not become a profession, and men be educated for it as well as for engineering. There is no knowledge the engineer can possess which is not equally valuable to the contractor, and those who are anxious to make a rapid fortune may succeed as contractors, while they will find it impossible as Engineers, to do so honestly.

Civil Engineers proper, as distinguished from mining and mechanical ones, are the most unfortunate of all classes in the matter of employment. The latter, having employment of a permanent character and being usually stationery, are in this respect more like lawyers and physicians; but the Civil Engineer is a lineal descendant of the Wandering Masons or 'Brethren of the Bridge.' His occupation is gone with the completion of the canal or railway on which he has been engaged; and as a rolling stone, whatever his salary, he gathers little moss. This fact although it forms no excuse, is an explanation why some of the profession, after a few years of employment and a greater number of forced idleness and approximate starvation, adopt the creed of the pickpocket, 'that the world owes them a living,' and resolve that on the first fitting opportunity they will take care of No. 1. There is often mingled with this decision a sense of neglect and injury received from society, which gives some color of retribution or at least retaliation to many of the frauds in which engineers have been the principal actors. No matter how regularly or how intelligently he may have discharged his duties, as soon as the work on which he has been engaged is completed, or so far advanced that his services can safely be dispensed with, the engineer is dismissed with empty compliments and an emptier purse, and some quack or favorite, with whom interest supplies the place of all qualifications is appointed to mismanage his work. If, absorbed in the duties of his profession, he has not made friends of the mammon of unrighteousness, he may have no right to claim a preference over those who have carefully attended to this important duty, by the neglect of all others; but it is not difficult to understand that – with necessity impelling and opportunity inviting them – some will be found who will take the first opportunity to render themselves independent of future injustice. These belong to rather a formidable class of public men, who view crime only by its immediate consequences, and consider it no great harm to plunder a corporation or a people, because the loss being distributed may not come home with inconvenience to a particular hearth.

The remedy for a state of things which brings disgrace on the profession is not easily administered. The engineer, though an indispensable agent, is generally a junior partner in the firm of Grab, Chisel & Co. It is neither in the Legislature nor in the press that reform can be ensured, for in both the firm is sufficiently represented to neutralize any spasmodic or 'bunkum' indignation.

The first step is, to put the profession on such a footing that it shall be self-sustaining; and this is to be done mainly by themselves. When engineers whose services are sought after assume the same position as lawyers and doctors, decline to be chartered by any party, but take as many clients or patients as they feel they can do justice to, it will not be in the power of the Government or a corporation to dismiss them to begin the world anew, when past the spring time of life, and laden with the support of a family. This position once established, the engineer is no longer necessarily a wandering Bedouin, but, by being able to have a fixed habitation he has some inducement to store, and having secured independence of position he may sustain independence of character. It is only men of some real or supposed reputation who are likely to be placed in positions where they can league with politicians and contractors, and become parties to the robbery of their employers. If you give these men an opportunity to earn an honest living, you may deprive the other knaves (on whom it would be hopeless to attempt a reformation) of the only accomplices by whose means they can successfully carry out their ends. Public bodies, therefore, must remember that when they insist on the exclusive services of an Engineer, without giving him in return any guarantee of his situation, they induce him to listen to proposals, which he might otherwise spurn, in order to provide for himself and his family, when suddenly dismissed by a chiselling Government or a soulless Corporation.

The government guarantee a life situation to their lowest clerks, but their engineers are hired, as their laborers, by the day. If they would hire them as they do their printers, commissioners and politicians, by the job, allowing them the same privileges, there would be some fairness in it, but they are neither guaranteed their posts nor allowed, like a political lawyer, to work for the state and the public at the same time.

The excuse for the temporary character of their engagement is – that engineers are paid out of appropriations, and not out of the civil list; and this same distinction is the clue to nearly all the political robbery of the last twenty years on both sides of the St. Lawrence. Appropriations are temporary: the civil list is permanent. In public works expenditure is literally covered up; when a work is completed, no man can say what it has cost, for cost depends upon the circumstances. Details are not easily traced, and many things are charged to an appropriation which have not had the remotest connection with the object for which that appropriation was made. In New York and Pennsylavania, which have been the great nurseries of thieving politicians, contractors, and engineers, the official salaries are so low, and the whole state appropriation (for nominal expenses of government) so small that besides the risk and difficulty attending it, few would think it worth their while to meddle with such paltry sums. Popular clamor having reduced the official salaries to the stipend of clerks, salary is looked upon rather as a badge of office, than as a consideration for services, and the control of appropriation forms the real reward of the successful party. Prohibited from any open interest in contracts, they cannot be deprived of the allotment of those contracts to sleeping partners. The State of New York escaped the bold and successful onslaught of these worthies only by a decision of her Courts, declaring unconstitutional the law under which the appropriations had been made; and the people, taking the alarm, have so hampered their state expenditure with restrictions, as almost to make it impracticable, vainly endeavouring to substitute legislation for common honesty. Pennsylvania rolled up her forty million debt under these auspices, until repudiation reared its head; and is there no risk of our galloping onward, with reckless and shameless stride, upon the same dangerous road?

The worst feature of this system, after those of the wide spread corruption, rapacity and national demoralization which it engenders, is – not that the public are robbed of so much money – but that works are undertaken which are utterly useless, and which, by their inevitable failure, destroy confidence in all future undertakings, and injure the commercial character and credit of the country. It matters little what or where the work is, so long as there is an appropriation for it.

Engineers engaged in Parliamentary contests are expected to support the side on which they are engaged *coute qui coute,* as unscrupulously, and with as much nonchalance as if bred to the law. This is a practice which requires peculiar qualifications, and a good deal of experience as a lobby member; great power of face and greater stomach; a confidential undertone with the serious, and a rollicking *abandon* with the junior or more convivial members.

From the exciting nature of this practice, as well as from the damage the reputation is apt to receive from frequent and continued exposure to such surroundings, it should be a specialty – and limited to the duly qualified practitioners.

Perhaps the best mode of shewing what the Engineer ought to be is to describe, first his position and what is required of him; and then, the initiation and prosecution of one of those piratical schemes where he figures as an accomplice.

When a contract is entered into, no matter how detailed may be the plans and specifications, or how specific the prices, to the Engineer almost without exception or restraint, is left the determination of the quantities and qualities and, therefore, of the actual cost of the work. In many cases, which cannot previously be provided against, he also determines the prices; but all of these are secondary to the power which he has by alterations, deviations, etc., of influencing the cost of the work, or opening the contract. Without infringing the *letter* he may violate the *spirit* of the contract, and enrich the contractor and himself at the expense of his employers. There is no legislative remedy for this; every attempt to circumscribe the power of the Engineer by new checks, is simply a transfer of that power from intelligent to ignorant hands; and ignorance, however honest, is a more expensive manager and an easier victim upon public works than knavery. The only safeguard is that which every merchant or banker feels he can alone depend upon – the character of the person employed. But to secure an honest Engineer, you must first establish honesty in the Corporation or Government which appoints him; because it is a melancholy fact that appointments have been made, not in ignorance, but *because* dishonesty was a primary qualification, a necessity, and because one Engineer could be made a scape-goat for many politicians, who could plead ignorance as laymen, and when called to account, exclaim, 'Thou can'st not say *I* did it.'

To secure this integrity in the appointing power there must be honesty and intelligence in the Legislature or the Corporation, and these only can spring from an enlightened, a moral and above all, a vigilant constituency. If the people, therefore, complain that they are plundered and deceived, they have themselves to thank for it, in their indifference to the character and motives of adventurers who, unasked, thrust themselves upon them, and by the aid of their prejudices, bigotry and a suborned press, obtain the control of their affairs.

The majority of popular representatives may be sufficiently honest, but it is a minority of the more able, bold, and often unscrupulous men who seize the reins; and in whom the mere possession of talent is accounted a sufficient covering for a multitude of sins. Obtuse honesty, therefore, may by ignorant sanction of acute knavery be the greater evil of the two; in other words it is better to have a knave than a fool for a legislator – for the knave knows his own interest (which may sometimes accord with that of the public) and the fool does not.

One way in which a great public enterprise may be initiated and carried through, or at least as far as the money goes, is at least instructive if not amusing. In Upper Canada each township is a sort of German principality, only democratic in its form of Government. The jealousy of the back townships is excited because the front ones have, or are to have, a railway. The Province having kindly undertaken the main line, the whole resources of the back townships are available for branch ones. The municipal loan fund act[1] – that wonderful contrivance which converts beautifully engraved paper into money – provides the means, and intending contractors, in the guise of apostles of progress, point out the way. *Reliable* men are elected, in some of whom the enthusiasm is indigenous, in others carefully counterfeited. All that the community can be induced to swallow is readily voted, but it is still far from the required amount. An eminent contractor then appears upon the stage, who offers to take all the available means provided, and the remainder in first mortgage bonds. In consequence of the doubtful value of these last the price is fixed at about double the expected cash cost of the road. The municipalities are told that their subscription is a mere matter of form, that the earnings of the road will pay the interest, and that it is only a loan of their credit, as an endorsation of their confidence in the enterprise, and not their money that is wanted. If there be any kicking they are told the eminent contractor will by his influence in

1 [The Municipal Loan Fund Act of 1852 was another of Francis Hincks' ingenious devices to permit the pledging of public credit for railroads. The Act authorized the sale of special Loan Fund debentures. From this pool of capital various municipalities might make withdrawals, after voting taxes to meet interest and sinking fund requirements, to aid the construction of local railways. *Inter alia*, see Skelton, *Life and Times of Sir Alexander Tilloch Galt*, pp. 109-12, and of course Keefer's essay on railroads below.]

the legislature, defeat their charter, will support a rival project, or by his influence with the government, prevent the sanction of their by-laws, and the exchange of their valueless debentures for Provincial Loan Fund ones. The contract is then entered into – of course wholly on the terms dictated by the contractor – and, where not tricked into conditions, they are bullied. The contractor agrees to do all the engineering, allowing the company to have an engineer of their own to determine the fulfilment, or otherwise of the previously settled contract; in other words, permitting them to lock the stable after it has been emptied. Through the contractor's representatives in the board of direction, an engineer is suggested to and appointed by the company, who afterward, but of course at too late a date, proves to be a partner, and the company are committed by the acts of their own officer. The contract was taken by the mile. When it was signed it was assumed that the earth works would average twenty thousand yards per mile, but the Engineer discovers they can be reduced to ten thousand – without having any grade steeper than the contract. This is done by running *around* all the hills instead of cutting *through* them, and by raising nearly all the grades to the maximum; and the longer the road is made the better it pays, so long as the work is kept light, for the price is *per mile.* Through the level land, instead of being raised by embankments, it is scantily ditched up from the sides, and the Company must look out if it be afterward flooded by the spring thaws or buried up in the winter snows, for it is 'according to contract.' By reducing the excavation one-half in quantity, the proportionate price at which it was estimated in the contract is doubled, and, as the mode of payment is one-half cash and the other half bonds, the cash portion of the estimate covers the cost of the work, and the contractor carries it on as long as the cash of the Company is forthcoming, accumulating, at the same time a fair share of their bonds, on which they are bound to pay him interest. When they have no more cash, and cannot pay their estimates or their interest he stops his work, still 'according to contract,' (unless the municipalities will come down with another vote of convertible debentures) and threatens to take possession of the work done, under the mortgage bonds in his hands.

If by extraordinary efforts and sacrifices the road is completed, it is almost a certainty that it will not, for the first three years, pay the interest upon the mortgage bonds, while the municipalities must take care of that upon their own debentures. The contractor, having received in cash all his outlay, has the road for his profit. If it will pay running expenses it will be run, and the municipalities will have the use of it, at moderate fares, as a return for their investment. The road has perhaps doubled the value of their property and thus paid for itself, and it would be unreasonable to expect it to pay twice.

I have thus endeavored to note some of the qualifications, as well as the conditions and vicissitudes incident to this practice of Civil Engineering. The mental and physical requirements may be summed up in the ancient prayer, '*mens sana in corpore sano*'; for a strong constitution is needed, not only in the exposures of the field, but to sustain the extreme mental tension which numerous and weighty responsibilities produce. There must also be an equable and self-reliant disposition, a steady perseverance in the plan laid down, despite the ignorance and opposition of those who cannot understand it, looking to the future instead of the hour for true appreciation and reward. Above all, if not only fame, but what is more important, conscientious self-approval, in the evening of life, are desired, there must be a jealous regard for personal integrity in a profession beset with such great trials and temptations – threatened poverty and then almost absolute control of large sums of money – ingratitude or misrepresentation, the offspring of ignorance on the part of those whom you may be doing all in your power to benefit. Those are incident to almost every walk in life: and as disasters and difficulties in construction make the experienced practical Engineer, so all artificial obstacles raised by ignorance, malevolence, or opposing interests, will disappear before a patient and resolute perseverance in the thing that is right.

T.C. Keefer's petition to the legislative assembly, April 1856

To the Honorable the Legislative Assembly,
in Provincial Parliament Assembled;

The petition of the undersigned, Thomas Coltrin Keefer, Civil Engineer, of the City of Montreal;

HUMBLY SHEWETH:

That Your Petitioner was employed in the years 1851 and 1852, as Chief Engineer of the 'Montreal and Kingston,' and 'Kingston and Toronto' Railway Companies. Both these Companies surrendered their charters in November, 1852, in favor of the Grand Trunk Railway Company of Canada, upon condition that the latter Company should assume the expenses of its predecessors.

Your Petitioner presented three accounts for services rendered to the Montreal and Kingston Company, all of which were duly certified by the Chairman of the Provisional Committee, and by the President of that Company. A deduction of more than twenty-five per cent was arbitrarily made from two of these accounts, and the balance only was paid. The third account was not acted upon, as belonging to the Bridge and not the Railway surveys. Your Petitioner believes he is as fully entitled to the whole amount of the two accounts certified by the proper officers of the Company, whose liabilities the Grand Trunk Railway was supposed to assume, as to the part which has been paid.

The third account, on which no action has been taken, was for services as Engineer in the survey for the Railway bridge over the St. Lawrence, at Montreal. In the charter granted for the construction of this bridge, the Company are bound to pay for so much of the plans and surveys as they may make use of, provided the amount shall not exceed the sum of five hundred pounds sterling.

Your Petitioner fears that this limitation of the liability of the Grand Trunk Railway Company may be used to his prejudice. If it be claimed that no use has been had of the surveys made by Your Petitioner, payment therefore may be refused altogether. Your Petitioner believes it was the intention of the Legislature that the projectors of the bridge survey, as pioneers of the enterprize, should be protected in their expenditure of time and money: that even if this survey had proved of no practical use to the Grand Trunk

Railway Company, the same principle by which they were bound to pay for Railway surveys, whether used by them or not, should be applied in the case of the bridge. But your Petitioner is prepared to prove that the contract made for the construction of this bridge, was based upon the survey made by him, none other survey having, at that time, been made. The existence of such a survey was necessary to a contract, and had there been no survey, it is extremely doubtful (looking to the subsequent change in the money Market,) whether any contract would have been made so as to have secured the commencement of the work as has now been done.

Your Petitioner has an account against the late Kingston and Toronto Railway Company, for one year's salary similar to the one partly paid on account of the Montreal and Kingston Company. He has been informed by the late Chairman of the former Company that, since the relinquishment of their charter, no meeting of the Directors could be obtained, but that he, the late Chairman, had in settling his accounts, brought the claim of your Petitioner under the notice of the Grand Trunk Railway Company, and had received a reply to the effect that the Directors of this Company 'could not recognize the claim of the Engineer.'

When your Petitioner's account for a precisely similar claim of one year's salary against the Montreal and Kingston Company was partly paid, a large reduction was arbitrarily made therefrom, ostensibly upon the ground that a similar account would be presented on account of the Kingston and Toronto Railway Company, which latter account, when presented, was ignored altogether.

Confident that the intention of the Legislature was practically to place the Grand Trunk Railway Company as the successor, in the same position, as to liabilities, which its predecessors would have occupied had they survived, your Petitioner prays that in any further legislation sought for by the Grand Trunk Railway Company your Honourable House will cause to be inserted a clause empowering all parties having legal claims, against the Directors or Provisional Committees of the late Montreal and Kingston, and Kingston and Toronto Railway Companies, to maintain the same against their successor, the Grand Trunk Railway Company of Canada.

And your Petitioner, as in duty bound, will ever pray.

THOS. C. KEEFER
Civil Engineer

Montreal, April 1856

Statement of the Honourable John Ross before the legislative council, Friday, 25 April 1856[2]

I am again obliged to trouble the House with some explanations regarding the appointment of engineers under the act of last session, to examine the Grand Trunk Railway works. It has become necessary in consequence of a report which I have read of an explanation given by the Inspector General in the House of Assembly, on the subject of the delay of the Company in the appointment of those engineers. I am quite sure that my late colleague did not intend to cast that blame upon me; but the report of his remarks as printed, would convey that impression. I endeavoured to see him yesterday but he was engaged; and I obtained the permission of His Excellency, the Governor General to make the statement which I shall now read, and to which my hon. friend, the Speaker, has obtained the concurrence of my late colleagues, as agreeing with their recollection of the fact. The statement is as follows:

I left Quebec in the early part of June, 1855, with my family, proceeded to Toronto, and thence to Boston, from whence I sailed on the 30th day of June for England. Up to this time nothing had been said about the appointment of engineers under the act of last session. During my absence I had no correspondence with any member or members of the Government regarding the appointment of engineers under the act referred to. On my return to Toronto, which was Sunday, the 9th [of] Dec., I was first in council on the 14th day of December, 1855, and the day following the subject of the appointment of engineers was spoken of, and Mr. T.C. Keefer and Mr. Wallis, it was stated, had been named. I had never heard of Mr. Wallis before, and was anxious to have names that would give confidence to the Board in England and to the public in Canada.

I am a personal friend of Mr. Keefer's, but thought he ought not to be appointed, as he was making a large claim upon the Company at that time, and still unadjusted with him. I proposed that Captain Swift, of Boston would be appointed, and it was thought it would

2 [For the best short introduction to the politics and politicians of this period, see J.M.S. Careless, *The Union of the Canadas: The Growth of Canadian Institutions, 1841-1857* (Toronto, 1967), pp. 166-223.]

cause too much delay. Sir Allan McNab suggested Mr. Reed, of the Great Western, and Mr. Spence, Mr. Benedict. After some little delay, Mr. Reed declined to act, and assigned as his reason, that the Great Western Board would not permit him to do so. Mr. Street was therefore applied to, and accordingly Mr. Benedict and Mr. Street were gazetted. The two gentlemen have, I believe, used all reasonable dispatch in prosecuting their examination in so far as they could do so in carrying out a thorough and careful inspection of the works, plant furnished, rolling stock, locomotives, checking out measurements, certificates and estimates. For the delay previous to the 14th December, I cannot assign any reason except that given by the hon. Inspector General, viz., the removal of the seat of Government, which happened during my absence. I have stated all the facts within my knowledge connected with the action of the Government since my return.

Letters of explanation to the Montreal Herald, May 1856

To the Editor of the Montreal *Herald*

SIR, – I have no desire to intrude my business affairs upon the notice of the public, but the fact that the Government have, through the President of the Grand Trunk Railway Company as their mouth piece, assigned as a reason for my non-appointment to examine the Grand Trunk, the existence of certain pecuniary relations between that Company and myself, I am obliged to ask the privilege of explaining this matter through your columns.

I have never had, or sought to have, anything to do professionally with the Grand Trunk Railway: but that Company having fallen heirs to the local Canadian Companies which preceded it, and for which I had acted, became the party to which I was obliged to look for the amounts due me by their predecessors. For the last three years I have been endeavoring to get the amounts due me on account of the Bridge over the St. Lawrence and the Railway from Montreal to Toronto, but so long as Mr. Hincks remained in power, he contrived to chisel me out of a settlement in retaliation for my having presumed to oppose his Grand Trunk scheme in 1852. I waited patiently for the end, feeling assured that the time would come when neither Mr. Hincks nor the Grand Trunk could afford to resist even the few friends whom I possessed. The following petition, which fully explains the nature of my claims, was first presented in the Session of 1854 and was referred, without being printed, to the Railway Committee, when Mr. Hincks, although then out of the Government, succeeded in burking it. The Session was adjourned, and when resumed, in 1855, the Grand Trunk Company again sought legislation – but now to the tune of £900,000 sterling. – I resumed my petition, this time taking the precaution to have it printed, with the intention of having my claims brought up in the debate, and at least an opportunity to test their validity provided for, if possible, in the relief bill. That I had not failed in my calculation may be inferred from the fact that as soon as my petition was printed (in May, 1855) the Company accepted my proposition, which was to refer the whole matter to the sole arbitration of Robert Stephenson, their own Engineer.

Considering the facts – 1st. That I have never received one farthing for my labors on the St. Lawrence Bridge, which were commenced nearly five years ago. 2nd. That Mr. Hincks, with characteristic insolence and vindictiveness, refused at first to pay me anything for my Bridge survey: declaring that we had no business to make it and that he would not give a button for the opinion of a Canadian Engineer upon such a subject – and that he only consented to render the Grand Trunk Company liable when he discovered that the contract for the Bridge had been based upon my survey. 3rd. That Sir Cusack Patrick Roney, who 'fretted his short hour' on the Grand Trunk stage, informed the President of the Kingston and Toronto Company that the Grand Trunk would not recognise my claim – although they were bound by law to pay the expenses of their predecessors; that, in short, the Grand Trunk Company have resisted a settlement of my claims as long as they felt themselves strong enough for any act of injustice, and only yielded from mercenary considerations when it was their interest so to do – I ask if it is not at least cool in the President of that Company to urge before his Excellency in Council, as an objection to my appointment, that I had unadjusted claims against the Company! How many members of that Council, besides its President, were Directors in the Grand Trunk Company? And as such were they not aware that my claims had been 'adjusted' by reference to arbitration? Is not 'the statement of facts as agreed upon' worthy of the Railway Executors of the departed Governor of Barbadoes?[3]

THOS. C. KEEFER

To the Editor of the Montreal *Herald*

SIR, – In the Toronto *Leader* of the 26th ult. there is a report of an explanation made by the Hon. John Ross respecting the appointment of skilled engineers, while he was both President of the Grand Trunk Railway Company and of the Executive Council. Mr. Ross says that immediately after his return from England, on the 15th December, he objected to my appointment because I was 'making a large claim upon the Company at that time and still unadjusted.' Mr. Ross says 'his hon. friend the Speaker had obtained the concurrence of his late colleagues to this statement, as agreeing with their

3 [The reference is to Francis Hincks. The standard biography is R.S. Longley, *Sir Francis Hincks* (Toronto, 1943).]

recollection of the fact.' As to the fact of my having an unadjusted claim against the Grand Trunk Railway Company, there were others at the Council Board who knew, as well as Mr. Ross, that that claim had been 'adjusted' a full year ago. If Mr. Ross means that the money has not been paid, that is true; but he knows that his Company have no power over the amount, and that it is as effectually 'adjusted' as is an account where a note of hand is given in payment. The assumption that his 'personal friend' could be influenced by any claims, adjusted or otherwise, can only be sustained by also assuming that the Grand Trunk Railway Company have the power to influence the arbitrator (Mr. Robert Stephenson) mutually agreed upon between us. If they had any such power, and if Mr. Ross' theory of adjustment be received as valid, I should expect my account would remain unadjusted until my death, or until the Province had sold out the last dollar of interest in the Grand Trunk, in order that I could be disqualified from making any professional report thereon.

A member of Parliament, as soon as he heard of the appointment of Messrs. Benedict and Street, made it his business to ascertain from the Hon. Mr. Cayley why I had been passed over, and was told, as the reason, that I 'had refused to act *with* the Board of Works.' As the law required the skilled Engineers to act *with* the Board of Works, it is not probable that I could have made so absurd a condition. I did refuse to act *under* the Board of Works, because I considered that that Department was on its trial – that the very naming of skilled Engineers by the Legislature proved that they had no confidence in the reports of Mr. Killaly; and I knew that if I consented to take my instructions from that Department, my hands would be tied, and I would be compromised, by having undertaken a duty which I would not be permitted to discharge.

If either of the reasons assigned by Messrs. Ross or Cayley influenced the Council, they were both equally without foundation. Had the Executive desired to know whether I would or would not have acted with the Board of Works, it would not have been difficult to make the enquiry.

About twelve months since – when the £900,000 grant was before the House – I was applied to, on behalf of Mr. Cayley, to know if I would act, solely or in conjunction with others, to carry out the provisions of that act. I replied to the hon. gentleman who wrote on Mr. Cayley's behalf that I was willing to act if the government really desired a *bona fide* examination and report; at the same time, I told him that our negotiation would amount to nothing; that the Grand Trunk Company would never permit such an examination, and that if they did, I would be the last person they would assent to. However, I was assured by influential supporters of Mr. Cayley, that it was only upon the condition of an examination, etc., by some Engineer, independent of the Board of Works and the Grand Trunk Company, that they had supported the grant, and that in fact there was a distinct understanding with Mr. Cayley that I should be selected for the duty.

I heard nothing more of the matter until September, when I received a telegraph from Quebec, from a member of the Government, enquiring if I would act. This telegraph was sent to Hamilton, although I had been for the previous week in Montreal; and by some unaccountable means, although all other letters were forwarded, this telegraph remained at Hamilton until I went up there, it being then a month old. I replied by letter, although as no answer had been sought for to this missing telegraph, I supposed something had transpired after sending it which made an answer unnecessary. When in Toronto, in January, I was informed by an authority I cannot question, that my name, associated with Mr. Wallace, of the Brantford Road, had actually passed the Council, but that upon the return of the President of the Grand Trunk Company, these appointments had been upset, at the instance, as I have been told, of the Chief Engineer of the Grand Trunk Company and Mr. Killaly.

I was shortly after called upon, in conjunction with the Chief Engineer of the Grand Trunk Company, to name a third arbitrator in the matter of the Toronto Esplanade. I named the Chief Engineer of the Board of Works, supposing a Company which had so many Government Directors would not object to an undoubtedly competent public officer. Mr. Page was agreed upon, but was afterwards objected to, on the ground that he had formerly acted for Cotton and Manning. Mr. Ross named only two parties – Messrs. Benedict and Street! Afterwards, on proceeding to Toronto, I learned that these same two parties were the Government nominees as 'skilled engineers.' I was, therefore, satisfied that their nomination was pure and simple, a Grand Trunk proposition; for if, in a matter in which that Company were interested to an amount exceeding fifty thousand pounds, they selected out of the whole province Messrs. Street and Benedict to be their umpire, I am justified in assuming that the appointment of these two gentlemen to investigate the affairs of the Grand Trunk was brought about by the same agency which nominated them in the matter of the Toronto Esplanade.

After this explanation, it is scarcely necessary to prove that neither of the conflicting reasons assigned by Messrs. Ross and Cayley for my appointment are *bona fide;* the fact is, my appointment was an impossibility, from my want of the necessary qualifications – viz., the possession of the entire confidence of the Grand Trunk Company.

If, as stated, I was once appointed, what becomes of the assertion that I had refused to act with the Board of Works? And even if not actually appointed, why was my name brought before the Council by Mr. Cayley, and objected to by Mr. Ross, if the former knew I would not act?

Mr. Ross says he proposed Capt. Swift of Boston, but forgot to explain that this gentleman is the confidential agent and in the pay of the Barings, very large shareholders in the Grand Trunk; that he has already been here, and that his opinions were known beforehand; and that under any circumstances he is not a disinterested party, as between the people of Canada and the Grand Trunk Company. He also says he desired names that would give confidence to the Board in England and to the public in Canada. The object of the act had no reference to the Board in England; but after the public in Canada are satisfied, any incidental satisfaction which the report of the 'skilled engineers' may give to the Board in England cannot be objected to.

I venture to predict that in the matter of these skilled engineers, the Government have commited a grave mistake. The very effort that has been made to secure the appointment of parties in the confidence of the Railway Company, will rouse the suspicions of the public. I know that the door of Government and Grand Trunk patronage is inexorably closed to me and I am content it should be so; but the public will require to be informed why the only professional business which Mr. Killaly attends to is the Grand Trunk, and why the Chief Engineer of the Department of Public Works is carefully excluded from all insight into the dealings of that Company with the Department? There would be no need of skilled engineers if the Government would order that engineer to examine and report. The public would have confidence in a report signed by Mr. Page, who is a thoroughly competent engineer, and a man of undoubted integrity, but it is greatly to be feared that these are fatal obstacles to his being selected.

I will take another occasion to explain the unadjusted claim which was the pretended cause of my rejection by the Government.

THOS. C. KEEFER

May 6, 1856

Editorial from the Toronto Leader, Thursday, 13 May 1856

Those who would assail the motives and character of others should be pretty well assured of their own antecedents. Indeed never so forcibly did a well known proverb recur to our mind as when perusing the production of a Mr. Thomas Keefer, which appeared in a leading Montreal journal and which we m[a]y republish for the benefit of our Upper Canada readers. By this document it would appear that in the Province there is but one virtuous and high-principled Engineer with capacity and experience sufficiently extended to cope with the difficulty of estimating the value of the work executed on the Grand Trunk Railway; while, on the other hand, Messers. Benedict and Street are held up to reprobation as incompetent, dishonest, and time-serving. We have taken the trouble to enquire who this new light is, whose non-appointment to office proves such a loss to the Province, and to examine into the fitness for the duties which he so much bewails he was not entrusted to undertake. And if ever there resulted a loose and impotent conclusion from sober query, we find it in this case. This Thomas Keefer is the author of two or three clever pamphlets, not devoid of vain boast, on our canal policy, and is at present the Engineer conducting the Montreal Water Works. With the exception of some insignificant sheds at Bytown, his name is unconnected with one single provincial work; and if we are correctly informed his railway experience consists in having attempted a southshore survey of the Grand Trunk from Toronto to Montreal, not one rod of which has been maintained; that is to say Mr. Keefer's survey was utterly valueless, the line having been constructed in a totally different locality to that pointed out by him. In this consists the experience in railway engineering which suggests to Mr. Keefer's modesty that he is the great SIR ORACLE of the day. But there is another fact which it would be well to recollect, when we notice his impertinence to Mr. Killaly. Who gave this gentleman the right to say that 'the legislature had no confidence in the reports of Mr. Killaly?' Is it a sense of superior ability and higher moral worth that leads him thus to assail the oldest Engineer in the Province, who has discharged with singular ability and tact the most difficult and delicate duties, and who, when Mr. Keefer was a boy at school, had attained a high reputation among his fellows. The charge against the Board of Works Commissioner, similar to the innuendos against Mr. Benedict and Mr. Street amounts to this, that if he is not a fool he is a knave. Pleasant indeed is it in these days of dishonesty to witness the virtuous indignation of disappointment. Yet if our memory serves us aright, we may trace to another motive the antagonism to Mr. Killaly. Some four or five years back, Mr. Keefer, then an Assistant Engineer on the Public Works, was directed to make a survey examination of the St. Lawrence Rapids, in order to give an estimate as to the cost of deepening them. The result was a report under his hand, that the project was perfectly feasible, and that the cost would be £10,000. It was Mr. Killaly's duty to comment upon Mr. Keefer's Report, and in doing so, he pointed out its many manifest contradictions, and gave it as his opinion that the amount named, was altogether insufficient, and, therefore, that no action should be taken in the matter. Will our readers believe that when those distinguished hydraulic engineers, Messrs. Maillefert and DeRaasloff, made an examination, two years later, they estimated the cost of this improvement at very little short of £200,000? Mr. Killaly can afford to despise any inuendoes of his former lieutenant; and we think that the public will understand that Mr. Keefer's efforts to advertise his claims to distinction are dictated by something more than mere selfish vaunting. He would have done well to recollect that his own character is now being assailed by his present employers, and that he is himself accused in no measured terms and in no vague manner of incompetence and incapability. It is not so long ago that we read in the Montreal papers that a culvert constructed by him under the Lachine Canal had fallen in, and that one of his arches had crumbled away. And it is equally a matter of notoriety that even the hon. Mr. Young, a long time his patron, did not consider that the work of Lake St. Peter would be benefitted by Mr. Keefer long interfering with the Superintendent, Capt. Belle's operations. And we are informed that the latter complained bitterly that Mr. Keefer published tables on the cost of dredging, compiled by him with great labor, as Mr. Keefer's own without acknowledgement; and that he further appropriated to himself the merit of discovering a new channel in the St. Lawrence, when he had received information of the fact from Mr. Belle. Indeed it is not only on this score that Mr. Keefer has been accused of taking other men's ideas and elaborating them. The most marked instance of this is in the Victoria Bridge, the site of which had been pointed out by at least half a dozen American and Canadian engineers, particularly Mr. Morton, on examination made at the request of the hon. John Young, who may rightly claim to be the originator of that great work. It was he who instructed Mr. Keefer to make the examination, and who obtained the necessary funds to pay him for his work, and whose advice, assistance, and information Mr. Keefer in no way acknowledged in his report.

Such is the man who imputes dishonest motives to his professional brethren, without adducing one solitary fact as a reason for doing so, or the least ground for the surmise, beyond that of an overweening estimate of himself – an estimate the more remarkable that we know no public man who participates in it. Far more wisely he would have acted had he remembered that if a remote reason be sometimes given in explanation of a line of conduct, it is as often dictated by delicacy as from any other feeling. What if Mr. Keefer be now told that never having been engaged on any railway works, being in short perfectly inexperienced, as to the value of the iron tubular bridge, and other railway works and rolling stock, it was deemed advisable not to call in his aid? What if he be reminded that from the beginning, having shown a positive opposition to the Grand Trunk enterprise, and by his own admission deeming it his duty to put Mr. Killaly 'on his trial,' it be thought inexpedient to select a man not only inexperienced but desirous of obtaining notoriety? The very hour at which his letter was penned, independently of its tone, showed that there was something more than a mere sense of personal injustice which dictated it. He has chosen the time when public clamour was strong, and when an enterprise, misjudged and misrepresented, is assailed from ignorance and by interested motives, and when journalists, whom we hold in high personal esteem, fail to consider the combination of circumstances which has brought about the crisis. We do not doubt but that the most superficial observer will see through Mr. Keefer's artifice, and they will understand why he was not appointed, and why Messers. Street and Benedict were – the latter were in no way committed, and had given no expression of opinion with regard to the Grand Trunk Railway – both gentlemen besides, were likewise experienced Railway Engineers; on both sides of the Lake Mr. Benedict is known, having had twenty years professional experience, and Mr. Street has only just successfully completed a line at our own door, the Toronto and Hamilton branch of the Great Western. It may be very well for this Montreal Water Works Engineer to stigmatise by inuendo those gentlemen as characterless and dishonest and to make it appear that Mr. Killaly is devoid of faith and honour. But like most tricks and schemes, the act will defeat itself; and judged by his own productions, Mr. Thomas Keefer will be deemed to be the last man to whom any enterprise ought to be entrusted. For the future we would counsel him quietly to pursue his avocations and not to interfere in matters on which his inexperience renders him unfit to adjudicate. His opinions have very bad insight, and it is a little too much to have such a man dealing out censure and to be reading us lectures on a sense of responsibility. By all accounts, he has quite enough to do to attend to his own position with the Montreal Corporation, and he might at least wait until he has completed the Water Works to the satisfaction of the citizens of that city and its completed cost is seen to tally with his estimate before he assails the character of others, and endeavouring to impede a large and important scheme. We do not, however, fear his efforts, for if they tally with the letter to which we refer he will find to his cost that they harm no one so much as himself.

T.C. Keefer's statement in reply and letter in defence published by the Globe, 14 May 1856

Having been virulently assailed in the editorial columns of the Toronto *Leader* – the paid mouth-piece of a clique of Railway practitioners, who affect to despise everything Canadian – except our debentures – I submit, as the best answer to this attempt to blacken my personal and professional character in the Capital City of my native Province – and amongst many old friends and school-fellows – the articles from the Montreal *Herald* which have called forth this labored, malignant, but pointless Grand Trunk denunciation.

That the publications which the *Leader* so flimsily professes to despise, have been keenly felt, is evident from the sharp cry of the wounded plotters through the columns of their organ. The *Leader*, with more shrewdness than honesty, labors to insinuate that my reply to the assaults of the Railway jobbers, is dictated by disappointed ambition. It is only necessary to refer to the fact, that I did not seek anything at the hands of the Government, but that the proposition came from them; moreover, as I never anticipated any other result than that which has taken place, the correspondence in the *Herald* which has given so much offence, would not have appeared at all, had not the same gentleman who has shewn so much discretion in publishing Mr. Brassey's letter, unnecessarily held me up to the country as an Engineer who might be influenced by Grand Trunk money. As an Executive Councillor he affected to fear the inveterate corrupting tendencies of the Company over which he presided – whose morality he was quick to discriminate, but helpless to reform – but to those who are familiar with the philosophy of the school to which he belongs, the reason assigned will be regarded as *lucus a non lucendo;* for had there been any possible grounds for the 'painful suspicion,' I should undoubtedly have received the hearty support of the President, Engineer, and pensioners of the Grand Trunk Railway.

The following letter was sent to the *Leader* – but its receipt is not even acknowledged in this day's issue (May 14):

Toronto, May 13, 1856

To the Editor of the *Leader*

SIR, – I believe it is the practice of impartial Journalists to publish the articles upon which they have occasion to comment. I think you will admit, that the personal attack in your paper of this day's date, entitles me to ask as a matter of justice at your hands, that you would be good enough to publish those productions of mine upon which you have so strongly animadverted.

I have the honor to be, Sir,

Your obedient servant,

THOS. C. KEEFER

The following reply to the attack in the *Leader* of the 13th May, appeared in the *Globe* of the next day:

To the Editor of the *Globe*

SIR, – I was invited to deliver last winter, an introductory course of lectures upon Civil Engineering, before the University of McGill College at Montreal; in doing which I took occasion to utter some wholesome, but, possibly to some parties, distasteful truths. It so happened that a short time after the last lecture had been delivered, the President of the Grand Trunk Company thought proper to drag my name before the Legislative Council and the country, as an Engineer who had been once thought of, as one of the parties to be appointed to examine the Grand Trunk Railway, but who, having been weighed in the balance – of an account due by that Company – had been found wanting. I am free to confess that the fact of my ever having had any pecuniary transactions with that Company, was in itself suspicious; I therefore felt it due to my own character fully to explain the whole affair, and at the same time to prove that there were other reasons, besides the discreditable one imputed to me by the President, why I had been rejected. Some extracts from these lectures – supposed to be applicable to the times – as well as my explanations were published in the Montreal *Herald* of last week, and it appears the latter at least have attracted the notice of the parties concerned, so that I have been honored with something over a column of mingled advice and abuse by one of the literary bravos, whose obedient steel is plunged in – ink, at the beck of the railway magnates, who have seized upon this unfortunate country and afflicted it with the '*Toronto Leader.*' The combined efforts of the Assistant Commissioner of Public Works the President and Chief Engineer of the Grand Trunk Company, (besides others too insignificant to mention) have resulted in the following indictment:

1st. That I once estimated the improvement of the Rapids of the River St. Lawrence at £10,000, while some other parties have estimated this work at £200,000. The *Leader* has understated my estimate about fifty per cent, and forgot to mention that the Engineer of the Board of Works also estimated this improvement at £25,000 or £30,000. A house, a ship, or a bridge, designed for the same purpose, will be estimated differently, if they are to be built of wood or iron – and with respect to the matter in question my plan involved no blasting under water – while the others were wholly or partially based upon this expensive, and in my judgment unnecessary operation. As a case in point, I may mention that in 1847, Mr. Killaly estimated the landing piers below Quebec as follows: Berthier £2,000; L'Islet £2,000; Cap Orrigneaux £2,000; Rivière du Loup £3,000; Father Point £1,500; total £10,500. I believe the cost has been at least ten times greater: but, no doubt, Mr. Killaly can explain the changes and alterations of plan, or other causes, which have occasioned the discrepancy.

2nd. That a Montreal paper once stated that a culvert built by me, under the Lachine Canal, had fallen in, and an arch had crumbled away. The culvert did not exactly fall in, but the water fell into it. This culvert was built upon a plan forced upon the Montreal Corporation by the Board of Works, which retained the right of supervision over it during construction, and it so happens that I protested in writing against it, as likely to let the water in, and my predictions were unfortunately verified. The story about the arch is all moonshine. No arch upon the Montreal Water Works has 'crumbled away,' or given way, as the *Leader* can easily satisfy himself, by enquiring of Mr. Walter Shanly.

3rd. That I deprived Captain Bell of the Montreal Harbour Commission, of the credit of some tables of dredging, compiled by him, and also of the discovery of a new channel. This is just the reverse of the facts. If the *Leader* had seen my report, he would have found that Capt. Bell's name is affixed to the table compiled by him, after a form furnished by me. Moreover, I believe I was the first person connected with the commission who gave that full credit to Capt. Bell, which he so well deserves, and which is to be found in my report. If Capt. Bell has 'complained bitterly' to anybody else, which

I cannot believe, he has always to me expressed his warmest acknowledgments of my notice of his labours. With respect to the discovery of the channel, I never claimed it – for the simple reason that there was no discovery. Captain Bayfield discovered all the channels of the St. Lawrence long before Capt. Bell or myself ever saw them.

4th. That I have endeavoured to deprive the American Engineers and the Hon. Jno. Young of the credit due to their labours in connection with the Victoria Bridge. This is also a wholesale perversion of the facts of the case. A preface was written to my Report upon the Bridge, for the very purpose of noticing the labours of my predecessors; and the only report of an American Engineer on the subject, is printed in the appendix. Lastly, my report was addressed to the Hon. Jno. Young, was printed under his directions and at his expense, and if there had been any such omissions in it as the *Leader* charges, he could and would have expressed his dissatisfaction, which he certainly did not do; nay more, he could have prevented its publication altogether.

This is the sum of the *Leader*'s attempt to break down my personal and professional character; and if he can find anything more to say upon the same subject, I have no doubt the exigencies of the Grand Trunk, or the revenge of its *victims,* will speedily produce it.

The *Leader,* in conclusion, gives two reasons for my appointment having been defeated by his owners; first, 'my having shown a positive opposition to the Grand Trunk enterprise from the beginning.' I am happy to be able to state, for the *Leader*'s sake, that this part of his article, at least, has some truth in it. I did oppose that enterprise in 1852, and have seen many good reasons for doing so since – but the Company cannot charge me with having since written one word to damage an enterprise to which we were so irrevocably committed; nor until they had first attacked me, and after they had pleaded their own bankruptcy, and demanded that we shall pay their debts, finish their works, and let them keep the road, the control of our commerce, and what Mr. Jackson calls the three P's, Power, Patronage, Profit. The second reason is, 'That I was perfectly inexperienced as to the value of the iron tubular bridges, &c.' Before reporting upon the Montreal Bridge, I made it my business to visit England and France, for the purpose of learning something of iron bridges; but the *Leader* has forgotten to inform his readers whether either Mr. Killaly or the two gentlemen appointed as 'skilled engineers,' have ever constructed any tubular iron bridges, and where.

I cannot accept the *Leader's* estimate of my professional ability, but there is one fact alluded to in his article which I feel bound, in consideration of its general economy of the truth, to acknowledge. He says that I made a survey of the Grand Trunk Railway from Toronto to Montreal, 'not one rod of which has been maintained.' I think this very likely – inasmuch as the contractors, having controlled the engineering, have probably followed the line where there was the least work, or the most land belonging to the faithful and to the privileged speculators. I found a route between this city and Kingston where the grades would not have exceeded thirty feet per mile. The Chief Engineer of the Board of Works in 1852, surveyed *for the Government,* the line since followed between Montreal and Kingston, and established the grades at *twenty-five feet* to the mile, and yet with a knowledge of that fact before him, the Assistant Commissioner of Public Works allowed a maximum grade of *fifty-three feet* per mile, to go into the contract, by which means the earth-works upon this section are about fifty per cent lighter than those upon the commonest American or Canadian roads. How much more than fifty-three feet has been used can only be discovered by the spirit level. Thus the unequalled surface of a route which it should have been our aim to have made unrivalled for speed and capacity, between tide-water and the interior, has been utterly disregarded, and all the natural advantages which the smooth and level valley of the St. Lawrence afforded, have been sacrificed to the profits of contractors. The truth is, Mr. Editor, I knew too much of the line between Montreal and Toronto to be allowed to inspect it 'under authority,' and hence the vigorous and successful exertions made to defeat my nomination in the Executive Council.

THOS. C. KEEFER

Editorial from the Toronto Leader, Saturday, 17 May 1856

In these days of political excitement we have not always time and space to the efforts after notoriety of such men as Mr. Thomas Keefer, who in his attack on the Grand Trunk Railway, resembles as much as anything we know, the fly on the wheel, with this difference, that while the ambitious little insect congratulated himself on the progress which he was making, our would-be arbiter is pluming himself on his power to annihilate a great national enterprise. His efforts however, tend no little to show his utter disqualification for the position to which he aspires. None know better than himself his inexperience in railway works, and that he has in no way attained results in the Province to entitle him to confidence. Where, we would ask, can he have obtained any extended experience? Was it in carrying out the specifications of his brother, Mr. Samuel Keefer, in Bytown, when constructing the slides in that place? Or is it to be traced to the pamphlets which he has written? The latter are clever enough in their way but hardly sufficient to extend to the author the right of assailing every other engineer in the Province, and to arrogate to himself the claim of being pre-eminently selected to perform duties, for which we repeat Mr. Keefer's antecedents in no way qualify him. We admit distinctly this gentleman's cleverness, as a writer of reports, but he has had no practical railway experience, and indeed has never until carrying out the Montreal Water Works – a connection certainly not without its dark side for him – being connected with any Provincial work, but in a subordinate position. If this be incorrect, the fact can easily be proved, and although we allow great latitude to writers of Mr. Keefer's school, we would remind him that, however much annoyed he may be, at being reminded of his deficiencies, and however strongly he may word his reply, that he will not answer the assertion, but in one way, and that is by stating how and where he was employed: What are the facts of the case? Mr. Keefer – unassailed – without provocation – attacks men who are his superiors in age, experience and attainments and declares them to be devoid of truth and honor. In a line of conduct of this character, he must expect to see his right of doing so, examined and weighted; and as is usually the case, when a character seeks notoriety, he sometimes gets a little more of it than he bargained for. Why, at this very moment it is averred that Mr.

Keefer's estimates for the Montreal Water Works before the work is completed, will be trebled, and his plans have been ably criticised as being wrong both in conception and detail. We do not say this to be the case, but a very eminent Water Works Engineer pronounced himself against them, and entered into calculations and comments which might have taught this person a little modesty. Or if this failed so to do he might have borne in mind his whole career. Among other things we hear much of the Victoria Bridge, which Mr. Keefer affects to treat as his own work, and the merit of which he has endeavoured to appropriate. Will he deny under his own hand that a correspondence did not pass between himself and the Hon. John Young on this point? Will he produce that correspondence? Our columns are open to him for that purpose, and if he will make it public we engage that he will make an impression, that even one of his interminable letters will not remove. In fact, Mr. Keefer's connection with the Victoria Bridge amounts to this. He was employed to make a survey of the site, and to take soundings. This he did with Bayfield's map before him, and with a knowledge of the labors of other engineers who had preceded him, not one of whose exertions he did justice to, as a high toned gentleman would. Let us take up his report as it stands, and the bulk of the merit may be affiliated to Sir William Logan and to the Hon. John Young. But with all this preliminary information, Mr. Keefer's location was rejected. Our readers perhaps have to be told that on none of Mr. Thomas Keefer's examinations was the work conceived. It was his brother, Mr. Samuel Keefer who placed the bridge where it is, being two thousand feet shorter and in a different part of the river than where it was located by Mr. Thomas Keefer. We hope therefore, that this will be the last time we shall hear of this individual claiming honours not his own, on which he bases his right to consideration to which he is not entitled, and his demand for employment for which he is unfit.

With regard to the single railway feat of Mr. Thomas Keefer, his attempted location from Toronto to Montreal of the Grand Trunk Railway – his comments upon it show his utter ignorance of the principles on which a location should be made. It must be evident that the grades of the road, viz., the change from one level to another, by which heights are ascended, depend upon the capacity of the locomotive to surmount them. In the infancy of these machines it was not thought advisable to have any but the slightest ascents, but now the improvement in engines has been such, that their capacity has been enlarged. The consequence is, that any grade which runs one foot in a hundred, that is fifty-three feet to the mile, is considered amply within the compass of a locomotive, and to indulge in useless work to obtain a less grade, is mischievous and ridiculous. Such grade is the maximum on the Grand Trunk Railway, and although Mr. Thomas Keefer with his usual disingenuousness tries to insinuate to the contrary, he must know from his intimacy with his brother, that such is the fact. This however, is a trifling matter, but what can we think of an engineer who makes it a reproach to Mr. Killaly, that he did not tie the line to a twenty-six feet grade? The answer is very plain that such a person is very inexperienced and knows nothing of what he pretends to be well informed upon. But when he says that he himself 'found a line not above 30 feet grade to the mile,' we have something tangible to go on. Of course the amount of work determines the grade. But if Mr. Keefer means a practicable line, we deny that such was the case. It is notorious that he left no trace of his labors behind him. His work was incomplete, and entirely valueless, and he knows better than anyone else, that the line was not taken because it could not be found. As a specimen of his work, it is only necessary to say that he shewed a straight line of seventy miles from the Ottawa west to Farren's Point, which we are informed on pretty good authority it was not possible to obtain, except at an expenditure that would be gigantic, and his crossing from the Island of Montreal to the main shore, was rejected simply because it was a bad one. The fact is, that Mr. Thomas Keefer has lived on the reputation of his pamphlets and his projects. As long as he quietly persued his professional career people let him alone. But there is another phase in his life. He has become the assailant of better men, and is impertinent and unfair to his professional brethren, stigmatizing them as dishonest and incapable. When he himself is examined he is found to be merely a person intent upon his own advancement, impudently intruding his name on all occasions before the public, and aping a reputation which he has done nothing to obtain. We do not deny him capacity and industry. Indeed we believe him to be a very useful person in his way. But he must clearly understand that he has no prescriptive right to assail every enterprise which he does not conduct, or to call in question men's character who personally and professionally are held in higher repute. If what we have said about him is not true, let him publish a contradiction from his brother, Mr. Samuel Keefer, that his location of the Montreal and Kingston line was a work of utility, and was not recognized for some other reason than that, first, it could not be found on the ground; secondly, that the places indicated did not correspond with the sections given; and thirdly, that it was not judiciously selected in point of general direction. Let Captain Bell state his gratitude to Mr. Keefer for the credit which the latter affects to have given him, and for the handsome way in which he acknowledged his dredging tables, and which, we repeat with the Report lying before us, Mr. Keefer appropriated to himself. Let him do this and we will be the first to recant what we have said. In the meantime we advise him to bear in mind that even to a lecturing engineer the old maxim of *ne sutor ultra crepidam* applies, and that he will do best by minding his own business, and not assail others unjustly and without reason. And while on this point, we would advise him in his next course of lectures to give the students information and knowledge, if he can do so, instead of uttering – as he boasts himself of having done – what he calls 'distasteful truths!' He is a very good hand at self-praise, and the lectures were doubtless an admirable medium for puffing himself off; but the judicious portion of the world will be long before it recognizes mere *bavardage* as a title to distinction. In the case of the Grand Trunk, of which he complains, it has been seen to fail, for his incompetence and inexperience were well known. He boasts of having always opposed the line. That is his business. It is ours to prevent his injuring a project which he affects to hate – to expose his misrepresentations, and to show the utter valuelessness of his opinions.

4 RAILWAYS

A chapter on Railways from T.C. Keefer's essay, 'Travel and Transportation,' in Henry Youle Hind, *Eighty Years' Progress of British North America*, Toronto, L. Stebbins, 1863, pp. 190-256

CANADIAN RAILWAYS

Canada owes her first railway as well as her first steamboat to Montreal. In 1831, when the news of the success of the Liverpool and Manchester road came across the water, measures were taken to obtain a charter, which was granted on 25th February, 1832, for the construction of a railway from Laprairie on the St. Lawrence to St. John's, a village above the rapids of the Richelieu River, the outlet for the waters of Lake Champlain. The length was sixteen miles, and the capital £50,000, in 1,000 shares of £50 each, or a little over £3,000 per mile. The work was commenced in 1835, opened with horses in July, 1836, and first worked with locomotives in 1837. It was a 'strap-rail' road until 1847, when the heavy T iron was laid.

The next movement was a premature one, in Upper Canada. A charter was obtained, 6th March, 1834, for a Railway from Cobourg to any point on Rice Lake; and though the distance is no greater than that between Laprairie and St. John's, no less than £400,000 capital was provided. In the same year a charter was granted to the London and Gore Railway Company, for a road from London to Burlington Bay, to be extended to the navigable waters of the Thames and Lake Huron. This was the legislative beginning of that important line the Great Western Railway.

The first railway actually constructed in Upper Canada was by the old 'Erie and Ontario Company,' and was designed to restore the ancient portage route around the Falls of Niagara, between Queenstown and Chippewa, which had been superseded by the Welland Canal. This line was chartered in 1835, and was opened in 1839, as a horse railway, the steepness of the grades near Queenstown being beyond the capacity of locomotive power of that day; and as it stopped at the bank of the Niagara, over one hundred feet above the water level, it fell into disuse. In 1852 the charter was amended, and the line altered so as to run from Lake Ontario at Niagara, to Suspension Bridge and the Falls of Niagara.

Between 1832 and 1845 over a dozen charters were granted in the two provinces, none of which, except the horse railway just mentioned, were followed up; and the Laprairie road continued the sole representative of the system, using locomotives for ten years, or until 1847. In 1845 the St. Lawrence and Atlantic Railway Company was chartered, to connect with the 'Atlantic and St. Lawrence,' an American company from Portland. This road, though an

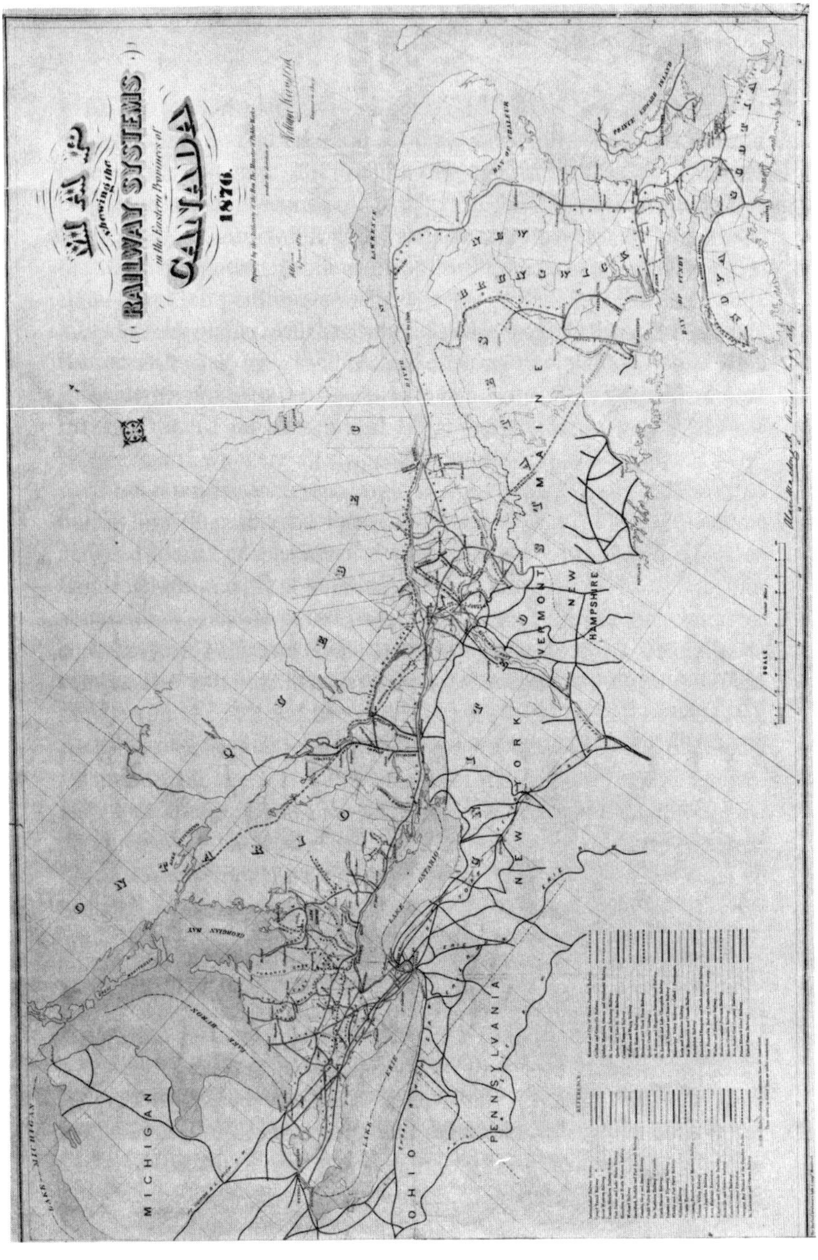

The railway systems in the eastern provinces of Canada, 1876, prepared by the authority of the Hon. The Minister of Public Works under the direction of William Kingsford, engineer in charge, Ottawa, 5 June 1876.

international rather than a Canadian one, became, by subsequent amalgamation, part of the Grand Trunk; and is, therefore, the beginning of that extensive line. It is worthy of remark, that up to this time the railway efforts of Montreal had been directed to divert the trade of Canada to American cities, her rivals as seaports. In 1846 the first look westward was made in the commencement of the Lachine Railway, but this was undertaken rather as a suburban portage road than as part of the main western line. Although some thirty charters had been granted up to 1850, the only roads on which any work had been done were the Laprairie, St. Lawrence and Atlantic, Lachine, St. Lawrence and Industry, in Lower Canada; and the Erie and Ontario in Upper Canada. Many of these charters have been allowed to drop; and, with the exception of the corporations named, nearly all those relating to roads since built, were extended and amended before any work was commenced. In 1850 the Ottawa and Prescott Railway was authorized, and the line was opened in December, 1854.

The first railway in Upper Canada on which locomotives were used was the Northern, from Toronto to Bradford, opened in June, 1853; yet in 1860, only seven years from that date, about three hundred locomotives were thundering and bellowing over the upper province, between the Ottawa and Lake Huron.

Of the fifty-six charters granted up to June, 1853, only twenty-seven were acted upon, and in twenty-five cases the roads have been completed; the other two (the Woodstock and Lake Erie and the Hamilton and Port Dover) are yet unfinished. By amalgamation or leasing, the Grand Trunk and Great Western have swallowed up nine out of these twenty-five chartered and completed roads, there being now only sixteen distinct railways in the whole province. Since 1853 only three new charters have been acted upon, viz., Preston and Berlin, Three Rivers and Arthabaska, and Peterboro' and Chemung Lake. The last is completed; the first was completed and opened for a time, but is not now in use, and the second is nearly completed.

The province has now 1,906 miles of railway, 1,800 of which have been opened within the last ten years, under the impetus given by the railway legislation of 1849-1852. Of these 1,906 miles, the Grand Trunk Company alone have 872 miles within the province, leaving 1,034 miles in all the other companies. Of these last, however, sixty miles, owned by four companies, are not now in

Railways of Canada: statement showing the dates of opening and length of each section, and the total length of all railways in operation, Jan. 1st, 1861, from report of Inspector of Railways

Corporate name of railway		Name of section	Date of opening	Length of section (miles)	Total length (miles)	Remarks
Great Western	Main Line –	Suspension Bridge to Hamilton	Nov. 10, 1853	43		Under one management
		Hamilton to London	Dec. 31, 1853	76		
		London to Windsor	Jan. 27, 1854	110		
	Branches –	Harrisburg to Galt	Aug. 21, 1854	12		
		Galt to Guelph	Sept. 28, 1857	15		
		Hamilton to Toronto	Dec. 3, 1855	38		
		Komoka to Sarnia	Dec. 27, 1858	51	345	
Grand Trunk	Main Line –	Toronto to Guelph	July, 1856	50		In Canada, and under one management
		Guelph to Stratford	Nov. 17, 1856	39		
		Stratford to London	Sept. 27, 1858	31		
		St. Mary's to Sarnia	Nov. 21, 1859	70		
		Toronto to Oshawa	August, 1856	33		
		Oshawa to Brockville	Oct. 27, 1856	175		
		Brockville to Montreal	Nov. 19, 1855	125		
		Victoria Bridge and approaches	Dec. 16, 1859	6		
		Montreal to St. Hyacinthe	Spring, 1847	30		
		St. Hyacinthe to Sherbrooke	August, 1852	66		
		Sherbrooke to Province Line	July, 1853	30		
		Richmond to Quebec	Nov. 27, 1854	96		
		Chaudière Junction to St. Thomas	Dec. 23, 1855	41		
		St. Thomas to St. Paschal	Dec. 31, 1859	53		
		St. Paschal to Rivière du Loup	July 2, 1860	25		
	Branch –	Kingston	Nov. 10, 1860	2	872	

Corporate name of railway	Name of section	Date of opening	Length of section (miles)	Total length (miles)	Remarks
Northern	Main Line – Toronto to Bradford	June 13, 1853	42		From Toronto to Lake Huron
	Bradford to Barrie	Oct. 11, 1853	21		
	Barrie to Collingwood	Jan. 2, 1855	32.14	95.14	
Buffalo and Lake Huron	Fort Erie to Paris	Nov. 1, 1856	83		
	Paris to Stratford	Dec. 22, 1856	33		
	Stratford to Goderich	June 28, 1858	45		
	From temporary terminus to Station in East st	May 16, 1860	1.27	162.27	
London and Port Stanley		Oct. 1, 1856		24	Lake Erie to London
Cobourg and Peterborough		May, 1854		28	Lake Ontario to Peterborough
Erie and Ontario		July 3, 1854		17	Lake Ontario to Chippewa
Ottawa and Prescott		Dec, 1854		54	From the St. Lawrence to Ottawa City
Montreal and Champlain	Montreal to Lachine	Nov., 1847	8		
	Caughnawaga to Moers' Junction	Aug., 1852	32		
	St. Lambert to St. John (old portion, July, 1836)	Jan., 1852	20		
	St. John's to Rouse's Point	Aug., 1851	21.76	81.76	
Carillon and Grenville		Oct., 1854		12.75	

Railways of Canada: – *continued*

Corporate name of railway	Name of section	Date of opening	Length of section (miles)	Total length (miles)	Remarks
St. Lawrence and Industry		May, 1850		12	Lanoraie to St. Industrie
Port Hope, Lindsay, and Beaverton	Main Line – Port Hope to Lindsay	Dec. 30, 1857	43		From Lake Ontario northward
	Branch – Millbrook to Peterborough	Aug. 18, 1858	13.50	56.50	
Welland		June 27, 1859		25	From Lake Ontario to Lake Erie
Brockville and Ottawa	Main Line – Brockville to Almonte	Feb. 17 & Aug. 22, 1859	51.25		
	Branch – Smith's Falls to Perth	Feb. 17, 1859	11.54		
	Tunnel from temporary station to Harbor	Dec. 31, 1860	.75	63.54	
Stanstead, Shefford, & Chambly	St. John's to West Farnham	Jan. 1, 1859	13		From Montreal and Champlain Railway to Co. of Shefford
	West Farnham to Granby	Dec. 31, 1859	15	28	
Peterborough and Chemung Lake	Peterborough to Snow Falls	July 6, 1859		4	
	Total miles in operation in 1860			1,880.96	

Corporate name of railway	Name of section	Date of opening	Length of section (miles)	Total length (miles)	Remarks
Preston and Berlin	From Galt branch of Great Western to Grand Trunk	Nov. 2, 1857		11	Omitted from the above table because not in use
Stanstead, Shefford, & Chambly	From Granby to Waterloo			15	Opened since 1860
	Total miles completed			1,906.96	

Of these 1,906.96 miles, sixty are not now (1862) in operation, viz: the Cobourg and Peterborough, Peterborough and Chemung, Erie and Ontario, and Preston and Berlin; of the remainder, the St. Lawrence and Industry, and Carillon and Grenville, are worked only in summer.

Railways of Canada: statement showing the cost, stock, bonds, loans, floating debt, and dividend accounts, of Canadian railways in 1860, compiled from the report of the Inspector of Railways

Corporate name of railway	Cost of road and equipments	Capital stock paid in	Funded debt: 1st preference bonds	Funded debt: 2d preference bonds	Funded debt: 3d preference bonds	Government loan	Floating debt	Interest paid on debt in 1860	Dividends paid in 1860
Great Western and its branches	$23,000,104.00	$16,158,641.00	$ 6,327,640.00	Included in 1st preference bonds		$ 2,791,947.00*		$ 528,254.00	3 per ct for six months
Grand Trunk and its branches	55,690,039.92	13,524,803.48	9,733,333.33	4,066,262.23	17,096,450.60	15,142,633.33	12,163,213.07	1,039,635.72†	
Northern (Toronto to L. Huron)	3,890,778.68	823,818.50	491,046.67	1,092,566.68	287,481.35	2,311,666.67		55,545.21	
Buffalo and Lake Huron	6,403,045.86	4,345,701.26	2,433,333.33	811,111.11			145,999.99		
London and Port Stanley	1,017,220.00	939,542.00	399,400.00	120,000.00			77,770.00		
Welland	1,309,209.92	710,299.60	486,666.67	243,333.33			211,851.93		
Erie and Ontario									
Port Hope, Lindsay and Beaverton, and branch					608,333.33				
Cobourg and Peterborough									
Brockville and Ottawa, and branch	1,901,000.00	207,000.00		648,000.00			280,000.00	4,968.00	
Ottawa and Prescott	1,432,647.21	300,630.35	486,666.67	300,000.00	243,333.34		179,332.37	2,321.90	
Montreal and Champlain, and branch	2,485,425.16	1,226,250.00	777,186.66	192,200.00	84,400.00		285,525.51	92,451.69	
Carillon and Grenville									
St. Lawrence and Industry	50,171.00	42,300.00					909.00	48.00	2 per ct
Stanstead, Shefford, & Chambly									
Peterboro' & Chemung Lake									
	$97,179,641.75	$38,278,986.19	$21,743,605.66	$7,473,473.35	$17,711,865.29	$20,246,247.00	$13,344,600.87	$1,869,224.52	

* The total amount borrowed from the Province by the Great Western Railway, on account of the Guarantee Law was, $3,755,555.18. In July 1858, this company repaid $957,114.45 of this amount.

† Exclusive of rents and mortgages.

NOTE: The length of roads for which there are no returns of cost in the above table is 172¼ miles, including eleven miles of Preston and Berlin, not running. The cost of these roads cannot be far from $5,000,000, and the total cost of Canadian Railways is over $100,000,000. The expenditure 'on capital account,' is much greater than the 'cost of road and equipments.' In the case of the Grand Trunk Railway, the total expenditure is about $70,000,000 – the difference representing interest and discount accounts, loss in working, &c. Of the Grand Trunk cost, $1,621,231.69 was on the Portland Division, and therefore not in Canada.

Railways of Canada: statement showing the earnings, expenses, income, mileage, no. of employes, and no. of locomotives and cars on Canadian railways in 1860, compiled from report of Inspector of Railways

Corporate name of railway	Total earnings in 1860	Total expenses in 1860	Net income for 1860	Deductions from returns: Earnings per mile per week	Deductions from returns: Expenses per mile pr week	Deductions from returns: per centage of expens's to earn's	Total miles run exclusive of piloting, shunting, &c.	Total persons employed on line	No. of locomotives	No. of carriages: Passenger	No. of carriages: Freight
Great Western and branches	$2,197,943.34	$1,993,806.00	$ 204,043.00	$122.51	$111.13	91	1,261,604	2,049	89	127	1,269
Grand Trunk and branches	3,349,658.18	2,806,583.17	533,075.01	58.72	49.20	84	3,195,064	3,118	217	135	2,538
Northern	332,967.01	260,466.56	72,500.45	67.40	52.72	78	280,035	370	17	20	301
Buffalo and Lake Huron	315,763.99	264,191.29	51,572.70	37.48	31.36	83	334,457	458	28	24	255
London and Port Stanley	29,385.57	23,256.02	6,129.75	23.55	18.62	78	41,300	38	2	2	50
Welland	64,554.40	51,274.35	13,280.06	49.64	39.44	79	47,810	104	4	4	87
Erie and Ontario							11,220		1	4	10
Port Hope, Lindsay and Beaverton, and branch	53,694.04	40,111.01	13,583.03	18.28	13.64	75	73,806	66	5	3	65
Cobourg and Peterborough									4	2	66
Brockville and Ottawa, and branch	53,801.10	34,427.25	19,373.85	16.30	10.42	64	53,715	74	3	8	79
Ottawa and Prescott	75,362.16	51,465.11	23,897.05	26.83	18.33	68	67,911	92	5	8	79
Montreal and Champlain	232,803.44	136,349.62	105,708.82	53.45	31.31	59	185,633	202	16	15	173
Carillon and Grenville	7,937.25	5,762.18	2,175.06	11.77	8.54	72	6,000	11	2	5	5
St. Lawrence and Industry	8,796.00	7,819.00	978.00	14.08	12.50	88	12,440	24	2	5	5
Stanstead, Shefford, and Chambly							43,720	Leased by the Montreal and Champlain			
Peterboro' and Chemung Lake								Worked by Cobourg and Peterboro'			
	$6,722,666.48	$5,675,511.56	$1,046,316.78	$ 63.65	$ 53.73	84	5,614,715	6,606	395	362	4,982

The improvement in the gross receipts of the first three roads since 1860, is as follows:

	1861 Gross earnings	1861 Earnings per mile	1862 Gross earnings	1862 Earnings per mile
Great Western	$2,266,684	$6,570	$2,686,060	$7,786
Grand Trunk	3,517,829	3,226	3,975,071	3,647
Northern	414,100	4,359	409,399	4,309

operation. Canada has more miles of railway than Scotland or Ireland, or any of the New England States, and is only exceeded in this respect by five States in America, viz., New York, Pennsylvania, Ohio, Indiana, and Illinois. Of her total railway expenditure, which exceeds one hundred millions of dollars, about thirty millions have been supplied by the government and municipalities. The preceding tables show the leading statistics of Canadian railways, from official sources, as far as returns have been made.

GRAND TRUNK RAILWAY

Canada had scarcely completed her magnificent system of canals when the rapid extension of the American railways, projected in all directions over the great grain region lying between the Mississippi, the Ohio, and the lakes, warned her that a new and formidable rival had appeared; and that further and greater exertions would be required – not merely to enable her to continue a competitor for western trade with the whole Union, but to maintain her own proper status in comparison with the individual commonwealths of the North. Stretching for nearly one thousand miles along the frontier of a nation ten times more numerous – herself the chief representative on this continent of the first empire in the world – this province has had imposed upon her duties and temptations, far greater in proportion than those of the most important of the associated States commercially opposed to her. Without a perennial seaport, and with her early trade restricted by imperial navigation-laws and custom regulations, she had no foreign commerce accumulating capital; and wanting this commerce and this capital, and confined to her own market, as well as discouraged by the traditionary colonial policy of the mother country, besides being always overstocked with the products of cheaper labor and capital, she could have no manufactures, and consequently no capital for investment in railways. Moreover, she did not possess that trade and travel which could make railways profitable, and thus invite external aid. But, *noblesse oblige* – the force of position made railways a necessity, if their construction could in any legitimate way be brought about; the more so, because it would have been impossible without them to have kept at home her most valuable population – the young, vigorous, and ambitious natives, 'to the manner born,' while in sight of a people speaking the same language, and having abundant facilities for developing an almost unbounded fertility, open to all comers.

When Montreal, therefore, was arrested half-way in her single-handed attempt to push a railway to Portland, and even the Great Western, which had been years under contract, could not move, the legislature, on the 30th of May, 1849, passed an act by which the province guaranteed (as a loan) the interest only, on the sum required to complete any railroad of seventy-five miles or more in length, of which one-half had been already made by the proprietors.[1] This act, which was of material service to the Portland and Great Western railways in their preliminary stages, was insufficient, and did not produce any commencement of the intermediate sections of the Trunk line between Montreal and Hamilton. In 1851 a bill was passed, providing for the construction of a main trunk line, and restricting provincial aid to the same. This act of 1851 looked to possible aid from the imperial government, in the form of a guaranteed loan – an offer having previously been made by Earl Grey to assist the colonies in that manner, to the extent required to construct a military line between Halifax and Quebec. A proposition was to be made to extend this boon to the continuation between Quebec and Hamilton, in order that Canada as well as the lower colonies might be traversed by the road built with Imperial aid; and in this event the trunk line was to be undertaken by the province as a public work – or so much of it as the Imperial guarantee might be obtained for. The bill provided, in the second place, that if this guarantee were not obtained, the province would undertake the work on her own credit, provided the municipalities would bear half the expense; and as a last resource, if both these plans failed, the local companies, which had been formed on the strength of the guarantee to attempt the different sections, were to be allowed to try their hand. This bill also extended the provincial guarantee to the principal as well as the interest on one-half the cost, and to this

1 This step was a repetition of the legislation of Upper Canada in 1837, before the Union – that province having voted the Great Western Railway £3 for every £1 of private stock subscribed, to the extent of £200,000. In default of repayment, the receiver-general could levy on the Gore and Western Districts.

extent substituted provincial debentures for railway bonds, while it allowed the aid to be issued when companies had expended half of the cost, including land, instead of *completing* half the length of their lines.

The imperial government having declined to aid the particular route demanded by the colonists, no attempt was made by the Canadian envoy[2] to carry out the second plan of the bill of 1850 – that is, to construct the Grand Trunk as a public work, in connection with the municipalities.

This change of programme was in consequence of propositions made to him while in London by English contractors of great wealth and influence.[3] It may be said in defence of this step, that the municipalities were not, like the province, irrevocably committed; that uncertainty existed as to the co-operation of some of them, and that, in any event, time would be required fully to embark them in the scheme. On the other hand, it was charged that the Canadian envoy broke off negotiations with the imperial government at the instigation of the contractors – who had already been at the colonial office in the position of competitors with the colonies for the privilege of controlling an expenditure of such magnitude, to be guaranteed by the British treasury. It was also believed that a powerful though indirect influence, wielded by these contractors, materially contributed to the adverse position assumed by the new colonial minister on a question to which the imperial government had, by his predecessor, been so far committed. The course of the Canadian envoy can only be defended on the assumption that a refusal was inevitable, and that a proper appreciation of his position led him to anticipate it. No more unfavorable impression would probably have remained, had not his name subsequently appeared as the proposed

2 [The Canadian envoy referred to here was Francis Hincks, the Inspector General.]

3 It is important to note, that if Canada did not construct her Trunk Railway without involving Englishmen (and women) in ruin, it was because Englishmen would have it so. Moreover, the demand came from such a quarter, that to those familiar with the resources of these 'operators,' it might have been extremely difficult for her to have gone into the money market on her own account, against their opposition.

recipient of a *douceur* from the contractors, in the shape of £50,000 of paid-up stock in the capital of the company, which, however, he repudiated when it was announced.

Previous to 1851, Canadian securities had no status of their own in England, the canal loans having been negotiated under an imperial guarantee. When provincial bonds had no regular quotations, it is not surprising (however much so it may now appear), that as late as 1851, the bonds of the city of Montreal were sold in London at thirty per cent. discount. At the great exhibition of 1851, Canada made her *début* so favorably, that the keen frequenters of 'Change Alley consented to *chaperon* the interesting stranger – confident that a good thing could be made out of so virgin a reputation – especially after the imperial government had a second time proposed to indorse for her.

No machinery could be better devised for launching a doubtful project, such as was the Grand Trunk Railway of Canada, viewed as a commercial undertaking, than that possessed by the colossal railway contractors, the modern and unique results of the railway era. Extensive operations, involving purchases of land from the nobility and gentry, and weekly payments of wages to the middle and lower classes, over hundreds of miles of country; large orders to iron masters, wood merchants, and engine and carriage builders, in all parts of the kingdom; with banking transactions, and sales of securities of the heaviest description in the capital itself, gather round the eminent contractors a host of dependents and expectants, in and out of Parliament, by a skilful, and, it is to be feared, sometimes unscrupulous use of whom, fortunes are made, and appointments, and titles even conferred. It does not follow that all, or even the majority of those who are thus made use of, are in any degree culpable. Setting aside the effect of pressure from constituents, many an honest man is moved by an unseen lever; and none know better than railway practitioners the value of a man *qui facit per alium* where he cannot *per se*.

Although some opposition was experienced from the promoters of the local Canadian companies – who had borne the burden of the project hitherto, and now saw another about to reap its benefits; and from the few who clearly foresaw the cruel injury which would be inflicted on the innocent, and the consequent responsibility of Canada, there was little difficulty in reconciling the provincial legislature and the municipalities to the abandonment of the joint provincial and municipal plan of constructing the road. The latter were shown that they could now devote their means to local improvements; and to those required members of the legislature who failed at once to perceive the great advantages to the country at large attendant upon the importation of so much English capital, the question was brought home individually in such a way that all scruples were removed. To prepare the scheme for the larger appetite of the London market, its proportions were extended from the 500 miles between Quebec and Hamilton, to upwards of 1000 miles, extending from Lake Huron to the Atlantic; although provision had already been made for the former by the Great Western, and for the latter by the New York and Boston lines approaching Montreal. Amalgamations with existing lines in Canada, and the lease of a foreign one, were made upon the most reckless and extravagant terms; and lastly, having whipped in the requisite financial indorsation in London, the scheme was successfully launched by the contractors most opportunely, just before the Crimean war. As the prospectus showed a probable dividend of eleven and a half per cent, the stock rose to a premium! For this premium a discount was substituted, as soon as exertion was slackened by success, which rapidly increased on the breaking out of the war, and became hopelessly confirmed as soon as the London, Liverpool, Manchester, and Glasgow merchants read the postscripts of their Canadian mercantile correspondents; nor could any subsequent effort of the company, with the aid of all the great names now fairly harnessed in, drag the unwieldy vehicle out of the slough into which, apparently by its own dead weight, it so rapidly sank. This sudden depression, before any trial of the scheme had been made, was the natural result of that reflection which ought to have preceded its reception; and is important in itself, as proving that the English shareholders were either self-deceived or deceived by their own countrymen, the promoters in London, rather than by any importance which they attached to the action of Canada; because no practical demonstration was waited for to prove the real value of the stock. The fact that they did not wait for this, proves by their own act that they were not warranted in believing the prospectus, although they have since founded a claim against Canada upon the faith they put in it.[4] A little reflection was all that was required to make that preposterous document harmless; and we can hardly be held responsible for their exercise of that reflection a few weeks *after*, instead of at the time of its publication.

Notwithstanding this early disrepute of the stock, the character of the subscription list and wealth of the contractors carried on the work until 1855, when the company came before the Canadian Parliament '*in formâ pauperis.*' This was repeated in 1856, when for the first time their contracts were submitted to public inspection. A grant of £900,000 sterling was voted in 1855, to enable them to go on; and in 1856 the province, which had hitherto stood in the position of a first mortgagee, to the extent of its advances to the company, gave up this position and went behind the shareholders, in order that the latter might issue preference bonds to fill the vacated space; and because they complained that Canada ought not to exact her rights to their prejudice. The ordinary bondholders – who, though they ranked after the provincial mortgage, no doubt counted upon similar forbearance when the proper time arrived, and therefore felt themselves virtually first mortgagees – were effectually floored by this preference *coup d'état;* nor can one fail to admire that lucky accident, or judicious foresight, which made one dollar of the original provincial aid, practically count as two to the future wants of the company: for the provincial lien could only have been considered as of prospective value by all parties, especially after the company, which had paid the interest upon it out of capital until 1857, formally declared their inability to continue to do so. This was caused not only by want of receipts, but by their having bound themselves to pay greater rents for leased lines than they could earn from them, so that the productive sections could not certainly do more than pay this deficiency, and complete, equip, and maintain the road. When thus virtually making the company a present of over £3,000,000 sterling, the legislature required them to expend £225,000 (or seven and a half per cent of this amount) upon branch lines connecting with the main Trunk, a stipulation which the company have described as one of the injuries inflicted upon them by the Canadians.

4 They really believed in men of their own country who did not believe in the prospectus, but who had other reasons for indorsing it; and this explains why their faith was of such short duration.

As section after section was opened, and no indications of the eleven and a half per cent presented themselves, the difficulty was accounted for, first, by the want of western connections, then by the non-completion of the Victoria Bridge, and lastly, the want of rolling stock. The western connections were obtained by promoting a company to construct a line in Michigan, at a cost at least one-third more than was necessary, and then leasing it at eight per cent upon this extravagant cost, *after* it had been demonstrated that it could not earn its own working expenses. The only possible explanation of such an extraordinary proceeding, at so late a date in the history of the company, is, that the parties who furnished the money did so in good faith, for the benefit of the whole enterprise, and that the work being situated in a foreign country, and constructed wholly on Grand Trunk account, they were entitled to protection. Also, that as this last and indispensable link was the golden gate through which the treasures of the boundless west were to pour over the Grand Trunk, and produce eleven and a half per cent dividends, eight per cent on their outlay was but moderate compensation to the corporate benefactors. The Victoria Bridge was completed, and then the want of rolling stock was the only reason assigned for the want of success; but when it was remembered that, by the Act of 1857, the conditions on which the province surrendered her lien only remain in force while the company 'supply the said railway with sufficient plant, rolling stock, and appliances to work the same efficiently,' and 'so long as they maintain and work the same regularly,' it was discovered that no more rolling stock was necessary at present; and at the same time the rumored threats of stopping the road, unless the postal subsidy were increased and capitalized, suddenly ceased altogether. When at last all efforts failed, the conviction forced itself on the hitherto infatuated proprietors, that the anticipated traffic was not to be had upon any Canadian route, except as a water-borne one which this rail way was unable to divert.

A failure so magnificent, complete, and disastrous has naturally led to recriminations; and forgetting the part played by Englishmen in the inception, and their almost exclusive execution and management of the undertaking, its British victims have attempted reclamations on the province, on the ground of the 'moral responsibility' incurred in accepting the tempting offers made her. A very large proportion of such claimants are effectually disposed of by the fact that, having acquired their stock at something like one-fifth its cost to the real victims, and other securities at proportionate discounts, long after the fallacy of the prospectus was admitted, they can have had no implied contract with Canada, 'moral' or otherwise. If we are bound to compensate, it can only be those who really put faith in us, and gave the first impulse to our railway, and not the bulls and bears of the stock exchange – perhaps the men who, having deceived and plundered their own countrymen, have bought back the depreciated securities, and now stand in dead men's shoes to intimidate and revile Canadians – every one of whom bears by taxation something more than a moral responsibility on account of the Grand Trunk. Canadians did not originate this scheme, and, left alone, they would have closed the gap in their Trunk line between Montreal and Hamilton without greater cost than they have contributed to the Grand Trunk, and without loss to any but themselves. This section was all that was necessary, in a national point of view, as it would have secured the connection of our chief seaports with the remote west. But a member of the British Parliament,[5] representing the wealthiest firm of contractors in the world, crossed the Atlantic, applied to the Canadian legislature for the necessary powers to bring out the gigantic scheme on the London market, and taught the inexperienced colonists how to take advantage of their position. The governor-general, either to immortalize his administration, or acted upon, however innocently, by those influences in London which control appointments and peerages, publicly implored the legislature not to shut the door in the face of such proffered relief; and prepared an elaborate statistical report, to accompany the prospectus, showing the progress and resources of the colony. It was not possible that a people ignorant of railways could resist such arguments or such temptations; nor is it remarkable that, knowing the marvellous effects of railways elsewhere, they should be unable to discriminate between the profitable and the unprofitable routes, especially when they were assured of success from such experienced and influential sources. Though they had just incurred a debt of millions for canals,

5 [Sir William Jackson, a partner in the firm of Peto, Brassey, Jackson and Betts, returned to Canada with Francis Hincks in 1852 to lobby on behalf of the revised Grand Trunk scheme.]

which were not directly remunerative, they embarked in railways to a much greater extent, assuming obligations which, could they have foreseen the results, they would not have done, even though English capitalists had offered to invest two dollars to their one.

CAUSES OF FAILURE

The Grand Trunk scheme embraces so large a proportion of the railway system of Canada, that its failure deserves investigation, and may be found in the following considerations:

1 We have seen that while private enterprise had taken up as intrinsically valuable, or supposed to be so, the railways leading from Montreal to Portland, Boston, and New York, and from Toronto and Niagara westward – the sections between Quebec and Toronto – the most prominent portions of the Grand Trunk, as prepared for the English market, were, though backed by a provincial guarantee, left by the Canadians until the last, because it was felt that no railway could successfully compete with such a navigation. The English projectors thought otherwise, because *their* railways had beaten *their* canals; but no analogy exists in the case of either system in the two countries. Their railways have a different traffic and climate, are better made and cheaper worked, while their canals are but enlarged ditches compared with ours. The original Canadian railway companies were organized on the basis of portage roads working in connection with the navigation, besides forming a through line for general purposes; but the Grand Trunk vainly essayed competition with the water, and disdained all connection with it between Montreal and Lake Huron.

2 While the Canadian envoy in May, 1852, looked only to a line between Montreal and Hamilton, the English scheme provided for an extension of both ends of a central line, itself never regarded as a promising one – the extensions, as a whole, being still more unpromising intrinsically than the centre; evidently counting upon a through traffic which should be more valuable than the local one. The weak point in the scheme was, that these extensions connected points already connected by better routes, and between which no regular traffic existed, or was likely to arise. The Canadian railway route between Detroit and Boston, as compared with that via

Albany, was an attempt to travel the arc of a circle (and a more arctic one at that) in competition with its chord. The scheme did not possess the elements of success, either as a whole or in its parts; the failure was, therefore, inevitable, and in proportion to the extension. The following statements which show the receipts and exports by sea, via the St. Lawrence, and the Grand Trunk Railway respectively, prove the hopelessness of the contest between the rail and the river; and the insignificance of the winter operations of the former, via Portland and Boston, in diverting exports from the latter:

Receipts of western grain and flour at Montreal, 1862:

	By water	By G.T. Railway	Total	Per cent by G.T.R.
Grain, bus.	11,367,710	802,128	12,169,838	6.59
Flour, blls.	772,381	402,221	1,174,602	34.25

Exports seaward of grain and flour from Montreal, 1862:

	By River St. Lawrence	By G.T. R'lw'y via Portland & Boston	Total	Per cent by G.T.R.
Grain, bus.	9,015,374	478,595	9,493,969	5.3
Flour, blls.	597,477	66,123	663,600	9.96

3 The enterprise, unpromising as it always was to competent and disinterested observers, was loaded down with improvident leases of foreign lines. The Portland railway was leased at six per cent upon its cost, and required the expenditure of over a million and a half of dollars to make it workable; yet with all the advantages of the Victoria Bridge and western connections, the company have not been able to earn more than two-thirds of the rent they agreed to pay. Nothing but the greatest infatuation could have led to the belief that such a road, with its heavy grades and curves, and a scanty local traffic, could, amid winter snows, do a through business, to warrant the price paid for it. The lease of the Michigan line we have already noticed: this was so much the worse, in that the company have not only been unable to earn any portion of the eight per cent rent, but have lost money in working it.

4 The purchase of the St. Lawrence and Atlantic line at cost, though the stock had been sold at fifty per cent discount, was made on the assumption that it was complete as far as it went; but, like the Portland end of the same line, another million of dollars or more was required to put it in efficient order. Besides this unexpected outlay on the existing road between Montreal and Portland, about six millions of dollars were subsequently required, to make up deficiencies in the contract provision for those portions of the line constructed under the company's own auspices. Whatever allowance may be made for heated imaginations, when estimating the prospective business of the road, and deluding themselves with the notion that it would, as a whole, earn dividends of eleven and a half per cent, when none of its parts had previously been considered as practicable without subsidies, the railway men of the prospectus must have known that this could not be done with three per cent of sidings, and the limited number of locomotives and carriages provided by the contracts; and that the working expenses could not be kept down to forty per cent of all the receipts which could be earned by such an equipment. The prospectus assured subscribers that the cost of the railway was defined by contracts, whereby 'any apprehension of the capital being found insufficient is removed,' and which 'secured a first-class railway, including sidings, ample rolling stock, and every requisite essential to its perfect completion'; and that, 'for the capital stated, the proprietors are assured of a railway fully equipped and complete in every respect, and free from any further charges whatever!' The capital estimated by the prospectus was \$47,500,000; the company, in 1860, showed a balance sheet of \$70,000,000; of this amount, about \$56,000,000 is charged to capital account as the 'cost of construction,' the remainder is interest, rent, loss in working, &c., although eighty-five miles of the original road have not been constructed: and after expending millions in supplying omissions in the contracts and estimates, the working expenses instead of forty, have exceeded eighty per cent of the gross receipts.

5 Not only did the contracts fail to provide 'every essential to the perfect completion of the road,' but the provisions they did contain were either not enforced or so loosely complied with, that the efficiency of the road has been impaired, its working expenses

increased, and all the available resources of the company have been required to supply deficiencies, and to repair damages consequent upon this state of things. The bad quality of rails east of Toronto, with the deficiency of ballast and sleepers under them, have led to a destruction of rolling stock and property (fortunately hitherto unaccompanied by loss of life) which is unprecedented in the history of railways. No doubt the force of circumstances, in a great measure, compelled the company to accept a road very much inferior to that originally intended. The English contractors had agreed to take two-thirds of their pay in stock and bonds, and when these became depreciated by the discredit of the company, they were in for a loss in discounts, which was largely increased by the inexperience of some of their agents, who, conducting large expenditures in a country new to them, and having it in their power to place the company in default and suspend the work, were masters of the situation, and naturally desirous, while carrying through their enterprise, to diminish their loss as much as possible.

The system under which the road was constructed was a vicious and illegitimate one, the order of things being reversed from that in well-regulated corporate enterprises. The only way in which an honest and efficient construction of any railway can be guaranteed, is that where *bona fide* shareholders elect their directors, who appoint the engineer and solicitors, and invite competition before the contract is given out. Thus those who expect to become the owners of the property have some control over its formation. But in the case of the Grand Trunk, the contractors assumed the risk of floating off the shares and bonds in consideration of getting a contract upon their own terms, with a board of directors, and an engineer and solicitor, of their own selection (and deriving their fees and salaries through them), to carry them through those all-important preliminary stages when the future shareholders are irrevocably bound, and in too many cases have their interests sacrificed, to those of the contractor. And here there was the additional evil of a political element. The contractors wielding a gigantic scheme which traversed almost every county in the province, virtually controlled the government and the legislature while the expenditure continued. The only supervision under the contract which would have affected their interests, was that which the government and their majority in the legislature could have insisted on. It was the interest of the company that in level country the road should be raised so as to keep it out of water and snow; that in hilly country it should be carried as high over the valleys and as deep into the hills as was prudent, in order to diminish the gradients and therefore the cost of working; and that the stations should be as near the business centre of the towns as possible, particularly in places on or near the competing navigation. But it was the interest of the contractors to keep the road as near the surface everywhere as the contract permitted, no matter how much it might be smothered in winter and flooded in spring – how undulating it was, or how frequent and severe the gradients became; and to place the stations where land was cheapest, or, so as to purchase political support thereby, or obtain a speculation in building lots. It is in vain that magnificent tubular bridges and way-stations of stone are pointed to as evidences of superiority, when the very back bone of the railway, the track on which its receipts are to be earned, is defective in location and construction. Better that the stations had been but temporary sheds, and that their cost had been put into the road-bed, for these can be rebuilt at any time; but the latter must lie as it is, with all its imperfections on its head.

It does not rest with the English public to charge upon Canada all the disastrous results of the Grand Trunk. The prospectus was not prepared in the province, nor did any member of her government see it until it was issued. Canada was not a stockholder in the company; but as the indorser for it, not of it, put four of her ministers on a board, composed of eighteen directors, of whom six were in London and twelve in Canada, eight of the latter being really nominees of the English contractors. The Canadians, as novices in railway matters, could not be censured if they even believed all they were told by the promoters of the railway; nor could they be worse than other people if they gave it a trial without believing in it; but there must have been many men, and many editors in London well versed in railways, not only English but American, who thoroughly appreciated the scheme, as one originated and promoted for the money which could be made out of it by men whose mission it is to prey upon their fellows. If these were silent, Englishmen must blame their own watchmen for not warning them; besides, had they sought the real merits of the scheme, they would have found them in the discussions of the Canadian press and Parliament. These were of such a character as to relieve Canada of any 'moral responsibility,' and contrast favorably with the intelligence or candor of the English press on the same subject. A proposition to attach the contracts to the prospectus was made, but voted down by the contractors' majority in the Canadian legislature. Why, when this was seen, did not the English press call for the contracts when the prospectus appeared, and tell their readers whether the capital would be sufficient, and analyze the scheme from American data? and why did they not show that the contractors could, through their appointment of the company's engineer, solicitors, and directors, give the subscribers any road they pleased, instead of the one described in the prospectus?

Among the minor causes which heightened the failure of the Grand Trunk, and deprived it of much of that sympathy of which it stands so much in need, have been the general extravagance and blundering in its management, and the ridiculous presumption of some of the officials, in a community in which there is so little of a real aristocratic element and so little room for a sham one. In an enterprise of such magnitude, the salaries of its higher officials, no matter how liberal they were, would seem to have little influence on results; and if these results were confined to the mere question of the difference in salaries they would be unimportant, particularly where the incumbents are worth what they cost. But, in the case under notice, the effect of princely salaries to chief officers was to establish a general scale of extravagance, and a delegation of duties and responsibilities, so as to turn the head of the recipients, and involve the company in needless outlays, and losses greater than all the salaries paid upon the line. The railway satrap sent out by the London Board, whose salary is only exceeded by that of the governor-general, naturally considers himself the second person in the province; and, as a consequence, the special commissioner sent out from the same source, with the salary of the President of the United States, to obtain more money from the province under the veil of a postal subsidy, would deem himself the second person on the continent, and therefore assume a position commensurate with his importance, and indulge in threats of destroying the credit of the province. The salary of this commissioner is reported at \$25,000, his charge for expenses \$12,000, and the cost of his special trains at \$6,000, making a total of \$43,000 on account of one year. If only half of this be true, it is sufficient to prevent Canadians increasing their own taxes in order to afford the company the means of continuing such extravagance. Men so much better paid than their confrères naturally value themselves much higher; can only be approached through successive doors, or be communicated with through successive deputies, in a diminishing scale, until the man who does the work is reached; and can only travel by special trains or in exclusive carriages, provided with every luxury on an imperial scale, and with equal indifference to detail. Perhaps no circumstance has tended more to make the management unpopular, and the liberality sought for on account of postal subsidy impossible, than this abuse of special trains and carriages by officials of the company intoxicated with the novelty of their position. The bishops, and the judges of assize; the most venerable and respectable inhabitants of the country, as well as tourists of the highest rank, are content to travel by ordinary trains and in the usual carriages; but the upper servants of the railway company have burned the fuel, worn the rails and rolling-stock, deprived their fellow employés of the needed Sunday's rest, and thrown the whole freight traffic of a single line out of time (thus jeopardizing life and property), in order that they may show their little brief authority. Passengers have been turned out of a sleeping-car in the dead of the night by the breaking of a wheel, and crowded into the only remaining carriage of the train except one, which, though large enough for fifty, was sacred to a few railway magnates whose duty it was – and pleasure it should have been – to treat the ejected passengers as their guests, but who resolutely kept out the vulgar herd. It seems absurd in such nabobs to plead poverty before our legislature, or expect the men whose wives and daughters have been so treated to support their petitions.

MUNICIPAL RAILWAYS

The municipalities, relieved from contributing to the Trunk Railway, were thus at liberty to embark in branch lines, and some rushed headlong in, seduced by men who saw how the thing was done in the Grand Trunk. Contractors controlled the board of directors and appointed the engineer; a scamped road, barely practicable for traffic, was made, on which the whole receipts for the present generation must be applied before it can be considered completed. To enable the municipalities to carry out their local improvements, the province virtually indorsed their bonds by exchanging them for others, in which it acted as a broker, undertaking to collect from the borrower and pay over to the lender. The by-laws by which counties, cities, and townships voted their loans or subscriptions to public works, required the approval of the governor in council before they could take the benefit of the Municipal Loan Fund Act. This provision was intended as a check upon extravagance, but the practical effect of it was to place the members from every county and city, seeking to avail themselves of the provisions of the act, at the mercy of the ministry of the day. Those who were most subservient obtained most money, and one village was allowed to borrow three hundred dollars per head for every soul of the population. Of course default was made in the interest on such loans, and one delinquent produced others; the province as indorser in the mean time paying for them, and in the end accepting, in lieu of the dues, an annual assessment of five per cent. Although loans of this doubtful character have been thus compromised, a rigid neutrality has been maintained toward those municipalities which, like Hamilton, embarked in good faith in similarly unfortunate enterprises upon their own unaided credit.

The following tables show that about six and a half millions of dollars have been contributed to railways by the municipalities in Upper and Lower Canada, out of the loan fund. Some three millions or more have been contributed by municipalities which did not borrow from the fund, so that the total investment by these bodies in railways cannot be far from ten millions of dollars.[6]

This flagrant disregard of obligations, by so many municipalities, is not to be ascribed wholly to the inability of some, and the example of such upon others; nor to any proneness to repudiation; for these bodies have made great and successful efforts to keep faith with other creditors, and have only failed in cases where the debt was overwhelming. Little effort was made to pay the loan fund, even during the most prosperous days of the corporations, chiefly because no attempt was made to collect: the example of the government in conniving at the default being the prime cause of its present

6 Unfortunately, the municipalities do not make any return to Parliament of their investments in public works. This is the case also with road companies and several other joint-stock corporations. No good reasons are advanced why these bodies should be more favored than banks and railways.

Table showing the amounts taken from the municipal loan fund by municipalities in Upper Canada for railway purposes only

Municipalities	Population in 1851	Population in 1861	Amount of loan	Arrears of interest due Dec. 31, 1861
Town of Port Hope	2,476	4,161	$ 740,000.00	$ 312,303.31
Township of Hope	5,299	5,883	60,000.00	25,862.56
Town of Niagara	3,340	2,070	280,000.00	148,974.02
Town of Cobourg	3,871	4,975	500,000.00	313,426.61
Village of Chippewa	1,193	1,095	20,000.00	7,109.71
Township of Bertie	2,737	3,379	40,000.00	8,873.36
Township of Brantford	6,410	6,904	50,000.00	2,428.11
Town of Brantford	3,877	6,251	500,000.00	186,754.87
Township of Wainfleet	1,841	2,316	20,000.00	1,446.37
Township of Canboro	1,151	1,252	8,000.00	330.80
Counties of Huron and Bruce	20,706	76,226	125,000.00	
Townships of Moulton and Sherbrooke	2,318	3,059	20,000.00	
Village of Paris	1,890	2,373	40,000.00	172.23
City of Ottawa	7,760	14,669	200,000.00	113,411.37
Town of Prescott	2,156	2,591	100,000.00	62,625.53
Town of Woodstock	2,112	3,353	100,000.00	47,824.29
Town of St. Catharine's	4,368	6,284	100,000.00	47,748.27
Township of Wood-house	2,894	3,703	10,000.00	31.04
Township of Norwich	5,239	6,383	200,000.00	101,508.96
Township of Ops	2,512	2,872	80,000.00	39,897.36
County of Elgin	25,418	32,050	80,000.00	35.95
City of London	7,035	11,555	375,400.00	155,412.56
Township of Windham	2,900	4,095	100,000.00	50,251.66
Town of Simcoe	1,452	1,858	100,000.00	52,276.99
Counties of Lanark and Renfrew	36,732	51,964	800,000.00	306,189.16
Town of Brockville	3,246	4,112	400,000.00	187,432.01
Township of Elizabeth-town	5,208	6,101	154,000.00	51,794.00
Village of Stratford		2,809	100,000.00	56,871.79
Town of Goderich	1,329	3,227	100,000.00	35,174.92
Town of Barrie	1,007	2,134	12,000.00	2,564.69
Town of Guelph	1,860	5,076	80,000.00	13,400.12
Town of Peterboro	2,191	3,979	100,000.00	27,274.12
Total			$5,594,400.00	$2,359,406.74

Table showing the amounts taken from the municipal loan fund by municipalities in Lower Canada for railway purposes only

Municipalities	Population in 1851	Population in 1861	Amount of loan	Arrears of interest due Dec. 31, 1861
County of Ottawa	22,903	27,757	$131,600.00	$ 84,740.19
County of Terrebonne	26,791	19,460*	94,000.00	60,498.17
County of Shefford	16,482	17,779	215,000.00	63,340.53
County of Stanstead	13,898	12,258	71,000.00	17,581.02
County of Megantic	13,835	17,889	5,840.00	3,580.57
St. Romuald de Farnham†			30,000.00	11,423.68
Township of Shefford†	2,512	3,712	57,500.00	21,895.59
Town of Three Rivers†	4,835	6,058	220,000.00	53,855.61
Township of Granby†	2,392	3,271	30,000.00	10,938.37
Township of Bolton†	1,936	2,526	13,000.00	2,834.39
Township of Stukely North†	2,194	2,820	16,000.00	3,763.29
Township of Stukely South†			10,000.00	2,364.00
Village of Fermont†			32,000.00	6,393.00
Total			$925,940.00	$343,208.41

* Boundaries changed since 1851

† Object of loan not stated; supposed to be for railways.

magnitude. To press a municipality was to drive it into opposition; and railway corruption had so thoroughly emasculated the leaders of the people, that they had not virtue enough left to do their duty. Moreover, at the time the money was borrowed supporters of the government had industriously sowed the impression that repayment would not be exacted, and this view gained ground after the lien on the Grand Trunk was abandoned. They could not see why the law of 1849, which treated all districts alike, should have been repealed for the benefit of the wealthier localities; and looked upon this move as an abuse of their political power by the majority. To these considerations, as well as to the feeling that the debt is due, in a great measure, by the people in one capacity to themselves in another, and not to individuals or a foreign government – and has moreover been pretty generally distributed over the province – may be traced this otherwise disgraceful exhibit. The dimensions of many of the loans, as compared with the borrowers, go to show that the latter did not expect and were not expected to repay; – nor could many of them have been sanctioned by the popular approval, had they been considered as *bonâ fide* debts. The manner in which the guarantee has been distributed, as shown in the following table, has likewise tended to foster this feeling.

	Great Western	Grand Trunk	Northern
Total cost of the road to 31st Dec., 1860	$23,000,104.00	$55,690,039.92	$3,890,778.68
Total amount received from the province in debentures	$ 3,755,555.18	$15,142,633.33	$2,311,666.67
Total miles built	345	872	95
Mileage entitled to guarantee	267	680	95
Amount received per mile of whole road in debentures	$ 10,800.00	$ 17,365.00	$ 24,333.00
Amount received per mile entitled to guarantee in debentures	$ 14,000.00	$ 22,200.00	$ 24,333.00
Per cent of cost supplied by the province	16.32	27.18	59.41

The debentures were sold at about twelve and a half per cent premium, which would increase these amounts one-eighth. The province has abandoned its claim on the last two roads; the Great Western has ceased paying principal or interest – the former from inability; the latter on the ground that its mail service has not been settled.

The Northern was not a part of the main trunk, but obtained provincial aid because it had been put under contract in view of the guarantee, before the repeal of the law of 1849; – a privilege which the Prescott and Ottawa as well as other companies might have obtained, had they added twenty-five miles or more in any direction to the length of their line (so as to make up the seventy-five miles required to secure them the guarantee), and contracted for the whole.

When the advance to the Grand Trunk was fixed at £3,000 sterling per mile, the railway commissioners established a similar limit for the Northern, or a total of £275,000 sterling, which was more than that company then hoped for from the province. On the twenty-first of June, 1854, after two-thirds of the line had been in operation eight months, the engineer of the company reported that the remaining third was rapidly approaching completion, grading and bridging finished – ties distributed and iron delivered, and one-half of the track laid; – that he expected to open the whole length in August, when the harbor at Collingwood would be sufficiently advanced to be used; and showed the expenditure, including road, harbor, station and depot services and equipments, to be £698,810 5*s.* 0*d.* sterling. He also rendered an account as follows:

Provincial guarantee, £275,000 stg. = currency at 9½ per cent	£334,583 6 8
Received by company, to date	284,166 13 4
Balance currency	£50,416 13 4

In the same month, the railway commissioners reported that the total amount to complete the works, including the rolling stock, was £716,530, of which the sum of £682,961 5*s.* 0*d.* had been expended, and recommended the advance of this balance, subject to the report of one of their own body, who was an engineer. This report was made on the twenty-seventh of September following, and it not only confirmed the advance, but declared that the road – which was so nearly completed, and which had been estimated by the board of which he was a member, three months before, at £716,530 – would now cost £1,156,592 7*s.* 7*d.* (or $4,626,369.52), the moiety of which, or full amount of guarantee by the provisions of the act, will be £578,296 3*s.* 9*d.*, of which the company has received (including the sum above recommended) £334,583 4*s.* 3*d.* leaving to be ultimately provided by the province the sum of £243,712, 17*s.* 1*d.* The company was paid the whole of this extra amount, £200,000 sterling, in debentures (over $1,000,000), within four months after this report was made. It is not often that a railway, or any public work, proves to have cost less than was estimated for it, seven years before, but the Northern is an honorable exception to the rule. The fiscal returns published by the inspector of railways, which are the company's own statements, show that the cost of this road and its equipments, up to the thirty-first of December, 1860, instead of $4,626,369.52, was $3,890,778.68, or $735,590.84 less.

The company has received	$2,311,666.67
One-half the cost as returned by them is	1,945,389.34
So it would appear they were overpaid	$366,266.33

Ottawa, Prescott, Brockville, Cobourg, Peterboro', Port Hope, Niagara, Brantford, St. Catherine's, Paris, London, Barrie, Guelph, Stratford, Goderich, and the counties and townships adjoining them, which have not displayed much alacrity in repaying the municipal loan fund, will doubtless claim that the railways which they have interested themselves in should receive some of that consideration which has been so liberally bestowed on the Northern.

The guarantee law of 1849 was very unguarded; so much so that contractors, by tendering at double the value, could make the half contributed by the province pay the whole cash outlay, and could thus afford to take payment in stock and bonds: this has been the result in the case of the Northern Railway. It became necessary, therefore, as we have seen, to restrict it to the main trunk line, and to provide not only for the approval of all contracts by the government, but that the estimates of work done and to be done should be submitted to it – well-meant but ineffectual provisos, as we have also seen. So, also, the manner in which the municipalities voted away their bonds, forced, after some three years' experience, a limitation of the amount for which the province would act as a broker. Some of the wealthier counties, careful of their credit, declined to pay eight per cent for money, and thus derived no benefit from the municipal loan fund (if benefit it can be considered), while they contribute through the consolidated fund to pay its losses.

During the Grand Trunk era of construction, from 1853 to 1859, the first Canadian age of iron, and of brass – the utmost activity was displayed in running into debt. The great success which attended the early years of the Great Western assisted every other Canadian road, and was doubtless the main instrument in preventing the Grand Trunk from being prematurely abandoned. Whatever loss of prestige or character the province may suffer from the almost universal failure of her railways, as investments, it is clear that in a material sense she has been benefited immensely by the early luck of the Great Western, and by the English infatuation about Grand Trunk; for without these the means for the construction of many miles now in use would not have been raised. The construction of the other lines simultaneously with Grand Trunk was equally opportune, because there would have been little prospect of getting them done after the bankruptcy of that road.

RAILWAY MORALITY

So much recklessness was displayed, in sanctioning by-laws, and in exchanging what were really provincial for municipal debentures, as to give color to the charge that contractors were not the only ones personally interested in these issues. The years 1852 to 1857 will ever be remembered as those of financial plenty, and the saturnalia of nearly all classes connected with railways. Before the invasion of the province at the east by a deputation from the most experienced railway men of England, bringing with them all the knowledge and appliances of that conservative country, it had been penetrated on the west by some contractors from the United States, bred in that school of politics and public works which brought New York to a dead stand and Pennsylvania to the goal of repudiation. These 'practical men' had built State canals with senators and even governors as silent partners, and were versed in all resources peculiar to a democratic community. The convergence of these two systems on the poor but virgin soil of Canada, brought about an education of the people and their representatives more rapid than the most sanguine among them could have hoped for. One bold operator[7] organized a system which virtually made him ruler of the province for several years. In person or by agents he kept 'open house,' where the choicest brands of champagne and cigars were free to all the peoples'

7 [The allusion here is to the legendary Samuel Zimmerman, the American promoter of the Great Western Railroad.]

representatives, from the town councillor to the cabinet minister; and it was the boast of one of these agents that when the speaker's bell rang for a division, more M.P.P.s were to be found in his apartments than in the library or any other single resort! By extensive operations he held the prosperity of so many places, as well as the success of so many schemes and individuals in his grasp, that he exercised a *quasi* legitimate influence over many who could not be directly seduced; or made friends of those he could not otherwise approach, by liberal purchases of their property, and thus, insensibly to them, involved their interests with his own. So he ruled boards of directors – suggesting, as the officers who should supervise his work, creatures of his own – and thus the companies found themselves, on settlement-day, committed by the acts of their own servants. Companies about to build a railway, and depending on the municipal loan fund, were led to believe that, if he were the contractor, there would be no difficulty in obtaining the government sanction of the by-laws to any extent, and therefore the exchange of bonds; or, if their charter were opposed, the great contractor only could set it all right. A few anecdotes will illustrate the impartiality of his levies.

An English contractor was, without competition, about to pounce quietly upon the contract for the Toronto and Hamilton Railway, when his American 'brother' demanded and received a royalty of £10,000 sterling, before he would allow a corporation to be so imposed upon: he was, however, subsequently obliged to disgorge this black mail, when seeking the co-operation of the same contractor in England for the celebrated but abortive Southern Railway scheme. The English contractors for Grand Trunk also were compelled, before they could risk the ordeal of the legislature, to promise the ever-present and never-to-be-avoided American one-third interest in their contract. This, considering the kind of payments and their prospective losses, the latter took the earliest opportunity to compromise for the consideration of £12,000 sterling.

The Toronto Northern road was let to a company of American contractors at a price per mile, payment being made chiefly in the company's stock and bonds, and the government guarantee debentures. It was necessary, in order to secure any portion of this latter item, that one-half of the work upon seventy-five miles should first be completed by the contractors. Having exhausted their means in reaching, as they hoped, this position, the contractors, through the company, called on the government for the advance; but, upon an inspection by the government engineer, the road was found to have been so 'scamped,' under the American engineer (who subsequently openly became a partner with the contractors), that the commissioner of public works refused to recommend the issue of the provincial bonds. Here was a fix! But the contractors sent for their American brother, who, for a brokerage of $100,000 of the first mortgage bonds of the company, undertook to obtain the guarantee. He went to his colleague in the government; the commissioner of public works was shunted out of office on a suddenly raised issue (which immediately thereafter was dropped), and just one week afterward the guarantee bonds were forthcoming. In connection with this incident, it is worthy of remark, that a member of the government shortly afterward paid away nearly £10,000 of the first mortgage bonds of the same company in the purchase of real estate.

The Great Western Railway, finding their traffic on the first opening of the road to exceed their expectations, sought, among other legislation, the power to lay a double track from Hamilton to London, and on applying to the government to promote their bill – instead of meeting with that encouragement which the proposal to expend so much additional English capital led them to expect – they were gravely assured that the government was powerless to give them their bill, in consequence of the influence of the enterprising Pennsylvanian in the house. The contractor's price for permitting the bill to pass was – the contract for the work to be done; and to this the company, seeing no escape, consented conditionally; that is, if the work were undertaken during the ensuing five years. Fortunately for them, before a commencement could be made, the double track was found to be unnecessary. Among other favors obtained by the legislation thus bartered for, was the power to disregard that provision of the railway act which requires trains to stop before crossing the drawbridge over the Desjardin's Canal. In less than two years thereafter, a train *which did not stop* plunged through this very bridge, and among the first recovered of the sixty victims to that 'accident,' was the dead body of the great contractor himself.

Lest it should be considered that there is any thing peculiar to Canada in these transactions, it may be mentioned that about the same period a Congressman was convicted at Washington of voting for a 'consideration,' and was expelled from the House of

Representatives. This man was declared to be the spokesman of a band, irreverently styled 'the forty thieves,' by whom he was authorized to negotiate for their votes with the highest bidder. The canal frauds of New York and Pennsylvania are matters of history. Venality and corruption in high places, mainly engendered in the contracts and expenditure for public works, have done, perhaps, as much as slavery, and that territorial covetousness which amounted to idolatry in the Union, to bring down the vengeance of Heaven upon our unhappy neighbors. Nor is this, what may be called, railway morality peculiar to this side of the Atlantic. The following extracts from Smiles' Life of George Stephenson reveal a similar history in English railways:

Folly and knavery were, for a time, completely in the ascendant. The sharpers of society were let loose, and jobbers and schemers became more and more plentiful. They threw out railway schemes as mere lures to catch the unwary. They fed the mania with a constant succession of new projects. The railway papers became loaded with their advertisements. The post-office was scarcely able to distribute the multitude of prospectuses and circulars which they issued. For a time their popularity was immense. They rose like froth into the upper height of society, and the flunky Fitz Plushe, by virtue of his supposed wealth, sat among peers and was idolized. Then was the harvest-time for scheming lawyers, parliamentary agents, engineers, surveyors, and traffic-takers, who were alike ready to take up any railway scheme, however desperate, and to prove any amount of traffic even where none existed. The traffic in the credulity of their dupes was, however, the great fact that mainly concerned them, and of the profitable character of which there could be no doubt. Many of them saw well enough the crash that was coming, and diligently made use of the madness while it served their turn.

The projectors of new lines even came to boast of their parliamentary strength, and of the number of votes which they could command in the 'House.'

Amongst the many ill effects of the mania, one of the worst was that it introduced a low tone of morality into railway transactions. Those who had suddenly gained large sums of money without labor, and also without honor, were too ready to enter upon courses of the wildest extravagance; and a false style of living shortly arose, the poisonous influence of which extended through all classes. Men began to look upon railways as instruments to job with; and they soon became as overrun with jobbers as London charities. Persons, sometimes possessing information respecting railways, but more frequently possessing none, got upon boards for the purpose of promoting their individual objects, often in a very unscrupulous manner; landowners, to promote branch lines through their property; speculators in shares, to trade upon the exclusive information which they obtained; whilst some directors were appointed through the influence mainly of solicitors, contractors, or engineers, who used them as tools to serve their own ends. In this way the unfortunate proprietors were, in many cases, betrayed, and their property was shamefully squandered, to the further discredit of the railway system.

Among the characters brought prominently into notice by the mania was the railway navvy. The navvy was now a great man. He had grown rich, was a landowner, a railway shareholder, sometimes even a member of Parliament; but he was a navvy still. The navvy contractor was greatly given to 'scamping.' He was up to all sorts of disreputable tricks of the trade; but he was greatest of all, perhaps, in the 'scamping' of ballast. The consequences were such as might have been anticipated. More bad and dishonest work was executed on the railways constructed in any single year subsequent to the mania, than was found on all the Stephenson lines during the preceding twenty years.

The navvy's great object was to execute the work so that it should pass muster and be well paid for. The contractor in such cases was generally a large capitalist; a man looked up to even by the chief engineer himself. But the worst feature of this system was, that the principal engineer himself was occasionally interested as a partner, and shared in the profits of the contract. In passing the contractor's work he was virtually passing his own; and in certifying the monthly pay-bills, he was a party to paying himself. What security was there, under such a system, for either honest work or honest accounts? The consequence was, that a great deal of slop-work was thus executed, the results of which, to some extent, have already appeared in the falling in of tunnels, and the premature decay and failure of viaducts and bridges.

Canadians, indeed, have had cause to blush at the spectacle of men filling the highest offices in their province, with a seat at the council-board of their sovereign, accepting fees and favors from contractors and officials of a railway company (between whom and them there should have been a gulf as wide as that which separates the judges of assize from the suitors before them), and laying the honor of their country in the dust, often at the feet of boorish and uneducated men, whose only recommendations were – the material one of ill-gotten wealth, and the immoral one of unscrupulousness in the use of it. May they never again see a member of their government wending his way to the wharf, after a *matinée* of champagne, supported by contractors and their suite, and departing amid the tipsy cheers of his associates; – or have to complain that ministers of the crown again have made men seeking favors from it their most intimate companions, their hosts and guests, their patrons and their protégés.

The evil effects of the past ascendency of railway influence is visible in the disregard paid by many of the companies to the law of the land. Every company chartered after the passing of the Railway Act of 30th August, 1851, is required to show a printed tariff in every passenger-car, and to submit all by-laws changing this tariff for the approval of the governor in council, and to publish the by-law and the order in council approving the same at least twice in the Canada Gazette before putting the same into operation; also to file in the registry office of each county traversed by the railway, a map and profile of the portion within that county; and one of the whole railway, in the office of the commissioner of public works; and to submit annually to the legislature *classified* statements of the passengers and goods transported by them. These provisions should either be enforced or expunged from the Statute-Book; for nothing can be more demoralizing in its example than long-continued disobedience by such conspicuous law-breakers. An unnecessary tenderness has also been displayed toward companies which are exempt by the date of their charter from the wholesome provisions of the Railway Act. Almost all the early charters contain a clause declaring that subsequent enactments by the legislature in the public interest shall not be considered a breach of the privileges granted; and therefore those railways which, like the Great Western, do not exhibit notice-boards at level crossings, and do not remove timber which may fall across the track, should be required to do so as much as those chartered a few years later. The number of level crossings (at every one of which, sooner or later, loss of life may be counted on) has been reduced on the Great Western by the fact, that the contractors were paid in proportion to the work done, and not by the mile, and because frequent crossings of this description would increase the danger *to the trains,* with the high speed aimed at in the location of that work. On other roads, where the contractor's interest was supreme, or where the companies were very poor, these crossings are more numerous, as being the least expensive.

THE GREAT WESTERN RAILWAY

This important road, second to the Grand Trunk only in its length, was first chartered sixteen years before it was commenced. The fine agricultural district between London and Woodstock is nearly equidistant from the three lakes, Huron, Erie, and Ontario; and as produce afloat on the latter is most valuable, being nearer its market, the original road of 1834 was one commencing at London and terminating on Burlington Bay; though power was also obtained to extend westward to the navigable waters of the Thames and to Lake Huron. Before the work was commenced, however, in 1850, the New York railways had reached the Niagara frontier, and the Michigan Central road connected Detroit with Chicago. The Great Western thereupon changed its character from that of a Canadian local and portage railway only, debouching on Lake Ontario (which was but a reproduction in iron of Governor Simcoe's road of the last century), to that also of an important section of the main line leading from Boston and Albany to Chicago, the shortest route for which is through the peninsula of Western Canada. The eastern terminus was therefore extended to Niagara, where a magnificent suspension bridge, worthy of the site, united it to the New York roads; and the western one was diverted from Lake Huron to Detroit, where a short ferry maintains uninterrupted communication throughout the year.

The estimate was made in 1847, by an American engineer, and was (exclusive of the Galt branch) only $4,954,080, which, however, did not include the important items of right of way and land damages or rolling stock. The following exhibit shows the expenditure of the company, and how it is made up, with the excess in the cost of the main line over the original estimate of 1847:

		£	s.	d.
Cost of main line and Galt Branch (with sidings fifty miles)	sterling	£3,651,524	19	7
Cost of Sarnia Branch		467,636	2	2
Cost of Galt and Guelph line		76,183	7	5
Cost of Hamilton and Toronto line		394,456	10	3
Cost of Steamboats Detroit Ferry		39,332	12	10
Cost of Steamboats Canada and America		48,820	5	6
Detroit and Milwaukee Loan		250,000	0	0
Total Expenditure in sterling		£4,927,953	17	10

Cost of main line and Galt Branch (not separated)				£3,651,524	19	7
Stuart's estimate, 1847	£990,816	0	0			
Cost of Galt Branch (estimated)	60,000	0	0			
Cost of Right of way (estimated)	188,371	0	0			
Cost of Rolling stock (estimated)	645,774	0	0	1,884,961	0	0
Excess of exp. on main line over original estimate				£1,766,563	19	7

This increased cost of track and buildings only, on the main line amounting to nearly $9,000,000, makes this part of the work cost nearly three times the original estimate, and is due to several causes:

1 It appears that millions of dollars were expended on these items *after* the line was opened for traffic. Until February, 1852, the expenditure was confined to the Central Division, between London and Hamilton (the original Great Western of 1834), and it was only then the company felt itself in a position to strike out for the larger scheme of the through line. Notwithstanding this tardy action, it was expected that the whole line would be opened in August, 1853. In November, 1852, there was a change of engineers, when it was found that the estimates of the previous June would be exceeded by £621,295 currency, and the new engineer protested against any attempt to open, in 1853, a line on which not a mile of track had been laid before the month of May in that year. Notwithstanding this opinion, so great was the pressure to bring about an opening at the earliest moment, that large sums were offered the contractors if they succeeded in passing a train by November 1st, 1853. One of the contractors, by laying the track in unfinished cuttings, at elevations varying from five to twelve feet above the permanent grade,

succeeded in passing a train on the 10th of November, for which performance he received a bonus of $50,000. The whole line was opened in January, 1854, but on the 1st of August of that year the engineer showed work yet to be done to the amount of $1,436,435. Of course the unfinished cuttings had to be lowered between the transits of trains; the ballasting was chiefly done under a similar disadvantage, and thus much of the work cost many times more than it could have been done for in the ordinary way. In this course the company exceeded the usual practice of American roads, where, for want of capital, the object is to expend only so much as is necessary to open a line, in order that the company may cease paying interest out of capital – have the means of paying the interest on further loans, and get these loans on better terms. It does not appear that the pressure for such premature opening arose from great difficulty in raising the amount required to cover the deficiency of original estimates, or that the earnings of the road were needed to meet the interest account. The company, which had then only received £200,000 sterling from the province, could have claimed millions of dollars as a six per cent. loan on account of the guaranteee.

2 The traveller, in riding over a perishable wooden bridge, nearly a quarter of a mile long and fifty feet high, which traverses an inlet near the shore of Ontario, sees the termination of it only a few rods from the line, where a better and cheaper crossing could have been obtained, and naturally wonders why the road was not placed there. At the western end he remarks that the track for miles runs in the water, with dry land everywhere parallel to the line and but a few yards from it, and is again nonplussed. The engineer who located the road had a weakness for straight lines; and from the manner in which the work was driven, it is probable that sufficient time was not given to amend the location of these long straight lines. Rather than sacrifice them, therefore, if a wide gulf or miles of water intervened, it was plunged into; or if a house stood in the line it must be removed, and the owner indemnified, *coûte que coûte.* Of course, the preliminary surveys in 1847 did not provide for such freaks of the location one, which was made some years afterward, and thus increased cost rolled up. An enormous amount has been expended in the location through Hamilton, and the 500 feet ascent westward from Lake Ontario (which is continuous for eleven miles), where the

road first worked itself, in the course of years, into a quiet bed through many fathoms of mud and ooze; then clings to the face of cliffs, or the rapid slopes formed by the shedding of their exposed faces; and, lastly, at the summit encounters a quicksand, at the bottom of deep and extensive cuttings. This location, which must have greatly increased the cost, was rather in the interest of the contractors than of the shareholders, and does not appear to have been contemplated in the original estimate of 1847. The contracts, some of which had been entered into four years before work was commenced, were item ones, and if at all profitable, this would be in proportion to the amount of work done. There is much reason to believe that alterations and additions to the plans, and also extra works, were ordered without the sanction or knowledge of the directors, more for the chief contractor's benefit than for that of the work; and to such an extent was this carried, that this road was styled his 'milch cow,' to be drawn upon at will.

In England capitalists object to item contracts because, under these, the final cost is not fixed; and, therefore, in preparing the Grand Trunk for that market, a price per mile was agreed upon; which, as we have seen, did not save that company from the necessity of adding many millions of dollars to its capital. The difference between an item contract and a per mile one, as usually carried out on this side of the water, is this. In the former there is always the temptation, by increasing the quantity and altering the quality of the work, to make a first-class road: in the latter it is just the reverse; every thing which is not in the bond (and sometimes much that is) is omitted. As to the two systems, it is but Scylla or Charybdis to a railway company, in the hands of dishonest men; and, like forms of government,

Whate'er is best administered is best.

The original estimate was, no doubt, most insufficient in many respects – but there is very little reason to doubt that the greater part of the excess of £1,766,564 sterling, is due to the causes we have mentioned.

This company was induced, by the example of American lines terminating on Lake Erie, to embark in the steamboat business; a disastrous experiment, as it has proved even on Lake Erie, where its chances were always best. Before so many through railway lines were established between the East and the West, passenger-steamers could be patronized; but the division of the business, and the dread of sea-sickness, no longer make it practicable to sustain such expensive boats as those floating-palaces, once the pride of the lakes. A much more serious undertaking into which the company has been led, was the subsidizing of the Detroit and Milwaukee railway. Whether this was a legitimate attempt to protect itself from the encroachments of the Grand Trunk, and to be able to avoid its proffered embraces, or whether (as is too often the case) the company was forced into it by controlling spirits, who had speculated in the securities of the subsidized road, and used their temporary power to give value to their major interest at the expense of a minor one, cannot yet be determined. Railway companies will always be exposed to such hazards, so long as their directors are permitted to hold a greater interest in any other company.

The Great Western is one of the best equipped and best managed railways on this continent, and traversing a rich and populous district, to which it offers a choice of market, will always have the best local as well as the best through business of any Canadian railway.

BUFFALO, BRANTFORD, AND GODERICH RAILWAY

While the Great Western was busily engaged in watching the proposed invasion of their territory on the north, by the Toronto and Guelph road and its extensions, they were assailed in the rear, and startled by the announcement that a company was formed, and had secured 'vested rights,' for a railway between Buffalo and Brantford. The general act, authorizing the formation of road Companies, had been amended in 1850, so as to extend to railways – a provision which, it appears, had escaped the notice of many railway companies. This virtually gave us the New York system of a General Railroad Law, under which any company may make a railway anywhere, by complying with certain conditions. This democratic measure is the horror of all orthodox existing companies; but while, in New York, the impossibility of getting capitalists to invest in competing lines has been ample protection, conservative legislation in Canada has entirely failed to produce the same result. The people of New York passed their General Railroad Law not only as a measure of justice to all districts, and a protection against monopolies, but chiefly in order to extinguish that corrupt trading in charters which has obtained in Canada, and which induced the legislature to repeal our General Railroad Law, immediately after the Buffalo and Brantford Company had been organized under it – saving those rights, of course. The mischief having been done in 1851, the Brantford Company, in 1852, was allowed to produce its line to Goderich, on Lake Huron.

This road originated in a desire, on the part of the populous city of Buffalo, to render tributary to herself the rich peninsula of Canada West; and also to divert the stream of eastern and western travel and freight away from the suspension-bridge route to her own hotels and stations. If the Great Western had not committed the mistake of giving Brantford the go-by, it is extremely doubtful whether Buffalo could have organized a Canadian interest strong enough to have carried out this measure. This road, which has an admirable track, and is splendidly equipped in stations and rolling stock, deserves a better traffic. Virtually connecting Lake Huron with Lake Erie, it can have, on this route, no through traffic – because this could only be supplied during the season of navigation, when there is slack water of unlimited capacity between its termini, with which it is impossible it can compete. Its local traffic, also, may be limited to that between way stations, since its principal terminus is in a foreign country, and liable to exclusion from Canadian traffic by international trade regulations and currency distinctions. The great want of this road is a terminus on Lake Ontario, in which case it would become available for the grain traffic from Chicago and Milwaukee, or Cleveland and Toledo, to Oswego, Ogdensburgh, New York, or Montreal. Now that the Grand Trunk is *hors du combat*, and better counsels prevail, the railways of the western peninsula will see that their great aim should be to build up the shipping interest on Lake Ontario. This lake is open by water communication both to New York and Montreal, and by the aid of water communication alone can our railways hope to deliver that back freight at their termini on Lakes Erie and Huron, which will induce vessels to bring grain to them instead of taking it on to Buffalo, where return cargoes always await them.

This railway has a value in its power of mischief, for it furnishes, in connection with the Grand Trunk, via Stratford and Sarnia, an opposition to the Great Western; and as it has at present no legitimate orbit, it may become merged in one of these larger bodies. The Grand Trunk, which has so long unsuccessfully wooed the Great Western, might hope to have in this an engine of coercion; while the latter may take it up as a means of self-defence, or to prevent the Trunk from establishing one leg on the Niagara frontier. It is, perhaps, superfluous to say, the Brantford road could be happy with either; but the legislature has fortunately been aroused to the danger of these amalgamations, and it is to be hoped we have seen the end of them. From Hamilton to Quebec, railway monopoly is shorn of its power by the water route, but a general amalgamation on the western peninsula would place the people there under a tyranny which could not and would not be endured.

GRAIN PORTAGE RAILWAYS

The Niagara peninsula separates the open stretch of inland navigation afforded by Lakes Erie, Huron, and Michigan, from Lake Ontario (which is 330 feet lower), by a distance of only thirty to forty miles. Although the Welland canal connects these waters by a fixed scale of navigation, it is found that the longer voyage on the upper lakes is most profitable when with a size of vessel too large for this canal; and that the saving in freight on grain from Chicago to this peninsula, in the larger vessel, is more than sufficient to cover the cost of elevating it by steam power and machinery, transporting it across by rail, and discharging it into the vessel on Lake Ontario. Time is saved, so that the wheat reaches the seaboard before the drafts by which it was purchased mature; the grain is improved and prevented from heating by the aeration it receives in passing through the elevators; and, most important of all, every craft afloat on and above Lake Erie is available to carry grain destined for Lake Ontario, instead of the limited number adapted to the locks of the Welland Canal.

The Welland Railway, which runs parallel with the Welland Canal, and thus takes advantage of its harbors, has demonstrated the importance of this traffic, having transferred upwards of eleven millions of bushels of grain from the upper to the lower lake since its opening in June, 1859. Instead of being a competitor with the canal, it has proved an auxiliary to it, as a lighter to grain vessels too deeply laden to pass the canal. Over half a million of bushels were thus 'lightered' from one end of the canal to the other in 1862; the total quantity transferred from Lake Erie to Ontario in this year, was 4,111,640 bushels.

This work, originally projected to connect a steamboat route between Port Dalhousie and Toronto with Thorold and the Great Western Railway, unites the two railways which skirt the opposite shores of the peninsula, and the numerous villages created by the water power of the canal, and thus has a self-sustaining local traffic as well as its through business. It has been successfully carried to completion by the same mind and will which produced the Welland Canal, and amid the same general predictions of failure. Following this lead, the Erie and Ontario road, which is now valueless, is to be extended to Lake Erie, and become a grain portage railway, besides forming part of the line between Buffalo and Toronto.

The Buffalo and Lake Huron Company also propose to acquire the half-completed Hamilton and Port Dover Railway, between their line and Burlington Bay. If a connection is made with Lake Erie at Dunville or Port Maitland, another grain portage railway is established for Lake Erie, in addition to their route from Lake Huron. All three of these roads will avoid the expense of harbor protection works, as all have the advantage of terminating in the best natural or artificial harbors to be found on these lakes. The difficulty which all, however, have to contend against, is the securing of a regular supply of tonnage working in connection with them, without which they are helpless, especially while the supply of routes to the seaboard exceeds the demand for them. Iron, from its cleanliness and greater carrying capacity in proportion to beam and draught, would make the best grain craft, but there is not capital here to supply them.

These, together with the larger portage roads, offer an opportunity for a legitimate and extensive increase of British commercial tonnage on the lakes, an object of vital importance in the defence of the province on its weakest side; and in this view, instead of mere private speculations, they become works of national importance.

THE INTER-COLONIAL RAILWAY

The proposal to unite the British North American Colonies by a railway was the suggestion of Lord Durham, the imperial commissioner sent out in 1838, to inquire into the Canadian Rebellion.[8] The initiative was taken by a proposition from Nova Scotia to have a survey made, at the joint expense of the three provinces; and this was undertaken under imperial direction, by Major Robinson and Captain Henderson, of the Royal Engineers, in 1846, and completed in 1848. In 1849, the colonies passed acts, guaranteeing to acquire the right of way through private property for this railway, and granting ten miles in width on either side of the road, wherever it traversed the public domain. They also pledged themselves to contribute £20,000 sterling each, per annum, toward making up any deficiencies of revenue. It was proposed to raise the capital on the security of a duty of seven shillings and sixpence per load (fifty cubic feet) to be levied on timber, the produce of the British North American colonies, then enjoying a protection in Great Britain. In May, 1850, Sir John Harvey, Lieutenant-Governor of Nova Scotia, made this proposition to Earl Grey, the colonial secretary, who promptly replied that her majesty's government were 'not prepared to submit to Parliament any measure for raising the funds necessary for the construction' of this railway. In July, 1850, a convention was held at Portland, Maine, for the purpose of pushing the American railway system eastward, through Maine, to Halifax, as the ultimate port of debarcation of mails and passengers for Europe. Nova Scotia, desirous of making her portion of this railway, like her electric telegraph – a public work – once more appealed (in August, 1850) to Earl Grey, to aid her with the imperial guarantee or indorsation, and offered to assume the whole burden of its cost. This application, with reference to a section of only provincial and not imperial importance, received no encouragement; whereupon the persevering little province, determining to make a final effort, dispatched a delegate, who arrived in England in November, 1850, and immediately opened his batteries on the colonial office, with such effect, that on the 10th of March, 1851, Earl Grey surrendered; agreeing to guarantee the interest on the cost of the Nova Scotia Trunk line, but only on condition that the other colonies, Canada and New Brunswick, should place themselves in the same position.

8 In a dispatch which arrived after the High Comr. had left the province, Lord Glenelg had suggested an inter-colonial road, and Lord Durham, instead of this, proposed the railway.

Of course the line was to go to Quebec or Montreal, instead of Portland. It was stipulated that the line should pass wholly through British territory, and should be approved of by the imperial government; but it was not required that it should necessarily be the one recommended by Major Robinson and Captain Henderson.

In announcing this decision to the delegate, the under secretary wrote, that 'Her Majesty's Government would by no means object to its forming part of the plan which may be determined on, that it should include a provision for establishing a communication between the projected railway and the railways of the United States.' The delegate read this to mean, that the guarantee would be extended to *two* lines through New Brunswick, the one to Quebec, and the other to Portland; thus connecting the maritime colonies both with Canada and the United States. On March 14th, 1851, dispatches were sent to all the governments, suggesting a conference at Toronto. New Brunswick, which had, in mean time, become excited on the question of the railway to Portland, passed resolutions, before her legislature adjourned, rejecting any proposition based on the conditions laid down by Earl Grey; evidently not feeling certain that the interpretation of the Nova Scotian delegate was to be relied upon. Delegates, however, from Nova Scotia and New Brunswick came to Toronto, in June, 1851, according to the suggestion of Earl Grey, when it was agreed that a line from Halifax to Quebec should be undertaken on joint-account. Crown lands on each side of it were to be conceded for the benefit of the road; the receipts to be common property until payment of cost and interest; after which each province should own the portion within her own territory. The legislature of Canada, then in session, at once adopted this agreement. The government of New Brunswick favorably received it, but in consequence of a change of ministry, no legislative action was then had. At the very time, however, when Nova Scotia was rejoicing over the acceptance, by her legislature, of the imperial offer, a dispatch was on its way out, which upset all that had been done. On the 27th of November, Earl Grey called the attention of the lieutenant-governor of Nova Scotia to an error into which he had fallen, in his speech when opening the extra session, by assuming that the imperial government intended to guarantee the amount necessary to construct the Portland line through New Brunswick, as well as that leading to Quebec. Earl Grey explained, that the passage which had led Nova Scotia's delegate astray, only meant that the imperial government would sanction, but not aid, the Southern, or European and North American lines, through New Brunswick – which, he was quite aware, was preferred by that province to the Northern, or Quebec and Halifax line.

The great preponderance of population, wealth, and political influence in New Brunswick, lies upon the Bay of Fundy and the river St. John, while Major Robinson's line ran along the Gulf of St. Lawrence. For this reason, New Brunswick would not contribute to the Halifax and Quebec line, unless she in turn was aided to make the line she preferred; and she saw clearly that the military considerations, set forth in Mr. Hawe's letter of the 10th of March, 1851, would keep the line either on the eastern coast or in the wilderness between it and St. John.

Canada, on receiving the interpretation of the original dispatch, and knowing that New Brunswick would now abandon the Quebec line, sent off three of her ministers to Fredericton to console her distressed sister, and at the same time to feel her pulse. As Earl Grey had not insisted on Major Robinson's eastern-shore line, although reserving the right of approval of the route, New Brunswick assented to 'try on' a Halifax and Quebec line which should follow the Southern or European and North American one as far as the city of St. John, and then ascend the valley of that river to Lake Temiscouata. Re-enforced by a delegate from the New Brunswick cabinet, the Canadians journeyed on to Halifax, where they found a new difficulty. Nova Scotia had no idea of standing a third of the cost, if the road should first *debouche* on the Atlantic Ocean at St. John, instead of at its rival, Halifax. Canada, acting as mediator and umpire, finally proposed that as New Brunswick would decidedly gain by the adoption of the southern instead of the northern route – getting her connection with Quebec and Portland where she wanted it, and with 100 miles less of her chosen railway to make at her own cost – she should assume five-twelfths and Nova Scotia one-fourth, Canada taking her old proportion of one third. At this stage the New Brunswick delegate put the question to his Canadian fellow-travellers, whether a proposal from English contractors to construct both roads, on receiving £90,000 to £100,000 per annum for twenty years from the colonies, besides a grant of 3,000,000 to 5,000,000 acres of land, would be entertained? The answer was, 'not for a moment'; whereupon New Brunswick, with dignified resignation, agreed to the new subdivision on Jan. 31, 1852. On Feb. 5, one of the Canadian delegates wrote from Halifax to Earl Grey, detailing the scheme as amended, and announcing that delegates from the three provinces would wait on him in London. To this, on Feb. 20, Earl Grey replied, declining to commit himself to the new route without more specific information, but expressing solicitude for a successful issue, and approving of the intended delegation to London. The Canadian delegate proceeded to London in advance of his colleagues, where he found Earl Grey out of office, and Sir John Packington as his successor. Sir John, on May 20, 1852, notified him that as all previous negotiations had been based on Major Robinson's line, or something near it, the route by the valley of the St. John was out of the question; and as the delegates were authorized to treat only for the latter, he must terminate the question by declining, &c. The provinces were thus left to carry out their own railways in their own way; they had, however, gained by the discussion. The mere proposal on the part of the British government to indorse their bonds, raised these in a market where they were not known; and before the adverse decision had been announced it had been anticipated, and Canada had thrown herself into the open arms of Messrs. Jackson, Peto, Brassey, and Betts, the great railway contractors.

Viewing the question as an imperial as well as an intercolonial one, it is evident that the first blunder committed by the colonies was in agreeing to pay the whole expenses of a railway survey which was to be made solely under imperial and military control. They thereby, at the outset, assented to the position that the imperial government had no substantial interest in the question, and at the same time they failed to ascertain the facilities for other routes, if such exist, than those recommended. Without impugning the ability of the royal engineers who conducted the exploration, there is little doubt that a more satisfactory survey could have been made by civil engineers, accustomed to similar surveys in the forests of this continent; and the want of some reliable knowledge of the practicability of other lines besides that recommended by Major Robinson, has been a stumbling-block in the way of every subsequent movement down to the present hour. It must also be admitted that the mother country drove a hard bargain with her offspring. Her own colonial secretary, Lord Glenelg, suggested the communication to her own high commissioner, Lord Durham, not as a military road solely, but as a political measure. When the colonies took up the idea, the mother country steadily refused all aid except that which, as had been proved to her in the case of Canada, was but nominal; while she exacted for this nominal aid sacrifices from the colonies which were real and important. She would not build the road, nor aid in building it, because it would not pay; and she would not permit the colonies to build it where they believed it would pay, at least, its working expenses. She had already guaranteed a loan for the cost of the canals of Canada, which were constructed wholly on commercial principles, and with the route of which she did not interfere, though military considerations were wholly disregarded in the case of the Beauharnois Canal. She acknowledged an imperial interest to which she attached but a nominal value; she felt for the colonies, but would not feel in her pockets for them.

Ten years have elapsed, and in the interim sections of the proposed Halifax and Quebec, and European and North American Roads have been constructed, the former by Canada and Nova Scotia, the latter by New Brunswick – and again the project is revived, by the renewed assent of the imperial government, to guarantee the funds for the construction of the diminished distance (reduced from 635 to 370 or 470 miles, according to the route to be selected); and as military considerations are now predominant, it is understood the selection of the route will be left to the imperial government.

For the revival of this project we are no doubt indebted to the exigencies of the Grand Trunk Company, aided by the re-establishment of the *entente cordiale* between the Colonies and the Colonial Office, consequent upon the visit of H.R.H. the Prince of Wales; by the subsequent civil war in the United States, and especially by the Trent affair. The Grand Trunk, at its wit's end to raise more money, and seeing the capitalization of a postal subsidy yet remote, sought to revive the intercolonial project in order to transfer to it as much of the unproductive sections east of Montreal as possible – no doubt at a bargain – and therefore the influential owners of this road brought about another Colonial conference. Some years back the Company, during one of its numerous and successful applications for relief, generously proffered their 118 miles east of Quebec as a gift to the Province (in consideration of the relief granted), to enable her, hereafter, to turn it in as part of her contribution towards the future Intercolonial Railway. As the Company were then subsidizing contractors to work this section, by paying them a handsome *bonus* in addition to all the receipts, the gift was not accepted. What it would now be valued at, it is difficult to imagine; but it is evident that the first preliminary toward the intercolonial project should be to establish its future relations with the Grand Trunk, and thus confine the expenditure of the capital to be raised wholly to the new road to be built, eastward of Rivière du Loup.

The provinces will, doubtless, build the road, at their own expense, on whatever route the mother country wishes it built, if solicited to do so by her – the loans being guaranteed, so that the money can be raised on terms not oppressive – because there will then be an implied pledge on the part of the empire, that if built as a military work, it will be used as such whenever occasion may require. In other respects its value to Canada will be more political and commercial than military, because, unless extended, with the same avoidance of the frontier, far beyond Quebec, it will be of little value in the defence of the province at large. Though it might bring men and munitions of war without interruption (except from snow) to Quebec, a fortress which does not require this protection, these could not reach Montreal or Western Canada by rail, unless the Grand Trunk Railway were maintained for a distance of nearly 400 miles between St. Hyacinthe and Toronto, every portion of which, except, perhaps, a few miles on the Island of Montreal, would be exposed to a sudden raid or a superior force.

In order to preserve the granaries of the province in case of threatened invasion, and supply the comparatively dense population of Western Canada with arms and munitions of war, as well as to enable us to contend for the superiority of the lakes, a railway from Quebec to Lake Huron, by way of Montreal and Ottawa, is required. If the latter city were made (as is practicable) a second Quebec, the water communication could always be kept open between them, thus reducing the imperative railway distance, in mean time, to less than half. Such a road would be a base line of operations for the defence of Western Canada; and by means of the present railways debouching at Prescott, Brockville, Cobourg, Port Hope, and Toronto, would serve to communicate with the frontier, while it would be, in its entire length, beyond the reach of an enemy. If now laid out as a railway, it could be used as a highway, on which the snow would seldom be wanting in winter, until time and money could be had for the better road. As it would pass almost wholly through the public domain and the best timber districts of Canada, it would pay indirectly, as a colonization road, creating wealth by rendering valuable timber which is now beyond reach, and is being annually diminished by fire; and giving increased value to the lands on both sides of it. In timber and lumber it would have a profitable local traffic in both directions, to the markets of Chicago and the Hudson river; and in spring and autumn, if extended to Montreal, a through grain traffic would arise, in which, the St. Clair flats being avoided, the largest class of vessels which can enter Chicago would be employed, and grain could be delivered at tide-water from Lake Huron, with one hundred miles less of railway carriage than by any other mixed route having but one transshipment.

Large sums of money have been annually expended without much system, and with comparatively partial results, on what are called colonization roads, which it would be wiser to concentrate on such a truly national object as the above – one which would promote immigration, develop the resources, and provide for the defence of the country. That such a road would yield the country a return commensurate with its cost there can be no doubt, and that it would be at least self-sustaining there is a certainty. The only thing therefore which should prevent its execution, is the burden of its cost until it has produced its fruit. To this it may be said, that more money would be spent and lost for the want of it, in one year of war, than would construct it; and that there is no way in which the colony could so powerfully contribute to her own defence, and to the integrity of the empire, without ultimate loss, and while pursuing the legitimate mission of peace. As a necessary extension and corollary to the intercolonial railway, the mother country might fairly be requested to promote such a work by similar assistance; and the province could have in her unsold provincial domain, thus rendered valuable, a reliable basis for a sinking fund to meet the interest, and to provide for the extinction of the principal, of the loan.

The importance of opening up this domain has been recognized in the charter of a company for the construction of a railway from

Quebec to Lake Huron, and the endowment of the same by a grant of 4,000,000 acres of the public lands. The demonstration of the failure of Canadian railways as investments, and the extent to which the provincial revenue is burdened by guarantees, left no other means of raising or attempting to raise the capital required, but that of a corporation based upon land grants; and if, as appears to be the case, large endowments of land will not secure the construction of the road, the project must either be abandoned or be taken up as a public work. However unpropitious the time may be considered for such a suggestion, it may be asserted that no public work already executed, or proposed, can surpass in importance that of a railway from Quebec to Lake Huron, as a national road. With such a base, and with our back to the unopened north, our flank could not be turned, nor our communication with the sea be cut off. Without it, the attempt to hold Western Canada against an invading force five times our superiors in numbers, and commanding, as they then could, the lakes, would be almost hopeless. If 4,000,000 acres is not sufficient appropriation for such a work, we can increase the quantity. The principle that the public lands are of little value until salable is self-evident; and it is equally true, as admitted by our free grant system, that a settler as a consumer, and subject of taxation, is more remunerative to the province than the unoccupied acres he would require. The interest question and municipal taxation will force the earliest practicable settlement of the lands, no matter into what hands they may fall. The United States Congress has granted no less than 25,000,000 acres to railways, besides 10,000,000 acres for other public improvements.

If the Intercolonial Railway be entered upon as a political and social measure only, it may terminate at Quebec; but if designed as a military one, it should be pushed to its legitimate conclusion, and that will not be found short of Lake Huron.

RAILWAY POLICY

The great want of the Canadian railways is a paying traffic. The Grand Trunk, in tapping the Western reservoirs, may feed itself under an almost constant head, and maintain an almost continuous descending stream, though this may not often be a paying one; but as the Western States do not import through Canada, there is no return traffic. The procession of empties, from the Atlantic to the

St. Clair, is 'a drawback' which will always be difficult to get round, and must have suggested melancholy trains of reflection in the mind of each successive manager. No price obtainable in competition with the water, or with the shorter lines and better gradients and lighter frosts and snows of the American routes, can compete with the latter, while these monopolize the carriage of the up freight, the merchandise and manufactures, on which the most profitable rates are collected. The through downward freight to the Atlantic, consisting chiefly of the cheap cereals, the flour and the lumber of the north, does not average more than about one-tenth of the value per pound of the cotton, tobacco, and sugar, the agricultural products of the south; and it is questionable whether on the whole of a year's business it has ever paid the railways more than the cost of carrying it. The downward or export tonnage, is usually three to one, as compared with the up or import freight; and to that extent the local business also involves a return of empties which has heretofore, to a considerable extent, been avoided on the American lines by the westward excess of the immigrant travel. The dream of a great railway traffic through Canada, between the Atlantic and the west, except on the portage lines terminating on Lake Ontario and the Niagara frontier, must therefore be abandoned; and we must turn our attention to the development of the local traffic of the country, and bring down our establishments from those of a foreign war of aggression on the more favored routes, with all its consequent extravagances and losses, to that of a peace and home establishment.

With regard to the passenger traffic, there yet remains the experiment of cheaper rates of fare, to test whether any increase of travel will produce a greater aggregate from this source, at the same cost to the companies. The rates charged are, when and where practicable, the maximum which the law allows, and are about fifty per cent higher than those on leading United States' lines. No doubt they are at this excess much less profitable, in consequence of the paucity of travel; but it is equally certain that the lower rates of the American routes have developed a much greater tendency to travel there than here. The manufactures of New England are the main source of the profitable local traffic of her railways, and this resource our roads do not possess. Besides the immigration and great business travel between the east and west, one of their profitable items is in the large amount of female travel between New England and her western colonies. The young adventurer returns from the prairies to take back a wife from his native hills; perhaps a sister accompanies them 'on speculation.' In the course of events the wife returns to her mother, or the mother goes to her daughter, and a third passenger appears on the stage.

On the one hand it is argued by the companies, that fifty passengers at ten dollars each, are more profitable than sixty at eight dollars; but if the number increase to seventy-five the reduction would pay. The increase would be the work of a little time, and might then possibly be attributed to the progress of the country, and not to the policy of lower fares. Such a bold experiment probably requires more faith and patience than our railways, in their present distressed state, can be expected to exercise. On the other hand it may be said that the trains must and do go, whether full or not; that even if no more money were received, they cost the company scarcely any more when full than empty; and that increased facilities beget both trade and travel, to the ultimate gain of the railway. The position assumed by the companies is, that there exists a certain amount of travel which must go, and that any reduction to this would be so much loss. Perhaps a compromise might be arrived at, and the experiment tried by a wise and gallant discrimination in favor of women and children. At present, a respectable woman in Montreal cannot pass her Christmas with relatives or friends in Toronto short of an outlay of twenty dollars. The fatigue of a sixteen hours' journey, and the risk of a broken rail (and neck), are such as to require decided temptations to travel; and it would be sound policy in railway companies to encourage a spirit of locomotion in that sex which is supposed to be attracted by every reduction in price, and which has both the leisure to travel, and the power of obtaining the ways and means from those who must remain at home. In their freight traffic the companies discriminate in favor of the long haul, and it is only in their passenger rates that the *pro ratâ* system is maintained. The principle that a half fare is better than none, is also admitted, where competition exists, in their through rates, between Chicago and Boston. It might be found equally wise to establish special through rates between distant cities in Canada, instead of treating them wholly as local points, and thus create a travel which does not now exist.

As to freight traffic, the rates must vary with the existence or otherwise of water competition, which is the only protection to the producer against excessive charges, there being no limitation by law to the freight tariff except the neglected sanction of the government. The greatest development of a legitimate and profitable freight traffic will be that which will arise from an abandonment of the attempt to compete with the water route, and the adoption of this as an auxiliary, particularly in the carriage of grain in bulk; which, from its mobility, can be shipped and transshipped by machinery, and with benefit instead of deterioration.

CANADIAN GAUGE

The gauge of the Canadian railways is five feet six inches, although this is not the exclusive one in use. The St. Lawrence and Champlain; Stanstead, Shefford, and Chambly; the Prescott and Ottawa; and the St. Lawrence and Industry roads, in all 147 miles, are of the American gauge of four feet eight and one-half inches.

Some energetic gentlemen in the city of Portland, ambitious of obtaining something of that railway aid which had contributed so much to the success of Boston, conceived the bold idea of tapping the St. Lawrence at Montreal by a railway over the route of the White Mountains, through the vast forests of Maine, New Hampshire, Vermont, and Canada. The distance is nearly three hundred miles, with an intervening summit of about one-third of a mile in height above the termini, the line having besides the frequent and severe curves and gradients usual to such a route. Having enlisted Montreal in the project, they took the precaution to bind the Canadians, under seals and penalties, to adopt the peculiar and exceptional gauge of five feet six inches; and an elaborate and sententious report was prepared, which proved to the unsophisticated Canadians, that by the simple adoption of this great improvement in gauge, Boston and New York would be distanced. When the Grand Trunk bill was passed, Lower Canada being in the ascendant, the Portland gauge was forced upon the province, the Lower Canadians being unanimous in its favor, because they had been led to believe that it would divert western trade from the New York route and send it down to Montreal.

The Great Western Railway, which was not restricted to a particular gauge by its charter, had decided on the American one, but was compelled to change it by threats from the government, both to withhold the guarantee, and also to charter a continuation of the Grand Trunk, on the Canadian gauge, from Toronto to Sarnia. To the latter intimation the company yielded, vainly supposing that they thereby acquired a right of protection from a competing line, especially as they formed a portion of the Trunk railway. But as soon as Grand Trunk became supreme in the provincial cabinet, the unfortunate Great Western had the disagreeable alternative of amalgamation or competition presented to them, and of the two evils they naturally chose the least. The Grand Trunk went to Sarnia, the guarantee following it, to the great benefit of the intervening counties, and of the contractors; and as it went to Sarnia, so it must also go to Rivière du Loup, in order that there might not be an undue preponderance of mileage in Upper Canada; and this is where the contractors and the counties got the better of the shareholders. The latter have, however, no cause of complaint against the province on this score, for, by their prospectus, they undertook to go to Sarnia, and not only to Rivière du Loup, but thirty-five miles beyond, besides constructing the Grand Junction, a work which has not been, and is not likely to be, commenced.

It has long since been demonstrated, that what is called the narrow or Stephenson gauge, of four feet eight and one-half inches, is wide enough for all practical purposes; and that any increased width is an unnecessary expense in first cost, and an increase of dead weight, and of resistance at curves in working.

In case of invasion, however, there would be this advantage in the Canadian gauge, that on all approaches – excepting that from Portland – the enemy must relay to his own gauge nearly the whole of our railways, before his own rolling stock could be used – unless indeed we should so blunder as to let ours fall into his hands.

HORSE RAILWAYS

The first railway company in Canada was organized the 29th of May, 1861, for the city of Toronto; and the materials being prepared, the Yonge street line was commenced on the 26th of August, and opened to the public on the 11th of September in the same year. The Queen street line was also commenced on the 16th of October, and opened the 2d of December. This company claim six miles of single track, eleven cars, and seventy horses; – which, with stables, car-houses, &c., are put down at a cost of $175,000 in stock and bonds. The cash outlay has probably been something under half of these figures.

The Montreal street railway was likewise commenced in September, 1861, and opened in the following November. The total length of track is six miles and a quarter; the cost of which, including eight cars, brick stable, forty stalls, and car-house, was $89,263.13; of which $42,500 was paid the contractor in stock. The company have besides, four one-horse cars convertible into close sleighs, three covered sleighs, five open sleighs, and sixty-three horses, with harness and other equipments, costing, together, $10,164.52: – making the total cost almost $100,000.

The street railway is an institution for the benefit of those who ride at the expense of those who drive; and is a flagrant violation of the rights of the minority, if not of the majority. The rights of a single owner are considered sufficient to prevent the closing or alienation of a highway; gas and water companies are only permitted temporarily to obstruct a street; but the horse railway is a permanent obstruction – practically dividing a wide street into two narrow ones, and a narrow one into two lanes.

These railways are a great relief to commercial cities, where the business centre is ever extending, and pushing the population into the suburbs; – and they therefore much increase the value of suburban property; – but it is questionable whether they will be found profitable as investments in Canada. It will be only occasionally that they can be worked in winter – and then only in Western Canada, so that during this period their permanent way is of no value; and the traffic by sleighs, always open to competition, will be barely sufficient to cover expenses. Where, however, they do not pay as investments they are often warranted, provided the traffic is sufficient to cover the working expenses, if laid down in connection with, and by the owners of real estate, in the suburbs. Still there should be some limit to the extent to which the streets of a town may be cut up for such partial and selfish purposes, as there is a tendency to obstruct streets with them where there is no plea of necessity, but chiefly to secure the franchise for the future. If proper discrimination were used, a few leading arteries could be laid down, in streets which are not thoroughfares, without much inconvenience to the public, and with nearly equal advantage to those who use them – a precaution which has not been taken either in Toronto or Montreal.